Why Do You Need This New Edition?

Why should you buy this new edition of *Writing Logically, Thinking Critically*?
Here are eight good reasons!

❶ **A new section of additional readings** addresses contemporary topics designed to engage you and challenge your reading and critical thinking skills.

❷ A new section at the end of the book, **A Quick Guide to Integrating Research into Your Own Writing,** supports you in one of the most challenging tasks you face: integrating source material responsibly and correctly into your own writing and avoiding plagiarism.

❸ **Integrated references to MyCompLab** throughout refer you directly to relevant sections of Pearson's MyCompLab, which can be packaged at no additional cost with this textbook.

❹ **An expanded discussion of media literacy** in Chapter 1, and new sections on this topic throughout the book, help you understand how to read images as well as texts with a critical eye.

❺ Chapter 3, "The Structure of Argument," now features a section on **summary writing** and its connection to close reading and critical thinking.

❻ Chapter 5, "The Language of Argument— Definition," includes a new section, **Shifting Definitions**, which traces the migration of meaning and how that migration reflects changes in the culture.

❼ Chapter 6, "Fallacious Arguments," now includes **red herring** in its list of fallacies.

❽ Chapter 8, "The Language of Argument—Style," now focuses more clearly on **parallel structure** and **repetition** as building blocks of style.

PEARSON

DATE DUE

MAY 0 8 2013	

Writing Logically, Thinking Critically

SIXTH EDITION

Sheila Cooper
Rosemary Patton

Longman

New York   San Francisco   Boston
London   Toronto   Sydney   Tokyo   Singapore   Madrid
Mexico City   Munich   Paris   Cape Town   Hong Kong   Montreal

Senior Sponsoring Editor: Virginia L. Blanford
Senior Marketing Manager: Sandra McGuire
Senior Supplements Editor: Donna Campion
Production Manager: Ellen MacElree
Project Coordination, Text Design, and Electronic Page Makeup: Nesbitt Graphics, Inc.
Cover Designer/Manager: Wendy Ann Fredericks
Cover Photo: Pete Atkinson/Photographer's Choice/Getty Images
Photo Researcher: Jody Potter
Senior Manufacturing Buyer: Dennis J. Para
Printer and Binder: R.R. Donnelley & Sons, Harrisonburg
Cover Printer: R.R. Donnelley & Sons, Harrisonburg

For permission to use copyrighted material, grateful acknowledgment is made to the copyright
holders on pp. 234–235, which are hereby made part of this copyright page.

Library of Congress Cataloging-in-Publication Data

Cooper, Sheila, 1946–
    Writing logically, thinking critically / Sheila Cooper, Rosemary Patton. — 6th ed.
      p. cm.
    ISBN 978-0-205-66856-4 — ISBN 978-0-205-66858-8 (exam copy)
      1. English language—Rhetoric. 2. Critical thinking. 3. Academic writing. 4. Logic. I.
Patton, Rosemary. II. Title.

PE1408.C5485 2009
808'.042—dc22
                                                2009004338

1 2 3 4 5 6 7 8 9 10—DOH—12 11 10 09

Longman
is an imprint of

www.pearsonhighered.com

ISBN 13: 978-0-205-66856-4
ISBN 10:   0-205-66856-9

He who will not reason, is a bigot; he who cannot, is a fool; and he who dares not, is a slave.

—LORD BYRON

A mind that is stretched to a new idea never returns to its original dimension.

—OLIVER WENDELL HOLMES

The vital habits of democracy: the ability to follow an argument, grasp the point of view of another, expand the boundaries of understanding, debate the alternative purposes that might be pursued.

—JOHN DEWEY

BRIEF CONTENTS

Detailed Contents vii

Guide to Readings...xii

Preface xiv

CHAPTER 1

Thinking and Writing—A Critical Connection 1

CHAPTER 2

Inference—Critical Thought 22

CHAPTER 3

The Structure of Argument 53

CHAPTER 4

Written Argument 77

CHAPTER 5

The Language of Argument—Definition 104

CHAPTER 6

Fallacious Arguments 131

CHAPTER 7

Deductive and Inductive Argument 157

CHAPTER 8

The Language of Argument—Style 200

A Quick Guide to Integrating Research Into Your Own Writing....................210

Additional Readings 215

Text Credits...234

Index 236

DETAILED CONTENTS

Guide to Readings xii

Preface xiv

CHAPTER 1

Thinking and Writing—A Critical Connection 1

Thinking Made Visible   1

Critical Thinking   2

    AN OPEN MIND—EXAMINING YOUR WORLD VIEW   3

    CRITICAL THINKING AS SELF-DEFENSE—MEDIA LITERACY   6

Writing as a Process   10

    INVENTION STRATEGIES—GENERATING IDEAS   11

    THE FIRST DRAFT   12

    THE TIME TO BE CRITICAL   13

Audience and Purpose   14

WRITING ASSIGNMENT 1   Considering Your Audience and Purpose   15

    E-MAIL AND TEXT MESSAGING   15

Reason, Intuition, Imagination, and Metaphor   17

    SUMMARY   20

    KEY TERMS   21

CHAPTER 2

Inference—Critical Thought 22

What Is an Inference?   22

    HOW RELIABLE IS AN INFERENCE?   23

What Is a Fact?   24

    FACTS AND JOURNALISM   25

What Is a Judgment?   26

Achieving a Balance Between Inference and Facts   31

    FACTS ONLY   32

    INFERENCES ONLY   33

Reading Critically   34

WRITING ASSIGNMENT 2   Reconstructing the Lost Tribe   35

Making Inferences—Analyzing Images   37

    EXAMINING AN AD   41

Making Inferences—Writing About Fiction   44

WRITING ASSIGNMENT 3   Interpreting Fiction   46

WRITING ASSIGNMENT 4   Analyzing Fiction   48

   SUMMARY   52

   KEY TERMS   52

CHAPTER 3

The Structure of Argument 53

Premises and Conclusions   54

Distinguishing Between Premises and Conclusions   55

Standard Form   56

WRITING ASSIGNMENT 5   Creating a Political Handout   59

Ambiguous Argument Structure   60

Hidden Assumptions in Argument   62

   DANGERS OF HIDDEN ASSUMPTIONS   64

   HIDDEN ASSUMPTIONS AND STANDARD FORM   65

   HIDDEN ASSUMPTIONS AND AUDIENCE AWARENESS   68

Summaries   69

   STRATEGIES FOR WRITING A SUMMARY   69

   AN EXAMPLE OF A SUMMARY   70

WRITING ASSIGNMENT 6   Summarizing an Article   70

Argument and Explanation—Distinctions   72

   SUMMARY   75

   KEY TERMS   75

CHAPTER 4

Written Argument 77

Focusing Your Topic   77

   THE ISSUE   77

   THE QUESTION AT ISSUE   78

   THE THESIS   79

   TWO KINDS OF THESIS STATEMENTS   81

Shaping a Written Argument—Rhetorical Strategies   82

   THE INTRODUCTION   82

   THE DEVELOPMENT OF YOUR ARGUMENT   83

   HOW MANY PREMISES SHOULD AN ARGUMENT HAVE?   84

   THE CONCLUSION   84

A Dialectical Approach to Argument   85

   ADDRESSING COUNTERARGUMENTS   85

   HOW MUCH COUNTERARGUMENT?   86

   REFUTATION AND CONCESSION   86

   ROGERIAN STRATEGY   87

   WHEN THERE IS NO OTHER SIDE   90

Logical Connections—Coherence 91
   JOINING WORDS 91
   MORE ON COHERENCE 93
Sample Essays 93
A Two-Step Process for Writing a Complete Argument 98
WRITING ASSIGNMENT 7 Arguing Both Sides of an Issue 98
WRITING ASSIGNMENT 8 Taking a Stand 102
   SUMMARY 103
   KEY TERMS 103

CHAPTER 5

The Language of Argument—Definition 104
Definition and Perception 104
   WHO CONTROLS THE DEFINITIONS? 104
   DEFINING OURSELVES 105
   SHIFTING DEFINITIONS 106
   DEFINITION: THE SOCIAL SCIENCES AND GOVERNMENT 108
Language: An Abstract System of Symbols 108
   THE IMPORTANCE OF CONCRETE EXAMPLES 111
   ABSTRACTIONS AND EVASION 114
   EUPHEMISM AND CONNOTATION 115
Definition in Written Argument 116
   APPOSITIVES—A STRATEGY FOR DEFINING TERMS WITHIN THE SENTENCE 116
   APPOSITIVES AND ARGUMENT 118
   PUNCTUATION OF APPOSITIVES 118
   EXTENDED DEFINITION 120
WRITING ASSIGNMENT 9 Determining Your State's Position on Gay Marriage 123
WRITING ASSIGNMENT 10 Composing an Argument Based on a Definition 124
   INVENTING A NEW WORD TO FILL A NEED 128
WRITING ASSIGNMENT 11 Creating a New Word 129
   SUMMARY 130
   KEY TERMS 130

CHAPTER 6

Fallacious Arguments 131
What Is a Fallacious Argument? 131
   APPEAL TO AUTHORITY 132
   APPEAL TO FEAR 133
   APPEAL TO PITY 133
   BEGGING THE QUESTION 134
   DOUBLE STANDARD 135
   EQUIVOCATION 136

FALSE ANALOGY   137

FALSE CAUSE   139

FALSE DILEMMA   140

HASTY GENERALIZATION   141

PERSONAL ATTACK   141

POISONING THE WELL   142

RED HERRING   142

SLIPPERY SLOPE   143

STRAW MAN   143

WRITING ASSIGNMENT 12   Analyzing an Extended Argument   151

KEY TERMS   154

CHAPTER 7

Deductive and Inductive Argument 157

Key Distinctions   157

(1) NECESSITY VERSUS PROBABILITY   157

(2) FROM GENERAL TO SPECIFIC, SPECIFIC TO GENERAL   158

The Relationship Between Induction and Deduction   159

Deductive Reasoning   164

CLASS LOGIC   164

RELATIONSHIPS BETWEEN CLASSES   165

INCLUSION   165

EXCLUSION   166

OVERLAP   166

CLASS LOGIC AND THE SYLLOGISM   168

THE SUBJECT AND THE PREDICATE   169

TRUTH, VALIDITY, AND SOUNDNESS   169

GUILT BY ASSOCIATION   171

MORE ON SYLLOGISMS   172

Hypothetical Arguments   176

THE VALID HYPOTHETICAL ARGUMENT   176

THE INVALID HYPOTHETICAL ARGUMENT   177

NECESSARY AND SUFFICIENT CONDITIONS   177

HYPOTHETICAL CHAINS   178

HYPOTHETICAL CLAIMS AND EVERYDAY REASONING   179

Inductive Reasoning   183

GENERALIZATION   183

THE DIRECTION OF INDUCTIVE REASONING   184

TESTING INDUCTIVE GENERALIZATIONS   185

CRITERIA FOR EVALUATING STATISTICAL GENERALIZATIONS   185

HASTY GENERALIZATIONS   187

THINKING CRITICALLY ABOUT SURVEYS AND STATISTICS   188

MISTAKING CORRELATION FOR CAUSATION   189

EPIDEMIOLOGY   190

CONSIDERING THE SOURCE   191

WRITING ASSIGNMENT 13   Questioning Generalizations   196

WRITING ASSIGNMENT 14   Conducting a Survey: A Collaborative Project   196

SUMMARY   197

KEY TERMS   198

CHAPTER 8

The Language of Argument—Style 200

Parallelism   200

THE STRUCTURE OF PARALLELISM   200

LOGIC OF THE PARALLEL SERIES   202

EMPHASIZING IDEAS WITH PARALLELISM   203

Sharpening Sentences, Eliminating Wordiness   204

CONCRETE SUBJECTS   205

ACTIVE AND PASSIVE VERBS   205

PASSIVE VERBS AND EVASION   206

WHEN THE PASSIVE IS APPROPRIATE   206

CONSISTENT SENTENCE SUBJECTS   207

SUMMARY   209

KEY TERMS   209

A Quick Guide to Integrating Research into Your Own Writing 210

WHERE TO BEGIN   210

THREE OPTIONS FOR INCLUDING RESEARCH   211

BLEND QUOTATIONS AND PARAPHRASES INTO YOUR OWN WRITING   211

MAKE THE PURPOSE CLEAR   212

PUNCTUATION AND FORMAT OF QUOTATIONS   212

OMITTING WORDS FROM A DIRECT QUOTATION—ELLIPSIS   213

PLAGIARISM   213

Additional Readings 215

"Is Google Making Us Stupid?" Nicholas Carr   215

"Blinded by Science," Chris Mooney   223

"When Human Rights Extend to Nonhumans," Donald G. McNeil Jr.   231

Text Credits   234

Index   236

GUIDE TO READINGS

CHAPTER 1

Thinking and Writing—A Critical Connection 1

"The Problem with New Data," Jon Carroll   4
NEWSPAPER COLUMN

"The Child's Draft," Anne Lamott   12
BOOK EXCERPT

"The Writer," Richard Wilbur   19
POEM

CHAPTER 2

Inference—Critical Thought 22

"The Facts of Media Life," Max Frankel   25
ESSAY

"The Totleigh Riddles," John Cotton   29
POEMS

"Mirror," Sylvia Plath   30
POEM

"Metaphors," Sylvia Plath   30
POEM

"On Me!" Philip Levine   31
POEM

"The Painful Images of War," Clark Hoyt   38
EDITORIAL

"Grace Period," Will Baker   44
FICTION

"Hostess," Donald Mangum   46
FICTION

"Hills Like White Elephants," Ernest Hemingway   48
FICTION

CHAPTER 3

The Structure of Argument 53

"AP Courses—Mounting Burden, Declining Benefit," Nathan Yan   70
STUDENT ESSAY

"Bush Remarks Roil Debate over Teaching of Evolution," Elizabeth Bumiller   73
NEWSPAPER ARTICLE

"Of God and the Case for Unintelligent Design," Lisa Fullam   73
NEWSPAPER ARTICLE

CHAPTER 4

Written Argument 77

"Could It Be That Video Games Are Good for Kids?" Steven Johnson   88
EDITORIAL

"College Athletes—Special Admissions?"   94
    STUDENT ESSAY

"A Case for Affirmative Action," Cynthia Tucker   97
    EDITORIAL

CHAPTER 5

The Language of Argument—Definition 104

"The Voice You Hear When You Read Silently," Thomas Lux   110
    POEM

"Let Gays Marry," Andrew Sullivan   121
    ESSAY

"Leave Marriage Alone," William Bennett   122
    ESSAY

"Radical" [1]   126
    STUDENT ESSAY

"Radical" [2]   127
    STUDENT ESSAY

"Slut," Maureen Dowd   127
    EDITORIAL

CHAPTER 6

Fallacious Arguments 131

"On Date Rape," Camille Paglia   152
    ESSAY

"Boxing, Doctors—Round Two," Lowell Cohn   152
    NEWSPAPER COLUMN

CHAPTER 7

Deductive and Inductive Argument 157

"Mechanics' Logic," Robert Pirsig   160
    BOOK EXCERPT

"To His Coy Mistress," Andrew Marvell   181
    POEM

"Dulce Et Decorum Est," Wilfred Owen   182
    POEM

"Preventive Medicine, Properly Practiced," Dr. Susan Love   194
    ESSAY

Additional Readings 215

"Is Google Making Us Stupid?" Nicholas Carr   215
    ESSAY

"Blinded By Science," Chris Mooney   223
    ESSAY

"When Human Rights Extend To Nonhumans," Donald G. McNeil Jr.   231
    ESSAY

PREFACE

Good writing is good thinking.

—NEW YORK TIMES MAGAZINE

Once again we have designed this new edition as the central text in a course devoted to composition with an emphasis on argumentation and critical thinking. We have updated essays, examples, and exercises for relevancy. We have also added some fresh cartoons, as we believe these visual images with punch lines reinforce the text. In response to helpful suggestions from those who have used previous editions, we have tightened, rearranged, and clarified material throughout the book. A feature of this text that makes it stand out among others in its field is the inclusion of fiction and poetry. For all readings, we provide a separate list for quick reference.

WHAT'S NEW IN THIS EDITION

- **More challenging readings.** Our closing section, Additional Readings, represents a major revision. In response to our readers' request for longer, more complex readings, we have added three essays with questions: "Is Google Making Us Stupid?" by Nicholas Carr, "Blinded by Science" by Chris Mooney, and "When Human Rights Extend to Nonhumans" by Donald G. McNeil Jr. All three address contemporary topics that will engage your students and challenge their reading and critical thinking skills.

- **MyCompLab.com.** The other major revision is the addition of "A Quick Guide to Integrating Research into Your Own Writing," which replaces the former Chapter 9. For a complete source of information on research and documentation, we refer you to Longman's MyCompLab.com. All users of *Writing Logically, Thinking Critically* may have access to this useful website if it is ordered packaged, at no additional cost, with this text. MyCompLab keeps up with the changing standards of research and documentation and provides the in-depth coverage that this book does not have the necessary space for. Instructors should request access to MyCompLab when ordering this text. We make reference to MyCompLab throughout this text when additional content would be useful. The new MyCompLab is a leader in online instruction, providing multimedia tutorials and exercises for writing, grammar, and research. Created after years of extensive research and in partnership with composition faculty and students across the country, the new MyCompLab provides help for writers and useful tools for instructors.

ADDITIONAL UPDATES AND REVISIONS

- In Chapter 1, "Thinking and Writing—A Critical Connection," we have expanded and updated our discussion of media literacy and clarified the relationship between thinking and writing.

- In Chapter 2, "Inference—Critical Thought," we added Hemingway's "Hills Like White Elephants" and a new exercise on inference. For media literacy, we've added an essay, "The Painful Images of War," and in Analyzing Images, we've updated the ads.

- In Chapter 3, "The Structure of Argument," we feature summary writing and its connection to close reading and critical thinking.

- In Chapter 4, "Written Argument," we describe all aspects of a well-written argument. We have updated topics in both examples and writing assignments and have highlighted crucial information, making it accessible to students.

- In Chapter 5, "The Language of Argument—Definition," we have added a new section, "Shifting Definitions," tracing the migration of meaning and how that migration reflects changes in the culture. We have also added a new definition essay, "Slut," by Maureen Dowd.

- In Chapter 6, "Fallacious Arguments," we have added the often-mentioned "red herring" to our list of fallacies.

- In Chapter 7, "Deductive and Inductive Argument," we have included a section on the hypothetical argument, expanding our coverage of deductive reasoning. We include two poems in this section: "To His Coy Mistress" by Andrew Marvell and "Dulce Et Decorum Est" by Wilfred Owen. We've also added a section on epidemiology to expand our discussion of inductive reasoning.

- We have greatly reduced Chapter 8, "The Language of Argument—Style," focusing on parallel structure and repetition as building blocks of style. We also emphasize sharpening sentence structure and eliminating wordiness.

- A brief new section at the end of the book, A Quick Guide to Integrating Research into Your Own Writing, provides clear, succinct guidance on using sources correctly and responsibly.

SEQUENCE

We suggest that instructors follow the sequence of chapters in order, with the exception of Chapter 8 (sentence polishing) and the end-of-book materials A Quick Guide to Integrating Research into Your Own Writing and Additional Readings, which can be referred to throughout the course. Some instructors, however, prefer to create their own order to suit the needs of their particular class.

As before, we assume that *Writing Logically, Thinking Critically* will be most effective in classes where the students have already completed an introductory semester or quarter of composition. But many find the book works well as the foundation in a first-year writing class. Some secondary school instructors have been enthusiastic about its success in their advanced composition classes. Upper-division college students preparing for the LSAT, the qualifying exam for law school, have also found the text useful.

PEDAGOGY

As in previous editions, we include a number of collaborative activities to encourage an interactive approach to learning. Most of the exercises and assignments can, in fact, be approached collaboratively, as can many writing projects in the business world. Writing assignments and exercises invite a broad range of responses that should cover the demands of writing across a diverse curriculum.

INSTRUCTOR'S MANUAL

We suggest you turn to the Instructor's Manual (0-205-66857-7) to find more strategies for each chapter and a few additional student essays related to select writing assignments.

ACKNOWLEDGMENTS

We remain grateful to our students, a few of whom are represented here. Thanks also to those instructors who have used *Writing Logically, Thinking Critically*, some of whom are among those who offered invaluable advice for this revision: Kamala Balasubramanian, Grossmont College; Chitralekha Duttagupta, Arizona State University; Jean S. Filetti, Christopher Newport University; Matthew Fleming, Cuesta College; Joy Lynch, Contra Costa College; Jeff Rice, University of Missouri; and Johnny Saraf, Santa Rosa Jr. College.

Sheila Cooper
Rosemary Patton

CHAPTER 1

Thinking and Writing—
A Critical Connection

It is doubtful whether a man [or woman?] ever brings his faculties to bear with their full force on a subject until he writes upon it.

—CICERO

It would hardly seem debatable that to write well we need to think clearly. And the evidence is strong for concluding that writing about ideas can help to clarify them. Taking this notion a step further, many would argue that the act of writing can create ideas, can lead writers to discover what they think. Language, according to many scholars, can give birth to thought, and written language provides a way to refine our thoughts since, unlike speech, it can be manipulated until it accurately reflects our thinking.

THINKING MADE VISIBLE

Consider writing then as thinking made visible, as thinking in slow motion, a process whereby we can inspect and reflect on what we are thinking about. Writing doesn't simply convey thought; it also forges it. It is a two-way street, both expressing and generating ideas. Writer Isaac Asimov expresses his satisfaction with the link between thinking and writing:

> Thinking is the activity I love best, and writing to me is simply thinking through my fingers.
> As novelist E. M. Forster put it, "How can I tell what I think till I see what I've said?"

Many writers have groaned over the pain of writing. In his poem *The Four Quartets*, T. S. Eliot writes of the "intolerable wrestle/With words and meaning." New York writer Fran Lebowitz is more graphic in her complaint: "Writing is torture. It is very hard work. It's not coal mining, but it's work."

After visiting the Galapagos Islands in the 1830s, evolutionist Charles Darwin wrote to his sister from his ship, the *Beagle*, about the special challenge of reasoning on paper, the kind of writing we emphasize in this book.

> I am just now beginning to discover the difficulty of expressing one's ideas on paper. As long as it consists solely of description it is pretty easy; but where reasoning comes into play, to make a proper connection, a clearness and a moderate fluency, is to me a difficulty of which I had no idea.

Although writing and thinking may be difficult, mastery and success in both can be well worth the effort. Indeed, clear writing is often essential. If we are not able to articulate a request, a complaint, or an endorsement in precise, forceful language, we may find ourselves settling for less than we deserve. If we can't write a persuasive application, the job or graduate school position may go to someone else. Linguist Robin Lakoff, in her book *Talking Power: The Politics of Language*, puts it this way:

> In a meritocracy such as ours, we believe that those who best demonstrate the ability to think and persuade should have the lion's share of power. Articulateness according to the rules goes a long way; and its possessors are assumed to possess intelligence and virtue as inseparable concomitants. People who say things right, who plead their cases well, will be listened to and their suggestions acted upon. They will make the money, win the offices, find love, get all the goodies their society has to give.

CRITICAL THINKING

If, as we maintain, there is a strong relationship between thinking clearly and writing well—if one skill strengthens the other—then integrating the two as a course of study makes sense. But what do we mean by "thinking clearly"? For our purposes, we have found it helpful to narrow our focus and concentrate on the phrase **critical thinking**. This term has assumed a central position in both academic and public life and is variously defined today.

In most contexts today, the term **critical** means censorious or faultfinding, but it comes to us from the Greek *kriticos* and Latin *criticus*, meaning able to discern or separate. It is this sense of critical that we have in mind—discerning or discriminating thought characterized by careful analysis and judgment. As student Denise Selleck describes it, "Thinking critically is the ability to understand a concept fully, taking in different sides of an issue or idea while not being swayed by the propaganda or other fraudulent methods used to promote it." She recognizes the importance of an **open mind** and the element of **self-defense** implicit in critical thinking.

An Open Mind—Examining Your World View

To have an open mind is to listen attentively to the views of others. It is, however, equally important to be aware of where our views come from. Cultures, subgroups within those cultures, and families within these groups tend to share what is called a **world view**, a set of assumptions about the world and the behavior of people in it. We may harbor prejudices about groups that cloud our thinking and restrict fair judgment. Many of these attitudes grow from the contexts of our lives that we take for granted—the opinions of parents and friends, our ethnic and religious backgrounds.

Where does the weakness in Jennifer's defense lie?

In the words of Professor Louis Menand, "Ideas are produced not by individuals, but by groups of individuals—ideas are social . . . ideas do not develop according to some inner logic of their own, but are entirely dependent, like germs, on their human carriers and the environment." Knowledge and ideas are not absolutes but are subject to the time, place, and circumstances in which they are expressed. For instance, up until the twentieth century, women were considered incapable of making rational decisions on political issues and thus were denied the vote. Today, most cultures recognize that such a view was **socially constructed**, not inherently true. Harvard professor Henry Louis Gates Jr. sees history as "a chronicle of formerly acceptable outrages":

> Once upon a time, perfectly decent folk took it for granted that watching two gladiators hack each other to death was just the thing to do on a summer afternoon, that making slaves of Africans was a good deal for all concerned. What were they thinking? You could say that posterity is a hanging judge, except that sooner or later capital punishment, too, will turn up on that chronicle of outrages.

We have an inborn tendency to filter out information that doesn't match our biases. We are inclined to remember news that matches our world view and dismiss facts that contradict it. In his book *True Enough: Learning to Live in a Post-Fact Society,* Farhad Manjoo, a staff writer at Salon.com, emphasizes this point. We resist information "that doesn't mesh with our preconceived beliefs." Manjoo cites two studies to illustrate this point. Students at Dartmouth and Princeton were shown a film clip of a football game between their two teams and asked to note instances of cheating. "Each group, watching the same clip, was convinced that the other side had cheated worse." A similar manipulation of facts occurred when Stanford students, one group favoring the death penalty and the other opposing it, "were shown the same two studies: one suggested that executions have a deterrent effect that reduces subsequent murders, and the other [study] doubted that [conclusion]." Each group of students "found the study that supported their position to be well-conducted and persuasive and the other one to be profoundly flawed."

To offer another example, when the *NewsHour* on PBS was showing photos of US soldiers killed in Iraq, many opposing the war saw this as humanitarian reporting honoring our troops, while some supporting the war thought it was a way of undermining the war effort.

Questioning our personal world view can be one of the most challenging steps in our growth as critical thinkers. In the following essay, newspaper columnist Jon Carroll points out that our world view, our opinions, can sometimes blind us to the truth.

The Problem with New Data
JON CARROLL

You may have heard that Dr. James Hansen, the man who first popularized the   1
notion that carbon dioxide levels and global warming were inextricably linked, has issued a new report saying that further studies have revealed that in fact other heat-trapping chemicals—methane, chlorofluorocarbons, particulate matter like coal soot, plus other smog-creating chemicals—are probably more responsible for the trend than carbon dioxide.

Any advance in scientific understanding is good news. Hansen's report is par-   2
ticularly interesting because it is contrary to his previous position, indicating that he is able to separate his professional ego from his scientific conclusions and change his mind right out in public.

This is less usual than it should be. We are all afraid of being wrong, and we   3
will tend to cling to our opinions in the face of mounting evidence to the contrary. In ideal science, all opinions are merely way stations on the road to the truth; in real-world science, though, opinions are the basis of reputation and income, and the difference between the establishment view and the revealed truth is not easy to discern from the outside.

And there's another reason why Hansen's conclusions are good news—it's a lot   4
easier to control the production of these new culprits than it is the production of carbon dioxide, which is the unavoidable byproduct of the burning of all fossil fuels, as well as the gas that emerges from our mouths every time we exhale.

And yet, Hansen's report was greeted with considerable trepidation. The   5
results might be misinterpreted; big polluters might twist the data; Congress might have a fig leaf to cover its natural inclination to let big corporations do whatever they want.

This is what happens when politics and science start to commingle. In politics,   6
opinions—they are called "positions" or "principles"—are the official yardstick

of integrity. People who change their minds are considered to be weak, are said to waffle.

Someone who has staked out a tough position on carbon dioxide would be   7
seriously uninterested in data suggesting it's not really the problem. Someone who supported the Kyoto Protocol—which identified carbon dioxide as the principal culprit—would feel the urge to attack Hansen, who would be identified as a "former ally."

Following the facts wherever they lead is always dangerous in the political arena.   8

In fact, Hansen has not changed his position on global warming at all. He is still   9
of the opinion that it forms a significant threat to the short-term (less than 100 years) ecological health of the planet. But he has a nuanced and evolving view of the causes.

"Nuanced" and "evolving" will, in the political world, buy you a cup of coffee,   10
provided you also have $2.

The urge to hang on tight knows no ideology. The gun lobby reflexively   11
brings up the slippery slope and the Second Amendment no matter what the issue, making something like trigger locks as controversial as universal confiscation of firearms.

Multiculturalists reflexively support bilingual education, despite new studies   12
suggesting that kids from different cultures learn better when a single language is the classroom standard.

Look into the heart of your opinions: What if early detection of breast cancer   13
had no real effect on mortality rates? What if secondhand smoke turned out to be no health risk at all? What if free condoms for every child lowered disease rates by 50 percent? What if air bags were bad, or good, or whatever is the opposite of what you currently believe they are?

It's the brain lock issue. We want to believe something because it fits with the   14
other things we believe, because the people we know believe it, because the people who believe the other things are loathsome.

Alas, the universe of facts is not a democracy. If it were, I'd vote for fried pork   15
rinds as a health food.

EXERCISE 1A

Examining Your World View

1. Professor Henry Louis Gates Jr. lists gladiators and slavery as two of the "acceptable outrages" that history chronicles. We added denying women the vote. As a class, add to this list.

2. Look closely at these "outrages"—gladiators, slavery, women being denied the vote, and others generated by your responses to question 1 above. In each case, ask which group held this view and what they had to gain from supporting this belief.

3. Gates predicts that one day capital punishment will be viewed as a "formerly acceptable outrage." Here's a chance to "deconstruct" a socially constructed

belief, to examine the roots of your own beliefs. As Jon Carroll says, "Look into the heart of your opinions." Write a paragraph stating your position on capital punishment and include the views held by your family, friends, and religion (if you belong to a religious group). Then compare paragraphs with a small group of your classmates. What have you learned about your world view? Putting such views into writing or even formulating what you think can be a challenge. There is no right or wrong answer here—just a critical exploration of your thoughts discussed with your peers.

(For a more complex discussion of Carroll's point about interpreting and reporting on science, see "Blinded by Science" in Additional Readings.)

Critical Thinking as Self-Defense—Media Literacy

In this age of information we are surrounded by facts, all of which are open to interpretation. Such interpretation requires critical thought. And if our democracy is to endure, we all have a moral responsibility to engage in deliberate, critical thinking. How else can we make informed decisions about political candidates and issues? But finding unbiased sources can be difficult.

Advertising and the media, with which we are confronted every day, require careful critical scrutiny if we are to protect ourselves from false claims, questionable judgments, and confusing or deceptive arguments designed to manipulate us for personal gain. We can be hard-pressed to distinguish factual information from promotion. Television infomercials push new products even as they masquerade as objective reports. Sandwiched in between the information we're seeking on the Internet, advertisers bombard us with an increasing array of products and services for sale, matching their ads to our Web searching habits.

With the explosion of websites, blogs, podcasts, RSS feeds, and **social-networking** sites—such as **Facebook, MySpace,** and **Twitter**—sources of information have multiplied dramatically. A **Google** search has become indispensable to finding information online, but caution is essential here because the sites listed are not necessarily given in order of reliability or of usefulness. You must exercise the same caution when consulting the online encyclopedia **Wikipedia** because entries are checked for accuracy only by users, not by experts, and so frequently contain errors. (For expanded discussion of evaluating sources, see "Research" on MyCompLab.com, and for a fresh perspective on our use of the Internet, read "Is Google Making Us Stupid?" in Additional Readings.)

Expanding their options today, most newspapers reserve considerable content for their websites. The *New York Times,* for example, prints a short digest of online articles each day, and most papers now make their content and archives available online. Many magazines and scholarly journals also provide online access. But there's a danger in this abundance. We can lose our way in the broad array of useful information mixed in with trivial gossip and entertainment.

In a letter to the *New York Times*, Edward Deitch (until recently at NBC News) comments on a front-page article that discussed online news sources.

> Re "Finding Political News Online, Young Viewers Pass It Along"
>
> It is one thing for young people (and even the not so young) to get caught up in the excitement of a charismatic presidential campaign and "to rely on friends and online connections for news to come to them."
>
> But it seems to me that in this age of news à la carte, when we can easily limit ourselves to just what we are interested in and have it served up to our computers, mobile phones and BlackBerrys, we must also redouble our efforts to look for the vital news of the day, from both here and around the world, that will affect our lives.
>
> That means we may have to click through a news Web site, sit through an informed news broadcast, or, yes, even spend a few minutes thumbing through the pages of a newspaper.
>
> Let's not confuse what excites us with what we need to know.

Headlines, lead paragraphs, unmediated blogs, and often careless or inflammatory responses in the blogosphere can be misleading or emphasize only one element in a complex story. Like individuals, all forms of media reflect a world view. Media watch organizations, whose goal it is to expose bias, have in fact their own bias or world view.

Addressing the issue of bias, a recent segment of public television's *NewsHour* focused on media coverage of the Middle East conflict. Included in the discussion were representatives from CNN, the *Boston Globe*, and two media watch groups. The representative from one of these watch groups claimed that "the media has tended to airbrush away Palestinian extremism," that certain Palestinians are portrayed as being moderate when they're not. The representative of the other media watch group claimed that the media was remiss in not criticizing "Israel's brutal occupation" of Palestine. Their world views are obviously different.

Many journalists faced with this kind of criticism struggle to be fair. The editor from the *Boston Globe* focused on the challenge of choosing unbiased language to describe the conflict: "The term 'occupied territories' is a matter of controversy. Some would rather say 'disputed land.' Some people will talk about an 'incursion' into the Palestinian territories. Palestinians tend to prefer the word 'invasion.'" (See Chapter 5 for further discussion of language and connotation.)

Or the media may make an explicit decision about what it will or will not cover, as it did in the aftermath of September 11 when it decided not to show film of victims jumping from the World Trade Center. In the case of the Middle East conflict, a CNN executive made explicit a policy of not giving suicide bombers and their families the same amount of coverage the network will give to the victims of terrorism "because there's no moral equivalence between the perpetrators of mass murder and the victims of mass murder."

As a reader and researcher, you must examine your sources for bias and its impact on the information you're seeking. For example, if you're writing a paper on global warming, it's important to know that magazines and Web information published by Greenpeace or the Sierra Club support environmental protections and thus emphasize the dangers of global warming. The American Enterprise Institute (www.aei.org) or the *National Review* (www.nationalreviewonline.com) are conservative organizations and are therefore more likely to downplay the dangers of climate change.

A good place to start looking at distinctions among increasingly important news websites is to compare sites recognized for a particular bias or slant. The Project for Excellence in Journalism (www.stateofthenewsmedia.org), once affiliated with the Columbia School of Journalism, attempts to be nonpartisan and discusses bias; the Daily Kos (www.dailykos.com) is generally considered very liberal; Media Research Center (www.mediaresearch.org) has a strong conservative slant. Nothing in these names suggests their bias. Onthemedia.org is another useful

source generally considered balanced. And new in news gathering is the trend toward nonprofit sites funded by philanthropists, such as Propublica.org. While its goal is "journalism in the public interest," it is helpful to know that its funders are loyal Democrats. At present, www.HuffingtonPost.com is dominating the Internet news sources. By the time you read this text, a whole new roster of sources will no doubt be populating the Web. The point here is that when you select a controversial topic, particularly one that involves a political issue, you should compare varied sources on your subject and ask teachers and librarians about the bias of a particular source if it isn't immediately evident. (Consult MyCompLab.com and "Blinded by Science" in Additional Readings for a more in-depth discussion of bias.)

EXERCISE 1B

Scrutinizing the Media

Read these two excerpts from different papers, the *New York Times* and the *San Francisco Chronicle*, reporting on the same Supreme Court decision.

High Court Upholds Buffer Zone of 15 Feet at Abortion Clinics

LINDA GREENHOUSE

Washington, Feb. 19—The Supreme Court today upheld a lower court's order keeping demonstrators at least 15 feet away from the doorways and driveways of clinics in upstate New York that were the targets of blockages and boisterous protests. The decision reaffirmed the Court's broadly protective approach toward maintaining access for patients entering abortion clinics. . . .

On the same date, the *San Francisco Chronicle*, relying on the *Los Angeles Times* for its information, reported:

Abortion Foes Entitled to Confront Patients Supreme Court Says It's Free Speech

DAVID G. SAVAGE
Los Angeles Times

Washington, Feb. 19—Abortion protesters have a free-speech right to confront pregnant women on the sidewalks outside clinics and to urge them vehemently not to go ahead with the procedure, the Supreme Court ruled yesterday.

The 8–1 decision calls into doubt a wave of new city ordinances and judges' orders that have barred persistent protesters from confronting and harassing doctors, nurses and patients outside clinics. . . .

1. How are the two articles different?

2. What conclusions might you draw about the writers who presented the two differing slants on the abortion clinic ruling quoted above?

3. Look for a single news story that is reported in different ways. Compare two different print versions of a story from the same date, as we illustrate. Quote from these two stories and describe how different sources present the same facts.

WRITING AS A PROCESS

What is written without effort is in general read without pleasure.

—SAMUEL JOHNSON

Where do you begin when faced with a writing assignment? Many students turn to the five-paragraph essay format—introduction, three supporting paragraphs, and conclusion—and choose material that will fit easily into this preconceived mold. Writers rely on this formula because they fear that without it they will produce an incoherent essay. They assume that if they follow it, their writing will at least be organized. Even inexperienced writers must learn to let go of this "safety net" because, although it may save them from anxiety and a disorganized essay, it can also determine the content of the essay; if an idea does not fit easily into the mold, the writer must discard it. This rigid structure prevents writers from exploring their topic, from following thoughts that may lead to interesting insights, and from allowing the material, the content, to find the shape that best suits it.

The most common misconception that student writers have is that good writers sit at their desks and produce in one sitting a polished, mechanically correct, cohesive piece of writing. If students are unable to do this, they conclude that they cannot write and approach all writing tasks with dread. As a first step toward improving their writing, students must discard this myth and replace it with a realistic picture of how writers write. Hemingway, in Paris writing his first collection of short stories, *In Our Time*, spent whole mornings on single paragraphs. While no one expects students, whose goal it is to produce a competent essay, to spend this kind of time on their writing, students, like most writers, must realize that writing is a complex intellectual act, that it involves many separate tasks, and that the mind is simply not able to handle all of these tasks at once. As writer Henry Miller saw it, "Writing, like life itself, is a voyage of discovery." Let's look at the distinct tasks involved in the act of writing a paper on this voyage:

Generating ideas

Conducting research (if necessary)

Focusing a topic

Establishing a thesis

Organizing the essay

Organizing paragraphs

Providing transitions between sentences and paragraphs

Choosing appropriate diction (word choice)

Polishing sentences for fluency

Correcting grammar, usage, spelling, and punctuation

Each of these tasks could, of course, be broken down further. What is the solution to this problem, this mental overload that writing forces on us? The answer is that it must be done in stages.

Writing is a **process** that breaks down into roughly three stages—**creating**, **shaping**, and **correcting**. A common error students make is to focus their energy on what should be the last stage (correcting) at the beginning, when the focus should be on the creative stage of the writing process. The effect of this misplaced attention is to inhibit creative thinking. It is essential that the writer give ample time to the first stage, to generating ideas, to following impulsive thoughts even if they may initially appear unrelated or irrelevant. At this stage a writer must allow himself to experience confusion, to be comfortable with chaos; he must learn to trust the writing process, to realize that out of this chaos a logical train of thought will gradually emerge. Most important of all, writers must learn to suspend all criticism as they explore their topic and their thinking.

Invention Strategies—Generating Ideas

Two concrete methods for beginning this exploration of your topic are brainstorming and freewriting, one or both of which you may already be familiar with.

To **brainstorm**, simply put the topic of the writing assignment at the top of a blank piece of paper or your screen. Then jot down words or phrases that come to mind as you think about this topic—as many words as possible, even if you are not sure they relate directly. After brainstorming, look at your list: circle ideas that you want to develop, draw lines through those that are decidedly unrelated or uninteresting, and draw arrows or make lists of ideas that are connected to one another. At this point you should be able to go to the next stage, organizing your essay either by writing an outline or simply by listing main points that you want to develop into paragraphs. Brainstorming is particularly effective with two or more people.

In **freewriting**, you begin by writing your topic on a blank sheet, but instead of jotting down words and phrases, you write continuously, using sentences. These sentences do not have to be mechanically correct, nor do they have to be connected. The only rule of freewriting is that you may not stop writing; you may not put down your pen or leave the keyboard for a set length of time. After freewriting for five to ten minutes, read over your freewriting, circling ideas that you find interesting or insightful. Now you may do another freewriting on the idea or ideas you have circled, or you may try to formulate a **thesis** or list ideas you want to develop. (For a detailed discussion of your thesis, see Chapter 4.)

These methods have two things in common. They are relatively painless ways to begin the writing process, and they allow you to circumvent your own worst enemy, self-criticism—the voice that says, "That's not right," "That's not what I mean," "This doesn't make sense." Critical evaluation of your writing is necessary but self-defeating if you are critical at the beginning. In addition, freewriting may offer surprising access to ideas you never knew you had.

If your paper requires research, you will want to start reading relevant journals and books and exploring Web sites. You may have started this process when searching for a topic. As you read you will need to take notes either on note cards, in a reading journal, or on a computer where you can store them until you are ready to print them out. No matter the source, be sure to record the data necessary for documentation (see *Integrating Research into Your Own Writing* and documentation under "Research" in MyCompLab.com). We suggest you try to brainstorm and freewrite on writing assignments throughout this text.

The First Draft

After exploring a topic in this way and examining data if you have done research, you will have a sense of what you want to say and will be ready for a first draft.

Successful writer Anne Lamott, in her book *Bird by Bird: Some Instructions on Writing and Life*, discusses the role of first drafts. Her advice grew out of her own experience as a writer and from writing classes she has taught. The title refers to a family story in which her brother, when 10 years old, was overwhelmed by a school report on birds that had been assigned three months earlier and was now due. Their father, a professional writer, put his arm around his almost weeping son and counseled, "Bird by bird, buddy. Just take it bird by bird." Good advice for writing and for life. See if you can start treating your first drafts as what Lamott calls "the child's draft" in the following excerpt from her book.

The Child's Draft

Now, practically even better news than that of short assignments is the idea of shitty first drafts. All good writers write them. This is how they end up with good second drafts and terrific third drafts. People tend to look at successful writers, writers who are getting their books published and maybe even doing well financially, and think that they sit down at their desks every morning feeling like a million dollars, feeling great about who they are and how much talent they have and what a great story they have to tell; that they take in a few deep breaths, push back their sleeves, roll their necks a few times to get all the cricks out, and dive in, typing fully formed passages as fast as a court reporter. But this is just the fantasy of the uninitiated. I know some very great writers, writers you love who write beautifully and have made a great deal of money, and not *one* of them sits down routinely feeling wildly enthusiastic and confident. Not one of them writes elegant first drafts. All right, one of them does, but we do not like her very much. We do not think that she has a rich inner life.

Very few writers really know what they are doing until they've done it. Nor do they go about their business feeling dewy and thrilled. They do not type a few stiff warm-up sentences and then find themselves bounding along like huskies across the snow. One writer I know tells me that he sits down every morning and says to himself nicely, "It's not like you don't have a choice, because you do—you can either type or kill yourself." We all often feel like we are pulling teeth, even those writers whose prose ends up being the most natural and fluid. The right words and sentences just do not come pouring out like ticker tape most of the time. . . .

For me and most of the other writers I know, writing is not rapturous. In fact, the only way I can get anything written at all is to write really, really shitty first drafts.

The first draft is the child's draft, where you let it all pour out and then let it romp all over the place, knowing that no one is going to see it and that you can shape it later. You just let this childlike part of you channel whatever voices and visions come through and onto the page. If one of the characters wants to say, "Well, so what, Mr. Poopy Pants?," you let her. No one is going to see it. If the kid wants to get into really sentimental, weepy, emotional territory, you let him. Just get it all down on paper, because there may be something great in those six crazy pages that you would never have gotten to by more rational, grown-up means. There may be something in the very last line of the very last paragraph on page six that you just love, that is so beautiful or wild that you now know what you're supposed to be writing about, more or less, or in what direction you might go—but there was no way to get to this without first getting through the first five and a half pages.

The Time to Be Critical

In agreement with Anne Lamott, teacher and writer Donald Murray, in an essay on revision titled "The Maker's Eye," points out a key difference between student writers and professional writers:

> When students complete a first draft, they consider the job of writing done—and their teachers too often agree. When professional writers complete a first draft, they usually feel that they are at the start of the writing process. When a draft is completed, the job of writing can begin.

The time to be critical arrives when you have a complete draft. Now is the time to read with a critical mind, trusting your instinct that if a word, a sentence, or a passage seems unclear or awkward to you, your reader will most likely stumble over the same word, sentence, or passage. You are ready to reshape your first draft, adding and deleting ideas, refining your thesis, polishing sentences for fluency, and finally writing another draft. Writer Zora Neale Hurston described the process as "rubbing your paragraphs with a soft cloth."

Hurston didn't have the advantage of a computer with which to move words, sentences, and paragraphs around freely. Sometimes the writing of the first draft will tell you when you need to do a little more research, expand your explanation of a point, or check some of your facts to be sure of your evidence. Computers make it relatively easy to revise your work and make repeated drafts. Just remember to save your work as you go.

Finally, you will be ready to check your spelling (in the dictionary or with a computer spellchecker) and your punctuation (in a handbook or on MyCompLab.com) and to read your essay aloud to yourself or to a friend, always ready to write another draft if it becomes necessary.

Every stage in the writing process is important. To slight one is to limit the success of the final product. There are exceptions, of course. Some writers are able to compress some of these steps, to generate and organize ideas in their minds before ever putting pen to paper. But for most of us, successful writing results from an extended writing process that is continually recursive.

As Donald Murray notes in his essay on revision, "Most readers underestimate the amount of rewriting it usually takes to produce spontaneous reading." But we can take heart from novelist Kurt Vonnegut: "This is what I find most encouraging about the writing trades: They allow mediocre people who are patient and industrious to revise their stupidity, to edit themselves into something like intelligence."

A caution: The danger in the way we have described the writing process is that we make it seem as though it progresses in three neat steps, that it proceeds in a linear fashion from prewriting to writing to rewriting and correction. In fact, this process is messy. You may be editing the final draft when you decide to add a completely new paragraph, an idea that didn't exist in any of the previous drafts. Nevertheless, if you realize that writing involves many separate tasks, that it is chaotic and unpredictable, you will not be defeated before you begin by criticizing yourself for having to do what all writers do—struggle to find your way, to express your thoughts so that you and your reader understand them.

AUDIENCE AND PURPOSE

A major distinction between writing outside the classroom and writing for a class lies in the audience to whom we write, what novelist and essayist Virginia Woolf referred to as "the face beneath the page." Job-related writing tasks, for example, include a designated audience and a real purpose. An employee may write to another company proposing a cooperative venture or to a superior requesting a raise. Readers of a newspaper often express their opinions in persuasive letters to the editor. But in a class, students are asked to write papers for the teacher to critique and grade, usually with no specified purpose beyond successfully completing an assignment. Teachers cannot remove themselves from the role of ultimate audience, but for most of the major writing assignments in this text we have suggested an additional audience to lend some authenticity to each project and to guide you in your writing choices.

Although different academic disciplines require variations in format, all good writing of an explanatory or persuasive nature is built on a balance between three essential elements: **knowledge of the subject or argument**, an identified **audience**, and a clearly defined **purpose**. The task of thinking through an argument, its audience, and purpose introduces a significant critical thinking component to an assignment. Only when you take a conscious rhetorical stance toward your writing can you have an appropriate voice and give power to what you write. The goal for you, therefore, is to **define your subject or argument, identify your audience, determine your purpose** in writing to this particular audience, and thus establish a tone that fits the writing task.

For example, suppose you have found that the college preparation provided by your high school was clearly inadequate. You have decided to take steps to remedy the situation. You will have to write letters to several different people explaining your concerns, citing supporting examples, and suggesting possible solutions. You know the issues and your purpose is clear: explaining a problem and calling for action. But the tone of your letters will vary according to your audience. The language you choose and the emphasis of your argument will be different when you direct your argument to your high school principal and teachers expressing your concerns; to local, state, and national political representatives asking for help in the improvement of secondary education; and to colleges of your choice explaining weaknesses in achievement tests. (For more on the relationship between writer and audience, see the section on Rogerian Strategy in Chapter 4.)

WRITING ASSIGNMENT 1

Considering Your Audience and Purpose

Choose any public issue that disturbs you—be it small or large, campus, community, or cosmic—and write *two* short papers (one to two pages *each*), expressing your concern. Before you start this assignment, look back in this chapter to the suggestions under "Writing as a Process" and follow the stages outlined there.

1. In the first version, direct your writing to someone connected to, perhaps responsible for, the problem you are concerned about. Your purpose here is to communicate your concern or displeasure and possibly persuade the person responsible to take appropriate action.

2. In the second version, address an individual who is in no way connected to the problem you are disturbed about. Your purpose here is to explain the situation and to inform your reader of something he may know nothing about and is not necessarily in a position to change. This means you must include more background detail than was necessary in your first paper.

Label the two papers at the top (*1*) and (*2*) and clearly identify each audience.

E-Mail and Text Messaging

The informality encouraged by e-mail and text messaging requires us to carefully consider our audience.

Language flies through cyberspace, and text messages are transcribed in a whole new shorthand. Impressions are made quickly. "2moro" for "tomorrow" is fine in a text message to a friend but not in an e-mail to an instructor or a potential employer. Getting it right in an e-mail matters in the academic and business worlds, where persuasive writing remains important.

A recent *New York Times* article, which addressed the concerns of many corporations, stressed the high cost to American companies of poorly written e-mails. A university professor, who now heads an online business writing school, quoted an example of a request he received:

> i need help I am writing a essay on writing I work for this company and my boss wants me to help improve the workers writing skills

No punctuation, no attention to the sentence. How far is this employee going? How can he help others?

Writer Brent Staples claims that the information age "requires more high-quality writing from more categories of employees than ever before."

No wonder the cry for improved writing instruction in schools and colleges keeps growing louder. In April 2008, the National Assessment of Educational Progress reported that only a quarter of the nation's high school seniors tested as proficient writers.

EXERCISE 1C

Thinking About Your Audience

Write an e-mail introducing yourself to your instructor. You will need to include information useful to your instructor, such as why you are taking this class, what writing or logic courses you have already completed, what you expect to gain from the class, and anything else bearing on your participation during the semester or quarter. If your instructor wants you to be in direct contact by e-mail, send this assignment over the Internet; if not, turn in a printout.

REASON, INTUITION, IMAGINATION, AND METAPHOR

The heart has its reasons which reason knows nothing of.

—BLAISE PASCAL

While good critical thinking depends on reason and embraces scientific methods, it can also include intuition, imagination, and creativity as well as logic. Our theory of critical thinking welcomes originality, encourages personal opinion, embraces creative thinking, and considers paradox and ambiguity to be central to thinking and writing well. Playwright Tony Kushner learned from his Columbia University Shakespeare professor that "everything in Shakespeare was paradoxical and contradictory." From this Kushner began "to understand something about life, . . . that two opposites can exist simultaneously." He embraced the notion that theatre should present contradictions and thus encourage active critical thought.

The French philosopher Blaise Pascal, quoted above, declared that there were two extravagances: "to exclude reason and to admit only reason." Contemporary biologist Richard Dawkins, supporting this view, claims that scientists must also be poets and thinks that poets are well served by a knowledge of science. Poet John Ciardi joked about reason and the natural world:

> *Who could believe an ant in theory.*
> *A giraffe in blueprint?*
> *Ten thousand doctors of what's possible*
> *Could reason half the jungle out of being.*

Sometimes a metaphor—a figure of speech that helps us understand one thing in terms of another—can carry, through images and associations, an understanding beyond what explicit reasoning can convey. Seeing comparisons, exploring relationships, is fundamental to successful critical thinking. Useful in mounting an argument, an analogy states explicitly the terms of a metaphor and concludes that two ideas or events not necessarily the same but alike in some ways will be alike in others. For example, those opposed to the Iraq war draw an analogy between our failure in Vietnam and the likelihood of similar failure in Iraq. But argument by analogy can be tricky, as we explain in Chapter 6 under "False Analogy."

In their book *Metaphors We Live By*, linguists George Lakoff and Mark Johnson point out how deeply dependent on implicit metaphor we are when we think and speak, citing the relationship between the way we use the term *argument* and the metaphors of war associated with it. Here are a few of their examples.

He attacked every weak point in my argument.
He *shot down* all of my arguments.
His criticisms were *right on target*.

Advertising frequently relies on metaphor to deliver its message. Look at the ad below and note all the words that support the war metaphor. The advertising industry

CANCER.

IT'S A WAR.

THAT'S WHY WE'RE DEVELOPING

316 NEW WEAPONS.

America's pharmaceutical companies are developing 316 new medicines to fight cancer—the second leading cause of death in the United States. Gene therapies, "magic bullet" antibodies, and light-activated medicines are all new weapons in the high-tech, high-stakes war against cancer. Pharmaceutical company researchers have already discovered medicines that are allowing more and more cancer survivors to say, "I won the battle." We hope one day we can all say, "We won the war."

America's Pharmaceutical Companies

Leading the way in the search for cures

www.searchforcures.org

knows the power of such metaphors, and the medical profession casts many of its approaches to disease in the same language. Strong metaphors create images often more powerful than simple presentation of facts.

In the following poem, Richard Wilbur uses metaphor to describe his daughter's struggle to produce a story.

THE WRITER

In her room at the prow of the house
Where light breaks, and the windows are tossed with linden,
My daughter is writing a story.

I pause in the stairwell, hearing
From her shut door a commotion of typewriter-keys
Like a chain hauled over a gunwale.

Young as she is, the stuff
Of her life is a great cargo, and some of it heavy:
I wish her a lucky passage.

But now it is she who pauses,
As if to reject my thought and its easy figure.
A stillness greatens, in which

The whole house seems to be thinking,
And then she is at it again with a bunched clamor
Of strokes, and again is silent.

I remember the dazed starling
Which was trapped in that very room, two years ago;
How we stole in, lifted a sash

And retreated, not to affright it;
And how for a helpless hour, through the crack of the door,
We watched the sleek, wild, dark

And iridescent creature
Batter against the brilliance, drop like a glove
To the hard floor, or the desk-top,

And wait then, humped and bloody,
For the wits to try it again; and how our spirits
Rose when, suddenly sure,

It lifted off from a chair-back,
Beating a smooth course for the right window
And clearing the sill of the world.

It is always a matter, my darling,
Of life or death, as I had forgotten. I wish
What I wished you before, but harder.

EXERCISE 1D

Understanding Figurative Language

1. Consider this poem for a few minutes. To what two things does Wilbur compare the writing process? What do these images say about his view of the writing process?
2. Identify and explain a metaphor that describes your own writing process. Begin this exercise by brainstorming or freewriting to help discover this metaphor.

"I was on the cutting edge. I pushed the envelope. I did the heavy lifting. I was the rainmaker. Then I ran out of metaphors."

SUMMARY

This book emphasizes the relationship between thinking clearly and writing well and stresses the importance of expressing ourselves persuasively while thinking critically about what we read, view, and hear. As we think critically, we need to understand the world view of others and recognize our own world view. We must develop a posture of self-defense as we face advertising and the expanding world of new media.

When writing, we need to think about the **audience** and the **purpose** for which we are writing. For an essay to be successful, we need to follow a sequential **writing process** that avoids formulaic structure and doesn't rush directly to a finished draft. While our main concern is with analytical thinking and argument, we also embrace creative thought and the imagination.

KEY TERMS

Analogy   states explicitly the terms of a metaphor and concludes that two ideas or events not necessarily the same but alike in some ways will be alike in others.

Brainstorming   unrestrained, spontaneous generation of ideas.

Critical thinking   discerning or discriminating thought characterized by fairness, open-mindedness.

Freewriting   unrestrained, spontaneous, continuous generation of complete sentences for a set length of time.

Metaphor   figure of speech that imaginatively implies a comparison between one object and another.

Social network   a virtual community in which individuals can create websites such as MySpace or Facebook.

World view   a set of assumptions about the world and the behavior of people in it.

CHAPTER 2

Inference—Critical Thought

Question

What do you infer from this cartoon?

"I knew the woodpeckers were a mistake."

Answer

A pair of woodpeckers pecked holes in Noah's Ark, and as a result, the boat is sinking. We do not see the woodpeckers, but we know they are a pair because all of the other animals are paired. This tells us that the boat is not just any boat, but is indeed Noah's Ark. The cartoon's caption, combined with the image of the sinking boat, leads us to the conclusion that the woodpeckers are the culprits. We do not see them in action, but on the basis of the **evidence**, we make an **inference**.

WHAT IS AN INFERENCE?

An inference is a conclusion about the unknown made on the basis of the known. We see a car beside us on the freeway with several new and old dents; we infer that the driver must be a bad one. A close friend hasn't called in several weeks and doesn't return our calls when we leave messages; we infer that she is angry with us. Much of our thinking, whether about casual observations or personal relationships, involves making inferences. Indeed, entire careers are based on the ability to make logical inferences. In *Snow Falling on Cedars*, a novel by David Guterson, a coroner describes his job:

> It's my job to infer. Look, if a night watchman is struck over the head with a crowbar during the course of a robbery, the wounds you're going to see in his head will look like they were made with a crowbar. If they were made by a ball-peen hammer you can see that, too—a ball-peen leaves behind a crescent-shaped injury, a crowbar leaves, well, linear wounds with V-shaped ends. You get hit with a pistol butt, that's one thing; somebody hits you with a bottle, that's another. You fall off a motorcycle at 40 miles an hour and hit your head on gravel, the gravel will leave behind patterned abrasions that don't look like anything else. So yes, I infer from the deceased's wound that something narrow and flat caused his injury. To infer—it's what coroners do.

Such reasoning is the basis for the popular television series *CSI: Crime Scene Investigation*, in which a team of investigators use cutting-edge scientific tools to examine the evidence, make logical inferences, and catch the killer. Critical thinking has always been an essential part of a good mystery.

How Reliable Is an Inference?

The reliability of inferences covers an enormous range. Some inferences are credible, but inferences based on minimal evidence or on evidence that may support many different interpretations should be treated with skepticism. In fact, the strength of an inference can be tested by the number of different explanations we can draw from the same set of facts. The greater the number of possible interpretations, the less reliable the inference.

In the cartoon, given the woodpeckers and the sinking boat, we can arrive at one inference only: the birds made holes in the boat. But the inferences drawn in the other two cases above are less reliable. The driver of the dented car may not be the owner: she may have borrowed the car from a friend, or she may own the car but have recently bought it "as is." Our friend may not have called us for a number of reasons: a heavy work schedule, three term papers, a family crisis. She may not have received our messages. These alternate explanations weaken the reliability of the original inferences. Clearly, the more evidence we have to support our inferences and the fewer interpretations possible, the more we can trust their accuracy. (For more on inference, see "Blinded by Science" in Additional Readings.)

THE LANGUAGE OF INFERENCE

The verbs *infer* and *imply* are often confused, but they can be readily distinguished:

    to imply: to suggest, indicate indirectly, hint, intimate; what a writer, speaker, action, or object conveys.

> **to infer:** to arrive at a conclusion by reasoning from facts or evidence;
> what a reader, listener, or observer determines or concludes.
>   A writer, speaker, action, or object **implies** something, and readers, lis-
> teners, or observers **infer** what that something is. A final distinction: only
> *people* (and animals) can **make inferences;** *anything* can **imply meaning**.

EXERCISE 2A

Interpreting a Cartoon

Quickly determine the message the following cartoon implies. What inferences do
you draw from the evidence given? After writing a short response, compare your interpretation with those of others in the class. Are they the same?

WHAT IS A FACT?

> *You're neither right nor wrong because others agree with you. You're right because your*
> *facts and reasoning are right.*
> —INVESTOR AND COLUMBIA PROFESSOR BEN GRAHAM TO CEO WARREN BUFFETT

We make inferences based on our own observations or on the observations of others as
they are presented to us through speech or print. These observations often consist of
facts—information that can be verified. The boat is sinking. We see dents in the car.
You have not spoken to your friend in several weeks. "A crowbar leaves linear wounds
with V-shaped ends." Our own observations attest to the truth of these claims. But often
we are dependent on others' observations about people, places, and events that we cannot
directly observe. Take, for example, the claim that in Boston, on September 11, 2001,

Mohamed Atta boarded a flight that flew into the World Trade Center. Few of us observed this action firsthand, but those who did reported it, and we trust the veracity of their reports. Books, newspapers, magazines, television programs, and the Internet are filled with reports—facts—giving us information about the world that we are unable to gain from direct observation. If we doubt the truth of these claims, we usually can turn to other sources to verify or discredit them. As former United States senator Daniel Patrick Moynihan stated, "Everyone is entitled to his own opinion, but not his own facts."

Facts and Journalism

In "The Facts of Media Life," Pulitzer Prize–winning journalist and former *New York Times* executive editor Max Frankel comments on the growing number of journalists, some of them well known, who have forgotten that verifiable facts are the foundation of good journalism. (For more on the importance of facts in journalism, see "Blinded by Science" in the Additional Readings.)

The Facts of Media Life

In journalism, the highest truth is truth. Period.

The roster of fallen journalists grows apace: Stephen Glass, Mike Barnicle, Patricia   1
Smith, James Hirsch, a whole team of CNN investigators. But the year's toll is proof
not that many reporters often lie; it bespeaks a heroic battle by the news media to
preserve the meaning of fact and the sanctity of quotation marks. Reporters have
been losing their jobs for committing fiction, a crime that is no crime at all in too
many other media venues, notably film and television docudramas.

While news teams root out the tellers of tall tales, the rest of our culture argues   2
that a good yarn justifies cutting corners, imagining dialogue, inventing characters
and otherwise torturing truth.

What's wrong with a little mendacity—so goes the theory—to give a tale velocity?   3

It is unforgivably wrong to give fanciful stories the luster of fact, or to use facts   4
to let fictions parade as truths.

Happily, journalism's infantry slogs on, struggling to distinguish fact from fic-   5
tion. It wants to preserve the thrills of reality and believes that readers deserve the
honesty implicit in Frank McCourt's refusal to put quotation marks around the
reconstructed dialogue in his memoir of an Irish childhood, "Angela's Ashes."

It is a noble but uphill struggle. Admired intellectuals like Joyce Carol Oates   6
have scoffed at the distinction, observing that all language tends by its nature to
distort experience and that writing, being an art, "means artifice." But see how
much she, too, values separating fact from fiction: Oates defeats her own defense
of artifice with the supporting observation that Thoreau compressed two years into
one in "Walden" and "lived a historical life very different from the . . . monastic life
he presents in his book." How could she ever know in a world without fact?

Facts, unlike literature, do not promise truth. They only record what has been   7
seen and heard somehow, by someone, subject to all the frailties and biases of
their observers and interpreters. Yet they must be defended, particularly in a society that values freedom, because by definition, facts can be challenged, tested,
cross-examined. Wrong facts and the truths derived from them are always
correctable—with more facts. Fictional facts are forever counterfeit.

A film, *Shattered Glass*, was made about Stephen Glass, one of the "fallen journalists" identified by Frankel. The film depicts the rise and fall of this *New Republic*
reporter who also contributed stories to *Rolling Stone*. And the list of "fallen journalists" continues to grow with the addition of Jayson Blair of the *New York Times*, who
filed dispatches from various locations when he was actually in New York. He also
fabricated comments and scenes as well as taking material from other newspapers
and wire services. Needless to say, Blair lost his job as did one of his editors, and the
reputation of our country's most prestigious newspaper was damaged.

EXERCISE 2B

Questions for Discussion

1. What does Frankel mean by "the sanctity of quotation marks"? For more on
   this issue, see "Plagiarism" in "A Quick Guide to Integrating Research into
   Your Own Writing" (page 213).
2. Why did author Frank McCourt refuse to put quotation marks around the dialogue in his childhood memoir, *Angela's Ashes*?

WHAT IS A JUDGMENT?

When we infer that the woodpeckers are sinking the boat, we laugh but are unlikely
to express approval or disapproval. On the other hand, when we infer that the woman
in the car in front of us is a poor driver, we express disapproval of her driving skills;
we make a **judgment**, in this case a statement of disapproval. Or, when we infer from
a friend's volunteer work with the homeless that she is an admirable person, we
express our approval; that is, make a favorable judgment. **A judgment is also an
inference, but although many inferences are free of positive or negative
connotation, such as "I think it's going to rain," a judgment always expresses
the writer's or speaker's approval or disapproval.**

Certain judgments are taken for granted, become part of a culture's shared belief
system, and are unlikely to be challenged under most circumstances. For example,
most of us would accept the following statements: "Taking the property of others is
wrong" or "People who physically abuse children should be punished." But many
judgments are not universally accepted without considerable well-reasoned support

or may be rejected regardless of additional support and cogent reasoning. Frequently, a judgment is further complicated by potentially ambiguous language and even punctuation. Take, for example, the highly controversial wording of the Second Amendment to the Constitution:

Amendment II
A well-regulated militia, being necessary to the security of a free State, the right of the people to keep and bear arms, shall not be infringed.

Those in favor of gun control interpret this to mean that only "a well-regulated militia," not every individual, is guaranteed the right to bear arms. "Well-regulated" implies an official militia, not a private one free of government regulations. But those against gun control believe that the Second Amendment guarantees "the people," meaning all individuals, the right to bear arms. This interpretation of the Second Amendment led five of the nine United States Supreme Court justices to a recent decision (July 2008) that individuals have a constitutional right to keep a loaded handgun at home for self-defense.

EXERCISE 2C

Distinguishing Between Facts, Inferences, and Judgments

Determine whether the following statements are facts, inferences, or judgments and explain your reasoning. Note that some may include more than one, and some may be open to interpretation.

> *Example:* I heard on the morning news that the city subway system has ground to a halt this morning; many students will arrive late for class.
>
> "I heard on the morning news that the city subway system has ground to a halt this morning." [*Fact:* I did hear it and the information can be verified.]
>
> "Many students will arrive late for class." [*Inference:* This is a conclusion drawn from the information about the breakdown of the subway.]

1. The United States invaded Iraq in the spring of 2003.
2. Material on the Internet should not be censored by government or any other organization.
3. For sale: lovely three-bedroom house in forest setting, easy commute, a bargain at $475,000.
4. Forty-one percent of Californians who die are cremated—almost twice the national average of 21 percent.
5. Artist Winslow Homer didn't begin to paint seriously until 1862.
6. Eric has a drinking problem.

7. Critic Ben Brantley called the latest production of Shakespeare's *As You Like It* "exhilarating."

8. After I took those vitamin pills recommended by the coach, I scored a touchdown. Those pills sure did the trick.

EXERCISE 2D

Drawing Logical Inferences

Read these "traffic facts" taken from Tom Vanderbilt's *Traffic: Why We Drive the Way We Do (and What It Says About Us)*. What *do* these facts about how we drive say about us?

A. Traffic Facts
TOM VANDERBILT

- "Children at Play" signs don't reduce accidents.
- Drivers honk less on weekends. Men honk more than women, and both men and women honk more at women than at men.
- New cars crash more frequently than older cars.
- Half of all fatalities occur at a speed of less than 35 mph.
- 1 in 5 urban crashes occur when one of the drivers is searching for parking.
- Saturday at 1 p.m. has heavier traffic than weekday rush hours.
- Driving aggressively burns up more gas, increases crash risk and saves one minute on a 27-mile trip.
- Solo motorists drive more aggressively.
- FasTrak lanes have been shown to increase crash rates.
- Fifty percent of American schoolchildren walked or biked to school in 1969. Today it's 16 percent.
- Drivers seated at higher eye heights tend to drive faster. Studies show that SUV and pickup drivers speed more than the average driver.
- Car insurance premiums are tied not only to driving records but also to credit scores. The greater the credit risk, researchers find, the more likely someone is to be involved in a crash.

B. What inference can you draw from this fact taken from *Dry Manhattan* by Michael A. Lerner?

There were 15,000 saloons in New York when Prohibition started; within a few years, there were 32,000.

EXERCISE 2E

Solving Riddles, Reading Poetry

Use your inferential skills to solve these riddles by English poet John Cotton:

1.
Insubstantial I can fill lives,
Cathedrals, worlds.
I can haunt islands,
Raise passions
Or calm the madness of kings.
I've even fed the affectionate.
I can't be touched or seen,
But I can be noted.

2.
We are a crystal zoo,
Wielders of fortunes,
The top of our professions.
Like hard silver nails
Hammered into the dark
We make charts for mariners.

3.
I reveal your secrets.
I am your morning enemy,
Though I give reassurance of presence.
I can be magic,
or the judge in beauty contests.
Count Dracula has no use for me.
When you leave
I am left to my own reflections.

4.
My tensions and pressures
Are precise if transitory.
Iridescent, I can float
And catch small rainbows.
Beauties luxuriate in me.
I can inhabit ovens
Or sparkle in bottles.
I am filled with that
Which surrounds me.

5.
Containing nothing
I can bind people forever,

Or just hold a finger.
Without end or beginning
I go on to appear in fields,
Ensnare enemies,
Or in another guise
Carry in the air
Messages from tower to tower.

6.
Silent I invade cities,
Blur edges, confuse travelers,
My thumb smudging the light.
I drift from rivers
To loiter in the early morning fields,
Until Constable Sun
Moves me on.
—JOHN COTTON, *THE TOTLEIGH RIDDLES, TIMES LITERARY SUPPLEMENT*

Now apply the same skills to these two poems by Sylvia Plath (1933–1963). What does each describe?

7.
I am silver and exact. I have no preconceptions.
Whatever I see I swallow immediately
Just as it is, unmisted by love or dislike.
I am not cruel, only truthful—
The eye of a little god, four-cornered.
Most of the time I meditate on the opposite wall.
It is pink, with speckles. I have looked at it so long
I think it is a part of my heart. But it flickers.
Faces and darkness separate us over and over.
Now I am a lake. A woman bends over me,
Searching my reaches for what she really is.
Then she turns to those liars, the candles or the moon.
I see her back, and reflect it faithfully.
She rewards me with tears and an agitation of hands.
I am important to her. She comes and goes.
Each morning it is her face that replaces the darkness.
In me she has drowned a young girl, and in me an old woman
Rises toward her day after day, like a terrible fish.

8.
I'm a riddle in nine syllables,
An elephant, a ponderous house,
A melon strolling on two tendrils.
O red fruit, ivory, fine timbers.
This loaf's big with its yeasty rising.

> *Money's new-minted in this fat purse.*
> *I'm a means, a stage, a cow in calf.*
> *I've eaten a bag of green apples,*
> *Boarded the train there's no getting off.*

Turn your inference skills to this more serious poem by Philip Levine. What question did the boy have? What answer does the man find?

ON ME!

In the next room his brothers are asleep,
the two still in school. They just can't wait
to grow up and be men, to make money.
Last night at dinner they sat across from him,
their brother, a man, but a man with nothing,
without money or the prospect of money.
He never pays, never tosses a bill
down on the bar so he can say, "On me!"
At four in the morning when he can't sleep,
he rehearses the stale phrase to himself
with a delicate motion of the wrist
that lets the bill float down. He can't pace
for fear of waking his mom who sleeps
alone downstairs in the old storage room
off the kitchen. When he was a kid, twelve
or fourteen, like his brothers, he never knew
why boys no older than he did the things
they did, the robberies, gang fights, ODs,
rapes, he never understood his father's wordless
rages that would explode in punches
and kicks, bottles, plates, glasses hurled
across the kitchen. The next morning would be
so quiet that from his room upstairs
he'd hear the broom-straws scratching the floor
as his mother swept up the debris and hear
her humming to herself. Now it's so clear,
so obvious he wonders why it took
so long for him to get it and to come of age.

ACHIEVING A BALANCE BETWEEN INFERENCE AND FACTS

We need to distinguish inferences, facts, and judgments from one another to evaluate as fairly as possible the events in our world. Whether these events are personal or global, we need to be able to distinguish between facts, verifiable information that we can rely on, and inferences and judgments, which may or may not be reliable.

We also need to evaluate the reliability of our own inferences. Are there other interpretations of the facts? Have we considered all other possible interpretations? Do we need more information before drawing a conclusion? These are useful thinking skills that we need to practice, but how do these skills relate to writing? To answer that question, read the following paragraph and distinguish between statements of fact and inference.

> A white player's life in the National Basketball Association is a reverse-image experience all but unique in American culture. Although fewer than 13 percent of United States citizens are African-American, about 80 percent of the N.B.A.'s players are. Of the 357 players on N.B.A. rosters, 290 were African-American, including several of mixed descent. Every one of the league's 20 leading scorers was black, and all but 2 of its leading rebounders. Not one N.B.A. team has as many whites as blacks.
>
> —ADAPTED FROM "THE LONELINESS OF BEING WHITE" BY BRUCE SCHOENFELD

This paragraph contains one inference while the remaining statements are factual, capable of verification. Notice that the facts support and convince us of the inference.

INFERENCE	FACTS
A white player's life in the National Basketball Association is a reverse-image experience all but unique in American culture.	Although fewer than 13 percent of United States citizens are African-American, about 80 percent of the N.B.A.'s players are.
	Of the 357 players on N.B.A. rosters, 290 were African-American, including several of mixed descent.
	Every one of the league's 20 leading scorers was black, and all but 2 of its 20 leading rebounders.
	Not one N.B.A. team has as many whites as blacks.

Facts Only

Now, what I want is Facts. Teach these boys and girls nothing but Facts. Facts alone are wanted in life. Plant nothing else, and root out everything else. You can only form the minds of reasoning animals upon Facts: nothing else will ever be of any service to them. This is the principle on which I bring up my own children, and this is the principle on which I bring up these children. Stick to Facts, sir!

So says Thomas Gradgrind in Charles Dickens's novel *Hard Times*, an indictment against Victorian industrial society. Dickens knew that facts alone do not make for a good education nor for good writing and thus gave that speech to an unsympathetic character. Expository writing frequently consists of a blend of inference and fact, with the one supporting the other. If you were to write a paper consisting only of facts, it would be of no interest to the reader because reading facts that lead nowhere, that fail to support a conclusion, is like reading the telephone book. Jeff Jarvis, a book reviewer for the *New York Times Book Review*, comments on the dangers of this kind of writing:

> Objectivity, in some quarters, means just the facts, ma'am—names, dates, and quotations dumped from a notebook onto the page. But facts alone, without perspective, do not tell a story. Facts alone, without a conclusion to hold them together, seem unglued. Facts alone force writers to use awkward transitions, unbending formats or simple chronologies to fend off disorganization.

A facts-only approach can also have serious consequences in our schools' textbooks. A recent report on public education cites such facts-only textbooks as one of the causes of students' lack of interest and poor achievement.

> Elementary school children are stuck with insipid books that "belabor what is obvious" even to first graders. At the high school level, history—or "social studies"—texts are crammed with facts but omit human motivations or any sense of what events really meant.

Keep the danger of a facts-only approach in mind when you are assigned a research paper. Do not assume that teachers are looking exclusively for well-documented facts; they also want to see what you make of the data, what inferences you draw, what criticisms and recommendations you offer. Do not fall into the trap of one eager young college freshman, Charles Renfrew, who, proud of his photographic memory, expected high praise from a distinguished philosophy professor for a paper on Descartes. He suffered disappointment but learned a lasting lesson when he read the comment "Too much Descartes, not enough Renfrew." A photographic memory for factual information is an asset, but your own inferences and judgments fully explained are also important. Don't leave your readers asking "so what?" when they finish your paper. Tell them.

Inferences Only

It is possible to err in another direction as well; a paper consisting only of inferences and judgments would antagonize readers as they search for the basis of our claims, the facts to support our opinions. In his biography of William Shakespeare, *Will in the World*, noted scholar Stephen Greenblatt irritated some Shakespeare authorities and other readers by drawing on a sketchy collection of facts to reconstruct the life of the great playwright about whom little is known. Greenblatt tells a good story, but are his inferences supported by the facts?

For example, in trying to create a childhood love of the theatre for Shakespeare, Greenblatt cites the surviving record of another man of Shakespeare's time, Willis, who, at a young age, went with his father to the theatre in Gloucester, where the boy stood "between his [father's] legs." Greenblatt adds to this testament the fact that Shakespeare's father, the mayor of Stratford, 30 miles from Gloucester, hired players when his son would have been five, and concludes that Shakespeare, too, must have gone as a child to the theatre. "When the bailiff [or mayor] walked into the hall, everyone would have greeted him. . . . His son, intelligent, quick, and sensitive, would have stood between his father's legs. For the first time in his life William Shakespeare watched a play." Notice the shift from the qualifier "would" to direct assertion. But are the facts sufficient to support his inference? One critic would certainly answer in the negative. Oxford professor Richard Jenkyns ridicules Greenblatt's reasoning: "Some people have birthmarks, and so Shakespeare may have had one."

EXERCISE 2F

Thinking Critically About Your Own Thinking

Write a paragraph or two about a recent inference you've made. Include what facts the inference was based on. Discuss with your classmates whether the inference was logical given the facts that led to it and whether others might have made a different inference from the same data.

READING CRITICALLY

Finally, distinguishing between facts, inferences, and judgments and evaluating their reliability allow us to analyze information, to read critically as writers, as consumers, as voters. Whether it is an article we find on the Internet, an auto salesperson, or a political candidate, we need to be able to separate facts from judgments and to ask that the judgments offered be supported by the facts. If we read or listen without these distinctions in mind, we are susceptible to false claims and invalid arguments, often with serious consequences for us as individuals and for society as a whole. (To practice these skills, see Additional Readings.)

EXERCISE 2G

Reading Critically

In this excerpt taken from a newspaper article, carefully distinguish those statements that are factual from those that are not. (Note that the sentences are numbered.)

> On Wednesday, March 9, a Los Angeles court dismissed charges against two physicians who allowed a terminally ill patient to die.[1] For generations organized medicine has focused on saving lives, no matter what the price in

emotional trauma, physical pain, or economic cost, because we are a death denying society.[2] But keeping people alive in the face of a painful death should not be inevitable, as Drs. White and Rosenbaum maintained when they shut off artifical life-support for their brain damaged patient at the urging of his family.[3] Although doctors and nurses should remain bound by some rules of law and ethics, they should be able to treat their patients in the most humane way possible as long as they have the informed consent of the patient or of his/her family if the patient can't give it.[4] Thus doctors should not be penalized for allowing a terminally ill patient's life to end mercifully, especially if the patient is clearly "brain dead."[5] The definition of "brain dead" remains a controversial issue but not one which should halt humane medical decisions.[6]

Overall, do you consider this article to be based on fact or judgment?

In what section of the newspaper would you expect to find this article?

WRITING ASSIGNMENT 2

Reconstructing the Lost Tribe

"When we first started seeing each other, we would always use the same word for snow."

The cartoon above refers to the fact that Eskimos have many words for snow, their vocabulary reflecting their environment. Similarly, the Hmong of Laos have many words for mountains—their shapes, slopes, and elevations—to describe their environment. As anthropologist Clyde Kluckhohn points out, "Every language is a special way of looking at the world and interpreting experience. Concealed in the structure of language are a whole set of unconscious assumptions about the world and the life in it." Simply put, a language reflects its culture.

With that idea in mind, imagine that a previously unknown civilization has been discovered and that linguistic anthropologists, after observing the civilization for a while, have delineated the following characteristics about the society's language:

Three words for *terrain*, designating "absolutely flat," "rolling," and "slightly hilly."

No word for *ocean*.

Dozens of terms for grains, including eight for wheat alone.

Several words for *children*, some of which translate as "wise small one," "innocent leader," and "little stargazer."

Seven terms to describe the stages of life up to puberty; only one term to describe life from puberty to death.

The word for *sex* translates as "to plant a wise one."

Terms for *woman* are synonymous with "wife and mother."

Terms for *man* are synonymous with "husband and father."

Twenty words for *book*.

No words for violent conflict or war.

Nine words for *artist*.

Terms for *praise* translate as "peacemaker" and "conciliator."

Words designating *cow*, *pig*, *calf*, and *sheep* but no terms for *beef*, *pork*, *veal*, *leather*, or *mutton*.

Several words for precipitation, most translating as "rain," only one meaning "snow."

Several words for *leader*, but all are plural.

Four words meaning *theatre*.

The Topic

Write an essay in which you characterize the society that uses this language. (Consider giving a name to this tribe to help focus your sentences.)

As you analyze the language, you will be reconstructing a culture. Obviously, because the data are limited, you will have to make a few educated guesses and qualify conclusions carefully. ("Perhaps," "possibly," "one might conclude," "the evidence suggests," and similar hedges will be useful.)

The Approach

Examine and group the data; look for patterns.

Draw inferences, depending only on the data given.

Be sure to use all the data.

Cite evidence to support these inferences—be sure to base all your conclusions on the linguistic evidence provided. Do not draw inferences that you don't support with specific examples. Explain your line of reasoning—how and why the data lead to the inferences you have made.

The Structure

The **opening section** of any essay must provide readers with the necessary **background information.** In this case: What information do you have? How have you come by this information? What are you going to attempt to do with this information?

Each **supporting paragraph** should deal with one distinct aspect of the civilization. Arrange the paragraphs so you can move smoothly from one paragraph to the next.

Some possibilities for the **conclusion** of the essay: What general conclusion(s) can you come to about this society based on the more specific conclusions you have presented in the supporting paragraphs? Is there any overall point you want to make about this society?

OR

What do you find admirable about this society? Do you have any criticisms of the society?

OR

Do you have any questions about the society?

Of course, the conclusion can deal with more than one of these possibilities.

Audience and Purpose

You have a wide range of possibilities here; we leave the choice to you. Your paper may assume the form of a report, scholarly or simply informative, directed to any audience you choose. It may be a letter to a personal friend or fictional colleague. It may be a traditional essay for an audience unfamiliar with the assignment, explaining what the language tells us about the people who use or used it. **What is crucial for success is that you, as the reporter-writer, assume that *you have not seen this tribe and have no firsthand evidence of it. You will also assume that your reader does not have a copy of this assignment;* it is up to you to cite all the specific evidence (the terms given in the list) to justify your inferences.**

MAKING INFERENCES—ANALYZING IMAGES

When you support a judgment with factual evidence and reasoning, you are mounting an argument, as we explain in more detail in Chapter 3. But it is also possible to persuade with **visual images**. We live in a world of intense visual stimulation.

The Internet, television, print media, billboards—we are surrounded by images designed to persuade, telling us what to buy, what to think, how to vote. Thus it is important that we train ourselves in media literacy—to interpret visual images in much the same way that we develop our skills in making inferences as we read printed texts.

In the cartoons you looked at earlier in this chapter, we discussed the ways in which the illustrator led you to make inferences, to reach a conclusion that was implied by the picture. In a similar way, a news photo on the front page of a newspaper may suggest a particular way to interpret an event or view a political figure. Photos of war scenes often carry an antiwar message or promote one side in the conflict over another. Pictures of starving children may plead for humanitarian aid. An unflattering photo of a political candidate may be chosen to discourage voters.

You may remember a photo of former President Bush published by many newspapers in which he is shown peering from the window of Air Force One as it flies over New Orleans four days after that city had been struck by Hurricane Katrina. Bush was criticized for his late and detached reaction to the crisis, and this photo greatly contributed to that criticism.

During the Vietnam War, pictures of coffins being unloaded at US air bases fueled the war's unpopularity. Until recently, no such pictures were shown of the soldiers who have died in Iraq. In fact, photojournalists have not had as much freedom to document the war in Iraq as they had in Vietnam. Publication of photos of wounded or dead soldiers is a particularly sensitive issue, as journalist Clark Hoyt points out in the following editorial.

The Painful Images of War
CLARK HOYT

The New York Times

Two hundred twenty-one American soldiers and Marines have been killed in Iraq   1
this year, but until eight days ago, *The Times* had not published a photo of one of
their bodies.

   The picture *The Times* did publish on July 26, of a room full of death after a sui-   2
cide bombing in June, with a marine in the foreground, his face covered and his
uniform riddled with tiny shrapnel holes, accompanied a front-page article about
how few such images there are.

   The Times reported that the freelance photographer who took the picture,   3
Zoriah Miller, was barred from covering the Marines after he posted it and other
graphic pictures of dead Americans and Iraqis on his Web site. A second photo
accompanying the article, of a dead Army captain in a pool of blood in 2004, got
that photographer in trouble at the time, too.

The article by Michael Kamber, an independent photographer and journalist   4
working in Iraq for *The Times*, and Tim Arango, who writes about the media, highlighted a longstanding tension between journalists who feel a duty to report war in
all its aspects and a military determined to protect its own.

Although the written ground rules for reporters and photographers embed-   5
ding with military units do not forbid photos of the dead and injured, commanders
have used a variety of tactics to prevent them. That, combined with the declining
number of Western photographers in Iraq—*The Times* has two—has meant fewer
than half a dozen graphic photos of dead American soldiers in five years of fighting,
Kamber and Arango reported.

Gail Buckland, an author and professor of photo history at Cooper Union in   6
New York, said she tells students that because of the lack of a comprehensive
photographic record of the war in Iraq, they are "more impoverished today than
Americans were in the 19th century," when battlefield photographs by Timothy
O'Sullivan and others documented the Civil War. "The greatest dishonor you can
do is to forget," she told me. "Photographs are monuments."

But before war photographs pass into history, they are news and records of   7
events that are still raw for everyone involved—soldiers, families and journalists.
The experiences of *The Times* in recent years with searing pictures of injury and, in
one case, imminent death, suggest how emotional, complicated and unpredictable
the issues can be.

In January 2007, Robert Nickelsberg, an independent photographer working   8
for *The Times*, and Damien Cave, a *Times* correspondent, were embedded with an
Army company helping an Iraqi unit search for weapons in a dangerous Baghdad
neighborhood. Suddenly, there were shouts that a man was down: the sergeant
whom Nickelsberg and Cave had been chatting with minutes before had been shot
in the head. Nickelsberg said he and Cave helped evacuate Hector Leija of Ray-
mondville, Tex., and Nickelsberg followed the stretcher downstairs to an armored
vehicle, taking pictures the whole time. Leija died that morning.

The Times waited four days, until Leija's family had been notified of his death,   9
and then published a photograph of him on the stretcher, with another soldier's
hand covering the wound. The newspaper also posted a moving five-minute video,
narrated by Cave, documenting the grief and frustration of Leija's fellow soldiers
and their determination not to leave until, at great peril, they had recovered all
his equipment.

Michele McNally, the assistant managing editor in charge of photography,   10
said *The Times* was trying to both tell the story and be sensitive. But friends said
Leija's family was upset by the coverage, and the Army reacted with outrage,
although Nickelsberg said that no one in Leija's squad tried to prevent him from
taking the pictures and soldiers later thanked him and Cave for sticking with
them through a tough day. After the photo and video were published, Cave said,
the military told him and Nickelsberg that they—and *The Times*—would be
banned from embedding with the military. After lengthy discussions, the ban
was lifted.

Bill Keller, the executive editor, wrote a letter to the family expressing regret   11
for their pain, although he said he does not regret publishing the photo and

video. Cave said he sent a message of regret to the family through an interme-
diary and e-mail to Leija's brother. The family did not respond to any of the
communications. My efforts through intermediaries to talk with them were
unsuccessful.

The Times reported that Lt. Gen. Raymond Odierno was furious and accused   12
the newspaper of violating a ground rule requiring written permission from a
wounded soldier before his picture can be published—often an impossibility with
seriously injured people who are evacuated within minutes.

Joao Silva, an independent photographer working for *The Times*, said he did   13
not ask for permission in late 2006 when he took a dramatic series of photographs
of Juan Valdez-Castillo, a Marine lance corporal seriously wounded in Karma and
heroically rescued by Sgt. Jesse Leach. A graphic shot of Valdez-Castillo lying
bloody and bandaged by a muddy lane, with Leach tending to him, ran at the top
of the front page. An audio slide show of the full sequence of pictures was posted
on *The Times* Web site.

Far from objecting, the Marines asked for copies of the pictures to support a   14
recommendation that Leach receive a medal. The newspaper provided them, and
Leach got his medal. The difference, almost certainly, was life and death. Valdez-
Castillo lived. Leija died.

Jim Looram, a retired West Point graduate and Vietnam veteran, feels   15
strongly that images of dead soldiers should never be published during a war.
"I cannot describe to you what it is like to see a dead American soldier," he
said. Civilians cannot understand what happens on a battlefield, Looram said,
and it dishonors dead soldiers to try to convey through pictures what they
went through.

His daughter, Meaghan, is the *Times* picture editor who handled the pho-   16
tographs that accompanied the article by Kamber and Arango. She loves her dad
but disagrees with him on this. "Looking at photographs of the gravely wounded
or dead is a profoundly affecting and emotional experience," she said. "However, I
do feel that it is my duty as a journalist to see that a truthful account of the consequences of war is given."

Like Jim Looram, Tom Langseth is a retired Army lieutenant colonel. He wrote   17
last year to thank *The Times* after a graphic photograph of his severely injured
grandson appeared on the front page. The picture—and an audio slide show on
The Times Web site—showed how hard everyone worked to save his grandson
Tommy, Langseth told me last week. "It eased our minds a whole lot. We would be
less without it than we are."

I asked Langseth if he would have felt differently had his grandson not sur-   18
vived. "I don't think I would," he said. "But the first time I looked at it, it would
have killed me."

Painful as these issues are—C. J. Chivers, a *Times* reporter and former Marine   19
officer who wrote about Valdez-Castillo, told me he is "pretty tortured" about
them—I think *The Times* has an obligation to pursue stories and photographs that
report the entire experience of war, including death.

Keller said, "Death and carnage are not the whole story of war—there is   20
also heroism and frustration, success and setback, camaraderie and, on occasion,

atrocity—but death and carnage are part of the story, and to launder them out of our account of the war would be a disservice."

EXERCISE 2H

1. According to this article, what are the reasons for and against the publication of pictures of dead and injured soldiers? Which position does the writer of the article, Clark Hoyt, support?

2. Write a paragraph or two on your position on this issue. Before doing so, you may want to see some of the pictures described in the article at www.nytimes. com; search "Zoriah Miller."

Examining an Ad

In advertising, the visual image often provides the evidence leading to an inference that carries a judgment: a product is better than others of its kind. The judgment is sometimes obvious, sometimes implicit. This holds true whether you're reading a magazine, noting a billboard as you drive, or viewing commercials on television or the Internet. Figuring out the underlying suggestive messages of a product can be fun as well as instructive.

When you see an image of a luxury car speeding up a steep mountain road surrounded by gorgeous scenery, it doesn't take you long to realize that the auto company is suggesting you should buy their model because it is powerful and beautiful and will take you to dramatic places at a thrilling speed. Most of us drive cars. Most of us would willingly be transported to such a world.

When a beer commercial excites your interest with glamorous models having fun and scarcely mentions the brand, the argument is more subtly suggestive. Some ads are so subtle that you are left wondering what the product is or exactly how the image relates to the product. The hope here is usually that the inference is subliminal, below the viewer's conscious reasoning, the argument indirect. But with careful analysis, you can evaluate the visual clues and infer the message. A number of companies refused our requests to use their ads in this text. Can you figure out why? We appreciate those who cooperated and wonder why others wouldn't rejoice over multiple copies of free advertising.

In the ad on the next page, note how the product name, Pirelli (tires made in Italy), is reduced to a small corner. It is the image that carries the message. Even if you don't recognize Rio de Janeiro, or Brazil's famous soccer player, Ronaldo, standing in for the statue of Christ the Redeemer, which presides on the mountaintop above the city, you can see a figure of tremendous power filling the foreground, towering over an impressive landscape. With arms outspread, he suggests control of this landscape, a godlike figure dominating the world, as reassuring as he is powerful. The picture catches a reader's attention even before he has a chance to read the caption. Were you able to see the picture in color, you would recognize a mystical light emanating from the figure, the whole scene bathed in a warm reddish glow. The image is one of inspiration—inspiring both power and control, underscoring the combination of power and control any driver would want in a tire.

EXERCISE 21

Making Inferences About Visual Images

1. Using the analysis of the Pirelli ad above as your model, select one of the two ads that follow (the first for Paul Mitchell hair products, the second for Guess clothing) to analyze in a paragraph or two. Fully explain exactly how the advertisers are using the visual image to make their argument and sell their product. Do you find the ad effective? Why or why not?

2. Find a magazine or Internet ad that persuades with visual images and write an analysis of it. (A possible source: www.advertisingarchives.co.uk/) Attach the ad or a copy of it to your response. You may have a chance in class to try out your choice on classmates and see if they reach the same conclusion you do. If they don't, what does it say about the effectiveness of the ad?

3. Select a news photo that implies a judgment of an event or a prominent political or sports figure. Write a paragraph in which you discuss the editor's choice of photo. What is he implying with this choice?

The copy on the left side of this ad urges readers to "Create change and build a better future. Join the John Paul Mitchell Systems family of hairdressers worldwide to fight hunger and poverty, safeguard our planet's water, and give hope to children in need." On the right side we are told that "Each of us can make a difference. Only in salons and Paul Mitchell schools. www.paulmitchell.com" Also note that the man in the ad is Paul Mitchell.

MAKING INFERENCES—WRITING ABOUT FICTION

Many students are intimidated by assignments that require them to write about a poem, play, short story, or novel. What can they say about a piece of literature? Isn't there a right answer known to the author and the teacher but not to them?

Fiction is **implicit**; it does not explain **explicitly**. Writers of fiction—through character, plot, setting, theme, point of view, symbolism, irony, and imagery—imply meaning. Fiction is oblique. The work implies meaning; you infer what that meaning is. As you can see, interpreting literature requires **critical thinking**; it asks you to make inferences about the meaning of the work and to support these inferences with details from it as you have done with cartoons, statistics, poems, and ads earlier in this chapter.

Reading is the making of meaning, and the meaning we make depends on who we are. Our sex, age, ethnicity, culture, and experience all create the context for our reading. Given the multiple interpretations possible, there is not a single right answer but only well-supported inferences that add up to a logical interpretation.

A final point: a critical essay is not a continuation of class discussion but a formal piece of writing that can stand on its own apart from the class. To accomplish this, you may think of your audience as one who is not familiar with the work you are writing about. This does not require you to retell every detail of the piece, but it ensures that you include the relevant details, the facts, on which your inferences are based rather than assume your reader knows them.

The next three assignments will give you ample opportunity to practice the skills of reading closely and thinking critically while making and supporting inferences about literature. The three stories on which the assignments are based are quite short, so regardless of the one chosen by your instructor, you may want to read both and see how you do.

EXERCISE 2J

Making Inferences About Fiction

Read *Grace Period* by Will Baker and then explain the meaning of the title. Support your answer, your judgment, with facts, details taken from the story.

Grace Period
WILL BAKER

You notice first a difference in the quality of space. The sunlight is still golden   1
through the dust hanging in the driveway, where your wife pulled out a few minutes ago in the Celica on a run to the mailbox, and the sky is still a regular blue, but
it feels as if for an instant everything stretched just slightly, a few millimeters, then
contracted again.

You shut off the electric hedge trimmers, thinking maybe vibration is affecting   2
your inner ear. Then you are aware that the dog is whining from under the porch.
On the other hand you don't hear a single bird song. A semi shifts down with a
long backrap of exhaust on the state highway a quarter mile away. A few inches
above one horizon an invisible jet is drawing a thin white line across the sky.

You are about to turn the trimmers on again when you have the startling sense   3
that the earth under your feet has taken on a charge. It is not quite a trembling, but
something like the deep throb of a very large dynamo at a great distance. Simultaneously there is a fluctuation of light, a tiny pulse, coming from behind the hills. In
a moment another, and then another. Again and more strongly you have the
absurd sense that everything inflates for a moment, then shrinks.

Your heart strikes you in the chest then, and you think instantly *aneurysm!* You   4
are 135 over 80, and should have had a checkup two months ago. But no, the dog
is howling now, and he's not alone. The neighbors' black lab is also in full cry, and
in the distance a dozen others have begun yammering.

You stride into the house, not hurrying but not dawdling either, and punch in   5
the number of a friend who lives in the city on the other side of the hills, the county
seat. After the tone dance a long pause, then a busy signal. You consider for a
moment, then dial the local volunteer fire chief, whom you know. Also busy.

Stretching the twenty-foot cord, you peer out the window. This time the pulse   6
is unmistakable, a definite brightening of the sky to the west, and along with it a
timber somewhere in the house creaks. You punch the Sheriff. Busy. Highway
Patrol. Busy. 911. Busy. A recorded voice erupts, strident and edged with static,
telling you all circuits are busy.

You look outside again and now there is a faint shimmering in the air. On the   7
windowsill outside, against the glass, a few flakes of ash have settled. KVTX. Busy.
The *Courier*. Busy. On some inexplicable frantic whim you dial out of state, to your
father-in-law (Where is your wife, she should have the mail by now?) who happens
to be a professor of geology on a distinguished faculty. The ringing signal this time.
Once. Twice. Three times. A click.

"Physical plant."   8

Doctor Abendsachs, you babble, you wanted Doctor Abendsachs.   9

"This is physical plant, buddy. We can't connect you here."   10

What's going on, you shout, what is happening with the atmosphere—   11

He doesn't know. They are in a windowless basement. Everything fine there.   12
It's lunchtime and they are making up the weekly football pool.

It is snowing lightly now outside, on the driveway and lawn and garage. You   13
can see your clippers propped pathetically against the hedge. Once more, at top
speed, you punch your father-in-law's number. Again a ringing. A click.

This time a recording tells you that all operators are busy and your call will be   14
answered by the first available. The voice track ends and a burst of music begins. It is a
large studio orchestra, heavy on violins, playing a version of "Hard Day's Night." At
the point where the lyrics would be "sleeping like a log" the sound skips, wobbles, and
skips again as if an old-fashioned needle has been bumped from a record groove.

You look out the window once more, as the house begins to shudder, and see that   15
it is growing brighter and brighter and brighter.

WRITING ASSIGNMENT 3

Interpreting Fiction

Read the short story "Hostess," by Donald Mangum, and write an essay based on the inferences you make about the hostess, the narrator of the story. Include the facts on which these inferences are based and an explanation of why you made such inferences.

Audience

Someone who has not read the story.

Purpose

To read closely and characterize the hostess—what kind of woman is she?

Hostess

DONALD MANGUM

My husband was promoted to crew chief, and with the raise we moved into a double- **1**
wide, just up the drive. Half the park came to the house-warming. Well, Meg drank
herself to tears and holed up on the toilet, poor thing. "Meg? Hon?" I said from the
hall. "You going to live?" She groaned something. It was seeing R.L. with that tramp
down in 18 that made her do this to herself. Now there was a whole line of beer
drinkers doing the rain dance out in the hall, this being a single-bath unit. I was the
hostess, and I had to do something. "Sweetheart," I said, knocking. "I'm going to put
you a bowl on the floor in the utility room." The rest of the trailer was carpeted.

Dale, my husband, was in the kitchen with an egg in his hand, squeezing it for **2**
all he was worth. Veins stuck out everywhere on his arm. Paul and Eric were laughing. "What's going on in here?" I said.

Dale stopped squeezing and breathed. "I got to admit," he said, "I never knew **3**
that about eggs." I could have kicked him when he handed Paul five dollars. I
found the bowl I was after, plus a blanket, and took care of Meg.

Then Hank and Boyce almost got into a fight over a remark Hank made about **4**
somebody named Linda. They had already squared off outside when it came out
that Hank was talking about a Linda *Stillman*, when Boyce thought he meant a
Linda *Faye*. Well, by that time everybody was ready for something, so the guys
agreed to arm-wrestle. Hank won, but only because Boyce started laughing when
Kathy Sueanne sat in Jason's supper and Jason got madder than Kathy Sueanne did
because there wasn't any more potato salad left.

You won't believe who showed up then. R.L.! Said he was looking for Meg. **5**
"You think she wants to see you, R.L.?" I said. "After what you did to her with that
trash Elaine?" So he said he'd only kissed Elaine a couple of times. "Or not even
that," he said. "She was the one kissed *me*."

"You know what you can kiss," I said. He stood there looking like some dog **6**
you'd just hauled off and kicked for no good reason. "Well, come on," I said,

taking him by the shirt. I led him to the utility room to show him the condition he'd driven his darling to. I'm here to say, when R.L. saw that precious thing curled up in front of the hot-water heater he sank to his knees in shame. I just closed the door.

Back in the den, there was this Australian kangaroo giving birth on the televi-   7
sion. The little baby kangaroo, which looked sort of like an anchovy with legs, had just made it out of its mama and was crawling around looking for her pouch. The man on the show said it had about ten minutes to get in there and find a teat or it would die. He said a lot of them don't make it. I got so wrought up watching that trembly little fellow that I started cheering him on. So did everyone else. Well, to everyone's relief, the little thing made it. Then Gus wanted to know why everyone over there always called each other Mike. Nobody had any idea.

Eric ate a whole bunch of dried cat food before figuring out what it was and   8
that somebody had put it in the party dish as a joke. He tried to act like it didn't bother him, but he didn't stay too long after that. Melinda went out to her car for cigarettes, and a yellow jacket stung her behind the knee, so when she came in howling, Rod slapped this wad of chewing tobacco on the spot to draw out the poison, which made her howl even louder, till I washed it off and applied meat tenderizer and let her go lie in the guest bed for a while.

That's when something strange happened. The phone started ringing, and I   9
ran back to get it in Dale's and my bedroom, which was the closest to quiet in the trailer. I answered and just got this hollow sound at first, like you get with a bad connection over long-distance.

There was a mumble, then a woman's voice said, "She's gone." I didn't recog-   10
nize the voice, but I was sure what "gone" meant by the way she said it. It meant someone had died. Then she said—and she almost screamed it—"Someone should have been here. Why weren't you and Clarence here?"

Now, I don't know a soul in this world named Clarence, and this was clearly a   11
case of the wrong number. "Ma'am," I said as gently as I knew how.

"You'll have to talk louder," she said. "I can hardly hear you."   12

I curled my hand around my lips and the mouthpiece and said, "Ma'am, you   13
have dialed the wrong number."

"Oh, God, I'm sorry," she said. "Oh dear God." And here is the strange thing.   14
The woman did not hang up. She just kept saying, "Dear God" and crying.

I sat there listening to that woman and to all the happy noise coming   15
from everywhere in the trailer and through the window from outside, and when she finally brought it down to a sniffle I said, "Honey, who was it that passed away?"

"My sister," she said. "My sister, Beatrice." And it was like saying the name   16
started her to sobbing again.

"And none of your people are there?" I said.   17

"Just me," she said.   18

"Sweetheart, you listen to me," I said, trying to close the window for more   19
quiet. Sweet Christ, I thought. Dear sweet Christ in Heaven. "Are you listening, angel? You should not be alone right now. You understand what I'm telling you?" I said, "Now, I am right here."

WRITING ASSIGNMENT 4

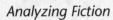

Analyzing Fiction

One critic said of Ernest Hemingway (1899–1961) that his writing is like an iceberg—
nine-tenths of it is beneath the surface. A writer having difficulty adapting one of
Hemingway's novels for the screen complained that the novelist wrote in the white
spaces between the lines. Hemingway's elliptical style stems, in part, from his frequent
use of the objective point of view. A writer employing this point of view is like a video
camera that only records what it sees and hears: It cannot comment or interpret or
enter a character's mind. This point of view demands that the reader make inferences
about the characters' behavior and motivations. Hemingway's "Hills Like White
Elephants" is just such a story. After reading the story and answering the questions
that follow it, write an essay about the conflict at the heart of this story.

Audience

Someone unfamiliar with the story.

Purpose

To infer the meaning of the story.

Hills Like White Elephants
ERNEST HEMINGWAY

The hills across the valley of the Ebro were long and white. On this side there was   1
no shade and no trees and the station was between two lines of rails in the sun.
Close against the side of the station there was the warm shadow of the building
and a curtain, made of strings of bamboo beads, hung across the open door into
the bar, to keep out flies. The American and the girl with him sat at a table in
the shade, outside the building. It was very hot and the express from Barcelona
would come in forty minutes. It stopped at this junction for two minutes and went
on to Madrid.

"What should we drink?" the girl asked. She had taken off her hat and put it on   2
the table.

"It's pretty hot," the man said.   3
"Let's drink beer."   4
"Dos cervezas," the man said into the curtain.   5
"Big ones?" a woman asked from the doorway.   6
"Yes. Two big ones."   7
The woman brought two glasses of beer and two felt pads. She put the felt   8
pads and the beer glasses on the table and looked at the man and the girl. The girl
was looking off at the line of hills. They were white in the sun and the country was
brown and dry.

"They look like white elephants," she said.   9
"I've never seen one," the man drank his beer.   10
"No, you wouldn't have."   11

"I might have," the man said. "Just because you say I wouldn't have doesn't   12
prove anything."

The girl look at the bead curtain. "They've painted something on it," she said.   13
"What does it say?

"Anis del Toro. It's a drink."   14

"Could we try it?"   15

The man called "Listen" through the curtain. The woman came out from the bar.   16

"Four reales."   17

"We want two Anis del Toro."   18

"With water?"   19

"Do you want it with water?"   20

"I don't know," the girl said. "Is it good with water?"   21

"It's all right."   22

"You want them with water?" asked the woman.   23

"Yes, with water."   24

"It tastes like licorice," the girl said and put the glass down.   25

"That's the way with everything."   26

"Yes," said the girl. "Everything tastes of licorice. Especially all the things   27
you've waited so long for, like absinthe."

"Oh, cut it out."   28

"You started it," the girl said. "I was being amused. I was having a fine time."   29

"Well, let's try and have a fine time."   30

"All right. I was trying. I said the mountains looked like white elephants. Wasn't   31
that bright?"

"That was bright."   32

"I wanted to try this new drink. That's all we do, isn't it—look at things and try   33
new drinks?"

"I guess so."   34

The girl looked across at the hills.   35

"They're lovely hills," she said. "They don't really look like white elephants. I   36
just meant the coloring of their skin through the trees."

"Should we have another drink?"   37

"All right."   38

The warm wind blew the bead curtain against the table.   39

"The beer's nice and cool," the man said.   40

"It's lovely," the girl said.   41

"It's really an awfully simple operation, Jig," the man said. "It's not really an   42
operation at all."

The girl looked at the ground the table legs rested on.   43

"I know you wouldn't mind it, Jig. It's really not anything. It's just to let the   44
air in."

The girl did not say anything.   45

"I'll go with you and I'll stay with you all the time. They just let the air in and   46
then it's all perfectly natural."

"Then what will we do afterward?"   47

"We'll be fine afterward. Just like we were before."   48

"What makes you think so?"   49

"That's the only thing that bothers us. It's the only thing that's made us unhappy." 50

The girl looked at the bead curtain, put her hand out and took hold of two of the strings of beads. 51

"And you think then we'll be all right and be happy." 52

"I know we will. You don't have to be afraid. I've known lots of people that have done it." 53

"So have I," said the girl. "And afterward they were all so happy." 54

"Well," the man said, "if you don't want to you don't have to. I wouldn't have you do it if you didn't want to. But I know it's perfectly simple." 55

"And you really want to?" 56

"I think it's the best thing to do. But I don't want you to do it if you don't really want to." 57

"And if I do it you'll be happy and things will be like they were and you'll love me?" 58

"I love you now. You know I love you." 59

"I know. But if I do it, then it will be nice again if I say things are like white elephants, and you'll like it?" 60

"I'll love it. I love it now but I just can't think about it. You know how I get when I worry." 61

"If I do it you won't ever worry?" 62

"I won't worry about that because it's perfectly simple." 63

"Then I'll do it. Because I don't care about me." 64

"What do you mean?" 65

"I don't care about me." 66

"Well, I care about you." 67

"Oh, yes. But I don't care about me. And I'll do it and then everything will be fine." 68

"I don't want you to do it if you feel that way." 69

The girl stood up and walked to the end of the station. Across, on the other side, were fields of grain and trees along the banks of the Ebro. Far away, beyond the river, were mountains. The shadow of a cloud moved across the field of grain and she saw the river through the trees. 70

"And we could have all this," she said. "And we could have everything and every day we make it more impossible." 71

"What did you say?" 72

"I said we could have everything." 73

"We can have everything." 74

"No, we can't." 75

"We can have the whole world." 76

"No, we can't." 77

"We can go everywhere." 78

"No, we can't. It isn't ours any more." 79

"It's ours." 80

"No, it isn't. And once they take it away, you never get it back." 81

"But they haven't taken it away." 82

"We'll wait and see." 83

"Come on back in the shade," he said. "You mustn't feel that way." 84

"I don't feel any way," the girl said. "I just know things." 85

"I don't want you to do anything that you don't want to do——" 86

"Nor that isn't good for me," she said. "I know. Could we have another beer?" 87

"All right. But you've got to realize——" 88

"I realize," the girl said. "Can't we maybe stop talking?" 89

They sat down at the table and the girl looked across at the hills on the dry side 90
of the valley and the man looked at her and at the table.

"You've got to realize," he said, "that I don't want you to do it if you don't 91
want to. I'm perfectly willing to go through with it if it means anything to you."

"Doesn't it mean anything to you? We could get along." 92

"Of course it does. But I don't want anybody but you. I don't want any one 93
else. And I know it's perfectly simple."

"Yes, you know it's perfectly simple." 94

"It's all right for you to say that, but I do know it." 95

"Would you do something for me now?" 96

"I'd do anything for you." 97

"Would you please please please please please please stop talking?" 98

He did not say anything but looked at the bags against the wall of the station. 99
There were labels on them from all the hotels where they had spent nights.

"But I don't want you to," he said, "I don't care anything about it." 100

"I'll scream," the girl said. 101

The woman came out through the curtains with two glasses of beer and put 102
them down on the damp felt pads. "The train comes in five minutes," she said.

"What did she say?" asked the girl. 103

"That the train is coming in five minutes." 104

The girl smiled brightly at the woman, to thank her. 105

"I'd better take the bags over to the other side of the station," the man said. 106
She smiled at him.

"All right. Then come back and we'll finish the beer." 107

He picked up the two heavy bags and carried them around the station to the 108
other tracks. He looked up the tracks but could not see the train. Coming back, he
walked through the barroom, where people waiting for the train were drinking. He
drank an Anis at the bar and looked at the people. They were all waiting reasonably
for the train. He went out through the bead curtain. She was sitting at the table
and smiled at him.

"Do you feel better?" he asked. 109

"I feel fine," she said. "There's nothing wrong with me. I feel fine." 110

EXERCISE 2K

Questions for Discussion

1. What is "the awfully simple operation" the man refers to? How does he feel
   about it? How does Jig feel about it? Is the man sincere in everything he says?

2. Why do you think Hemingway gave the woman a name but not the man?

3. What do you know about their life together? What is the relevance of the woman's comments about absinthe?

4. What is the significance of Jig comparing the hills across the valley to white elephants? Why does Hemingway use that comparison for his title?

5. How is the conflict between the couple resolved?

EXERCISE 2L

Analyzing a Film

As a final exercise in making and supporting inferences, rent the John Sayles film *Limbo*. The conclusion of the movie is open to interpretation; members of the audience are left to decide for themselves if the three individuals stranded on the island are rescued or murdered. What do you think? Write a short paper explaining your answer, citing as evidence specific details from the movie.

SUMMARY

In order to interpret the world around us and write effectively about it, we need to be able to distinguish **facts**, **inferences**, and **judgments** from one another and to evaluate the reliability of our inferences.

In written exposition and argument, and in the interpretation of visual images, literature, and film, it is important to achieve a balance between fact and inference, to support our inferences with facts and reasoning.

KEY TERMS

Explicit   clearly stated or explained, distinctly expressed.

Facts   information that can be verified.

Implicit   suggested or hinted at, not directly expressed.

Inference   a conclusion about something we don't know based on what we do know.

Judgment   an inference that expresses either approval or disapproval.

The Structure of Argument

You always hurt the one you love!

In logic, an argument is not a fight but a rational piece of discourse, written or spoken, that attempts to persuade the reader or listener to believe something. For instance, we can attempt to persuade others that an individual's carbon footprint contributes to global warming or that a vote for a particular candidate will ensure a better society. Though many arguments are concerned with political issues, arguments are not limited to such topics. We can argue about books, movies, athletic teams, and cars, as well as about abstractions found in philosophy and politics. Whenever we want to convince someone else of the "rightness" of our position by offering reasons for that position, we are presenting an argument.

What is the difference between an argument and an opinion? When we offer our own views on an issue, we are expressing an **opinion**. We all have them. We all should have them. But we should also recognize the difference between voicing an opinion and developing an argument. Someone might insist that using animals for medical research is wrong; a research physician might respond that this attitude is misguided. Both are expressing opinions. If they both stick to their guns but refuse to elaborate on their positions, then each may simply dismiss the opponent's statement as "mere opinion," as nothing more than an emotional reaction. If, on the other hand, they start to offer reasons in support of their opinions, then they have moved the discussion to an argument. The critic might add that animals suffer pain in much the same way that humans do, and thus experiments inflict cruel suffering on the animals. The physician might respond that modern techniques have greatly reduced animal suffering and that such experiments are necessary for medical breakthroughs. They are now offering support for their opinions. Don't be afraid of your opinions. Just be prepared to defend them with good reasoning. Think of opinions as starting points for arguments.

PREMISES AND CONCLUSIONS

The structure of all arguments, no matter what the subject, consists of two components: premises and conclusions. The **conclusion** is the key assertion that the other assertions support. These other assertions are the **premises**, reasons that support the conclusion. For example:

> Because gambling casinos pay a significant amount of taxes, Indian tribes should be allowed to build as many as they want on their land.

In this example, the conclusion—that Indian tribes should be allowed to build as many [gambling casinos] as they want on their land—is supported by one premise: gambling casinos pay a significant amount of taxes.

For a group of assertions to be an argument, the passage must contain both these elements—**a conclusion and at least one premise.**

Now look at the same argument with an additional premise added:

> Because gambling casinos pay a significant amount of taxes and provide employment for unskilled workers, Indian tribes should be allowed to build as many as they want on their land.

Which argument do you think is stronger?

Now look at the following letter to the editor of a news magazine:

> I was horrified to read "Corporate Mind Control" and learn that some companies are training employees in New Age thinking, which is a blend of the occult, Eastern religions, and a smattering of Christianity. What they're dealing with is dangerous—Krone Training will be disastrous to the company and the employee.

This writer thinks that she has written an argument against Krone Training, but her letter consists of a conclusion only, which is in essence that Krone Training is not a good idea. Because she fails to include any premises in support of her conclusion, she fails to present an argument and fails to convince anyone who did not already share her belief that Krone Training is "dangerous" and "disastrous." A conclusion repeated in different words may look like an argument but shouldn't deceive a careful reader. (See the fallacy of begging the question in Chapter 6.) Can you formulate a premise that would transform the letter into an argument?

DISTINGUISHING BETWEEN PREMISES AND CONCLUSIONS

In order to evaluate the strength of an argument, we need to understand its structure, to distinguish between its premises and conclusion. **Joining words**—conjunctions and transitional words and phrases—indicate logical relationships between ideas and therefore often help us to make this distinction. Notice the radical change in meaning that results from the reversal of two clauses joined by the conjunction "because":

> I didn't drink because I had problems. I had problems because I drank.
>
> —BARNABY CONRAD

The use of joining words in argument is especially important because they indicate which assertions are being offered as premises and which are offered as conclusions. For example:

> Instead of building another bridge across the bay to alleviate traffic congestion, we should develop a ferry system **because** such a system would decrease air pollution as well as traffic congestion.
>
> A ferry system would decrease air pollution as well as traffic congestion, **so** we should develop a ferry system rather than build another bridge.

In the first example, "because" indicates a premise, a reason in support of the conclusion that creating a ferry system makes more sense than building a bridge. In the second example, "so" indicates the conclusion. Both statements present essentially the same argument; the difference between the two sentences is rhetorical—a matter of style, not substance.

"Because" and "since" frequently introduce premises.

"So," "therefore," "thus," "hence," and "consequently" often introduce conclusions.

conclusion because *premise*

premise therefore *conclusion*

Note: "and" often connects premises.

Joining words are essential for conveying a logical sequence of thought. If logical connections are missing, the reader cannot follow the line of reasoning and either stops reading or supplies his own connections, which may not be the ones intended.

EXERCISE 3A

Joining Sentences for Logic and Fluency

Make this disjointed argument cohesive and logical by joining sentences with appropriate joining words. You don't need to change the sequence of sentences.

> Obstetricians perform too many Cesareans. They can schedule deliveries for their own convenience. They can avoid sleepless nights and canceled parties. They resort to Cesareans in any difficult delivery to protect themselves against malpractice suits. Cesareans involve larger fees and hospital bills than normal deliveries. Cesarean patients spend about twice as many days in the hospital as other mothers. The National Institutes of Health confirmed that doctors were performing many unnecessary Cesarean sections. They suggested ways to reduce their use. The recommendation was widely publicized. The obstetricians apparently failed to take note. In the 1980s, the operation was performed in 16.5 percent of US births. In the 1990s, 24.7 percent of the births were Cesareans. Today, the percentage is even higher.

STANDARD FORM

With the help of joining words and transitional phrases, we can analyze the structure of an argument and then put it into **standard form**. An argument in standard form is an argument reduced to its essence: its premises and conclusion. In other words, it is an outline of the argument. In the previous argument on Indian gambling casinos, each premise is indicated by the "because" that introduces it, the conclusion then following from these two premises. In standard form, the argument looks like this:

Premise 1   Gambling casinos pay a significant amount of taxes.

Premise 2   Gambling casinos provide employment for unskilled workers.

∴ Indian tribes should be allowed to build as many casinos as they want on their land.

Note: ∴ is a symbol in logic meaning "therefore."

Read this argument about college grading policies by Clifford Adelman, a senior research analyst with the Department of Education.

> If there are 50 ways to leave your lover, there are almost as many ways to walk away from a college course without penalty. What are prospective employers to make of the following "grades" that I have seen on transcripts: W, WP, WI, WX, WM, WW, K, L, Q, X and Z. What does "Z" mean? "The student 'zeed out,'" one registrar told me. At another institution, I was told that it stood for "zapped." Despite the zap, I was informed, there was no penalty.
>
>   But there is a penalty. The time students lose by withdrawing is time they must recoup. All they have done is increase the cost of school to themselves, their families and, if at a public institution, to taxpayers.

"Indian casino. I'd say Comanche."

This increasing volume of withdrawals and repeats does not bode well for students' future behavior in the workplace, where repeating tasks is costly. Many employers agree that work habits and time-management skills are as important as the knowledge new employees bring. It wouldn't take much for schools to change their grading policies so that students would have to finish what they start.

Though this argument is three paragraphs long, in standard form it can be reduced to four sentences:

Premise 1   The time students lose by withdrawing is time they must recoup.

Premise 2   They increase the cost of school to themselves, their families, and, if at a public institution, to taxpayers.

Premise 3   Work habits and time-management skills are as important as the knowledge new employees bring to the workplace.

∴ Schools should change their grading policies so that students would have to finish what they start.

The first paragraph provides the reader with necessary background information because the writer can't assume that his readers will know the specifics of current college grading policies. The second paragraph contains two of his three premises, while the final paragraph contains his third premise (and development of that premise) and his conclusion.

The conclusion of this argument—that schools should change their grading policy—is an inference, a judgment. Indeed, all conclusions are inferences. If they were facts, we would not need to supply premises to support them; we would simply verify them by checking the source. In this argument, the first two premises are factual and the third is an inference; one that, on the basis of experience, most of us would be inclined to accept.

Examine the following argument:

Baseball fans have long argued that the city should build a downtown baseball stadium. If the city doesn't build a new stadium, the team may leave, and a major city deserves a major league team. Furthermore, downtown's weather is superior to the wind of the present site, and public transportation to downtown would make the park more accessible.

In this example, four separate premises are offered for the conclusion.

Premise 1   If the city doesn't build a new stadium, the team may leave.

Premise 2   A major city deserves a major league team.

Premise 3   Downtown's weather is superior to the wind of the present site.

Premise 4   Public transportation to downtown would make the park more accessible.

∴ The city should build a downtown baseball stadium.

EXERCISE 3B

Reducing Simple Arguments to Standard Form

Put each of the following arguments into standard form by first circling the joining words and transitional phrases, then identifying the conclusion, and finally identifying the premises. List the premises, numbering each separate statement, and write the conclusion using the symbol ∴. Leave out the joining words and phrases, because standard form identifies premises and conclusions, but write each premise and the conclusion as a complete sentence.

Example: All politicians make promises they can't keep, and Jerry is nothing if not a politician. He will, therefore, make promises he can't keep.

> 1. All politicians make promises they can't keep.
> 2. Jerry is a politician.
> ∴ He will make promises he can't keep.

1. Because fast food restaurants contribute to the obesity epidemic in this country, they should be required to post the calorie count for their food on the menu.

2. Because donors to presidential campaigns wield too much influence over their candidates and because political ads on television are too costly, presidential campaigns for the major candidates should be financed by the government.

3. The student union building is ugly and uncomfortable. The preponderance of cement makes the building appear cold and gray both inside and out. Many of the rooms lack windows, so that one is left staring at the cement wall. The chairs are generally cheap and uncomfortable, while the poor lighting makes studying difficult, and the terrible acoustics make conversation almost impossible.

4. Abortion raises important moral questions, for abortion involves both a woman's right to privacy and the question of when life begins, and anything that involves personal rights and the onset of life raises serious moral questions.

5. Many biologists and physicians argue that life does not begin at conception. And the Supreme Court ruled in 1973 that to restrict a woman's right to have an abortion violates her right to privacy. These two facts lead us to believe that abortion should remain a woman's choice.

6. Capital punishment is not justified, since with capital punishment, an innocent person might be executed, and no practice that might kill innocent people is justified.

7. Because some killers are beyond rehabilitation, society should have the right to execute those convicted of first-degree murder. More uniform implementation of the death penalty may serve as a deterrent, and victims' families are entitled to retribution. Furthermore, the costs of maintaining a prisoner for life are too great, and no state guarantees that life imprisonment means no parole.

8. In his celebrated work *On Liberty*, a defense of freedom of speech, John Stuart Mill argues that "power can be rightfully exercised over any member of a civilized community" only to "prevent harm to others." Because he maintains that no opinion, no matter how disagreeable, can inflict harm, it follows that we don't have the right to suppress opinion.

9. It makes sense for properly trained airline pilots to carry handguns as a last-ditch defense against terrorist takeovers. A recent undercover test by the Transportation Department showed airport screeners missing a significant number of knives and other potential weapons, and there aren't enough sky marshals to protect the thousands of daily flights. Pilots must have the means to save lives.

10. The pope should allow priests to marry. Currently in the United States there is one priest for every 1,400 Catholics, and the average age of this one priest is 60. The Church needs more priests, and surely more young men would join the priesthood if celibacy were not required. And a majority of American Catholics are in favor of allowing priests to marry. In fact, before the 11th century, priests and popes did marry.

WRITING ASSIGNMENT 5

Creating a Political Handout

The following handout urges Californians to vote "no" on Proposition 174. This proposition (like other school voucher initiatives) would require the state to give parents vouchers to apply to their children's tuition if they choose private schools over public. This issue is debated at the national level as well. As you will recognize, the content of this handout is essentially an argument in standard form: premises in support of a conclusion. Each premise is then developed and supported by a sentence or two.

After evaluating the effectiveness of this handout, create one of your own in support of or in opposition to a current political issue, on campus or off. Pay special attention to the format and visual appeal of your document. Your computer program may allow you to add graphics to your design.

Five *Good* Reasons to Oppose the Vouchers Initiative

It provides no accountability.

- Though they would receive taxpayer dollars, the private and religious schools would be wholly unaccountable to the taxpayers—or to anyone other than their owners. Anyone who could recruit just 25 youngsters could open a "school." It would not need to be accredited, to hire credentialed teachers, or to meet the curriculum, health, and safety standards governing the public schools.

It undermines "neighborhood" schools, making large tax hikes likely.

- The initiative would strip our public schools of 10 percent of their funding—even if not one student transferred to a private or religious school—to give vouchers to students currently in nonpublic schools. Either the public schools would be devastated—or hefty tax increases would be needed . . . not to improve education in the public schools, but to pay for subsidizing private, religious, and cult schools.

It permits discrimination.

- Private and religious schools could refuse admission to youngsters because of their religion, gender, IQ, family income or ability to pay, disability, or any of dozens of other factors. In fact, they wouldn't even have to state a reason for rejecting a child.

It transfers taxpayer money to the rich.

- Rich parents already paying $10,000 to $15,000 or more in private school tuition would now gain $2,600 from the vouchers—a form of "Robin Hood in reverse."

It abandons public school students.

- The children left behind, in the public schools, would sit in classrooms that were even more crowded—and that had even less money, per student, for textbooks, science equipment, and other materials and supplies.

Vote No on Prop. 174
California Teachers Association/NEA • 1705 Murchison Drive • Burlingame, CA 94010

AMBIGUOUS ARGUMENT STRUCTURE

Sometimes the precise direction of an argument seems ambiguous; what is offered as conclusion and what is meant as supporting premise can be unclear. In such cases, it is important to look for what is most reasonable to believe, to give ***the benefit of the*** *doubt*. Try each assertion as the conclusion and see if the premises provide logical support for it, beginning with what seems most likely to be the intended conclusion.

Closely allied with the benefit of the doubt is the ancient principle known as *Occam's razor*. Named for William of Occam, a 14th-century European philosopher, this principle advocates economy in argument. As William of Occam put it, "What can be done with fewer assumptions is done in vain with more." In other words, the simplest line of reasoning is usually the best. Newspaper columnist Jon Carroll invoked Occam's razor when commenting on the O. J. Simpson murder trial: "I am not a juror; I am not required to maintain the presumption of innocence. I used Occam's razor, a tool that has served me well before. The simplest explanation is usually the true one; if a wife is killed, look to the husband."

Medicine too follows this principle, as Dr. Lisa Sanders tells us in *Diagnosis*, a *New York Times Magazine* column:

> . . . [Y]ou should strive to come up with the simplest possible explanation for the phenomena you observe. In medicine, that means we try to find a single diagnosis to explain all that we see in a patient. Occam's razor, it's called—the art of shaving the diagnosis to the simplest most elegant solution.

EXERCISE 3C

Reducing an Editorial to Standard Form

Put the argument presented in the following editorial into standard form.

Nurit Karlin

Solves Surplus Problem

To The Editor:

At last, someone else—Elizabeth Joseph (Op-Ed, May 23)—has put into words what I have been silently thinking for some time: Polygamy makes good sense.

Ms. Joseph writes from the perspective of a wife. I write from the perspective of a divorced working mother. How much more advantageous it would be for me to be part of a household such as Ms. Joseph describes, rather than to be juggling my many roles alone.

If polygamy were legal, the problem—and I see it as a problem—of the surplus of extra women would disappear rapidly. No matter how many polemics there may be in favor of the free and single life-style, a divorced woman can feel extra in today's society, more so if she has children, which can isolate her from a full social life. How much easier to share the burdens—and the jobs.

When more women can rediscover the joys of sisterhood and co-wifehood (which are as old as the Bible), and overcome residual jealousy as a response to this type of situation, I think our society will have advanced considerably.

Frieda Brodsky
Brooklyn, New York

HIDDEN ASSUMPTIONS IN ARGUMENT

Many real-life arguments come to us incomplete, depending on **hidden assumptions**, unstated premises and conclusions. Sometimes a missing premise or conclusion is so obvious that we don't even recognize that it is unstated.

Ken is lazy, and lazy people don't last long around here. [Missing conclusion: Ken won't last long around here.]
Since I've sworn to put up with my tired Honda until I can afford a BMW, I must resign myself to the old wreck for a while longer. [Missing premise: I can't afford a BMW now.]
The senator is a Republican, so he is opposed to gun control. [Missing premise: Republicans are opposed to gun control.]

Filling in the omitted assumptions here would seem unnecessarily pedantic or even insulting to our intelligence.

Literature, by its nature elliptical, depends on the reader to make plausible assumptions:

Yon Cassius has a lean and hungry look; such men are dangerous.

—SHAKESPEARE, *JULIUS CAESAR*

Shakespeare assumes his audience will automatically make the connection—Cassius is a dangerous man. But not all missing assumptions are as obvious or as acceptable. At the heart of critical thinking lies the ability to discern what a writer or speaker leaves **implicit**—unsaid—between the lines of what he has made **explicit**—what he has clearly stated.

What is left implicit in the following cartoon?

Dear Abby's readers took her to task for a response she made to a man who complained that because he shared an apartment with a man, people thought he was gay. She called this rumor an "ugly accusation." The implicit assumption here is that homosexuality is ugly, an assumption many of her readers—both gay and straight—objected to. One reader asked, "If someone thought this man was Jewish, Catholic or African American—would you call that an 'ugly accusation'?" Dear Abby apologized.

During the 2008 presidential race, when a McCain supporter yelled that she didn't trust Obama because "he's an Arab," Senator McCain corrected the woman: "No, ma'am. He's a decent family man, citizen." What is the hidden assumption here? In fairness to the Senator, we assume this was a misstatement rather than his belief.

A new kind of therapy called philosophical counseling is based on the belief that many personal problems stem from faulty logic, from irrational assumptions. One practitioner of this therapy, Elliot D. Cohen, gives as an example of such faulty reasoning the assumption that one should demand perfection from oneself and others. He teaches his clients critical thinking skills so that they can identify and correct such damaging assumptions.

Law professor Patricia J. Williams, in *The Alchemy of Race and Rights*, examines the implicit assumptions that led to the death of a young black man in New York. In this incident, three young black men left their stalled car in Queens and walked to Howard Beach looking for help, where they were surrounded by eight white teenagers who taunted them with racial epithets and chased them for approximately three miles, beating them severely along the way. One of the black men died, struck by a car as he tried to flee across a highway; another suffered permanent blindness in one eye.

During the course of the resultant trial, the community of Howard Beach supported the white teenagers, asking "What were they [the three black teenagers] doing here in the first place?" Examining this question, Williams finds six underlying assumptions:

Everyone who lives here is white.

No black could live here.

No one here has a black friend.

No white would employ a black here.

No black is permitted to shop here.

No black is ever up to any good.

These assumptions reveal the racism that led the white teenagers to behave as they did and the community to defend their brutality.

Dangers of Hidden Assumptions

Examine this seemingly straightforward argument:

John is Lisa's father, so clearly he is obligated to support her.

What's missing here? The premise that all fathers are obligated to support their daughters (or their children) is omitted. But would everyone find this premise acceptable under all conditions? Probably not. What about the age factor? Is Lisa over 21? What about special circumstances: Lisa's mother has ample means while John is penniless and terminally ill? Or Lisa was legally adopted by another family, John being her birth father?

The danger with such incomplete arguments lies in more than one direction. A writer may leave his readers to supply their own assumptions, which may or may not coincide with those of the writer. If the issue is controversial, the risks of distorting an argument increase. Or, writers may deliberately conceal assumptions to hide an unsound, often misleading argument. Watch for these in advertising and politics. If you are on the alert for such deceptions, you are better able to evaluate what you read and hear and thus protect your own interests.

Look at the unstated assumption in the following example:

Echoing the arguments of the National Physicians for Social Responsibility, a prominent archdiocese refused to participate in a federal civil defense program that taught ways of preparing for nuclear war. They objected to instructions for teachers and students that recommended that "if there should be a nuclear flash, especially if you feel the warmth from it, take cover instantly in the best place you can find. If no cover is available, simply lie down on the ground and curl up." Their objections were leveled not at the specific suggestions but at the underlying unstated assumption: that nuclear war is survivable. In the words of the Board: "To teach children that nuclear war is a survivable disaster is to teach them that nuclear war is an acceptable political or moral option."

Did the federal civil defense program deliberately conceal an assumption, or did it fail to think critically about the instructions issued to schools?

Some politicians are in favor of privatizing Social Security. They argue that individuals should have the right to invest their own retirement savings. But this argument is based on the following unstated assumptions—that everyone has the necessary knowledge to invest successfully in the stock market and that the stock market will perform well for each individual when he or she reaches retirement age. How realistic are these assumptions?

Hidden Assumptions and Standard Form

To help sort out the stated and unstated assertions in an argument, it can be illuminating to write out the argument in standard form. This means including the important hidden assumptions so the complete argument is before you and putting brackets around these assumptions to distinguish them from stated premises and conclusions.

Examples:

1. Harold is a politician, so he's looking out for himself.
    a. [All politicians look out for themselves.]
    b. Harold is a politician.
    ∴ Harold is looking out for himself.
2. Products made from natural ingredients promote good health, so you should buy Brand X breads.
    a. Products made from natural ingredients promote good health.
    b. [Brand X breads are made from natural ingredients.]
    ∴ You should buy Brand X breads.
3. Products made from natural ingredients promote good health, and Brand X breads are made from natural ingredients.
    a. Products made from natural ingredients promote good health.
    b. Brand X breads are made from natural ingredients.
    ∴ [You should buy Brand X breads.]

EXERCISE 3D

Identifying Hidden Assumptions

A. The following arguments are missing either a premise or a conclusion. Put them into standard form, adding the implicit premise or conclusion; then place brackets around the missing assumptions you have inserted. A word to the wise: as with all argument analysis, find the conclusion first and then look for what is offered in its support.

1. Maggie is a musician, so she won't understand the business end of the partnership.
2. Those who exercise regularly increase their chances of living into old age, so we can expect to see Anna around for a very long time.
3. I never see Sophie without a book; she must be highly intelligent.
4. Those who buy stock on margin lose their money eventually. Yet that is what Sam is doing.
5. That is not a star because it gives steady light.

6. The Western industrialized nations will resolve the energy crisis if they mobilize all the technological resources at their disposal. If financial incentives are sufficiently high, then the mobilization of resources will occur. The skyrocketing cost of energy—as a result of increased oil prices—has produced just such sufficiently high financial incentives. The conclusion is clear.

7. "Most professional athletes don't have a college degree and so have no idea how to handle the big salaries suddenly dumped in their laps." (Harry Edwards, college professor and financial consultant for professional athletes)

8. Having become so central a part of our culture, television cannot be without its redeeming features.

9. **CONVICTED:** U.S. Petty Officer 3/c **Mitchell T. Garraway, Jr.**, of premeditated murder in the stabbing of a superior officer. The military court must now decide his sentence; its options include the death penalty. The last execution carried out by the Navy took place in 1849. (*Newsweek*)

10. From a letter to the *Sacramento Bee* after an article reporting that a nursing mother had been evicted from a downtown department store cafeteria:

    It was inhumane to deny this woman the right to nurse her baby in the cafeteria because she was simply performing a natural bodily function.

    (Where will this argument take you once you supply the suppressed assumption?)

B. The following article appeared in the news section of several major newspapers. Read it carefully and supply the hidden assumption it seems to be leading us to. Why would the writer choose to make this assumption implicit?

Robert Redford's Daughter Rescued

SALT LAKE CITY—Shauna Redford, daughter of actor Robert Redford, was rescued when her car plunged into a river, authorities said yesterday.

They said Redford was wearing a seatbelt and suffered only minor injuries in the accident Friday. Redford, 23, of Boulder, was rescued from her partially submerged auto by three other motorists, who saw her vehicle crash through a guardrail into the Jordan River, eight miles south of Salt Lake City.

The Utah Highway Patrol said the three rescuers released Redford's seatbelt, pulled her from the car and carried her to the riverbank.

She was held at a hospital overnight for observation and released.

Last summer, Sidney Wells, 22, a Colorado University student who had dated Shauna Redford, was shot and killed in Boulder. Police said the killing may have been drug related.

C. Look closely at the following two cartoons from the *New Yorker* magazine archives. What do they suggest about relationships between men and women in the workplace in the 1950s? What hidden assumptions are they based on?

"Three more months and he reaches mandatory retirement age, thank God."

*"Notice, class, how Angela circles, always keeping
the desk between them. . ."*

Now look at this recent cartoon. What unstated assumptions about relationships between men and women are suggested here?

A SUCCESSFUL WEDDING PARTY
RETURNS FROM THE HUNT

Hidden Assumptions and Audience Awareness

Politicians and advertisers may deliberately suppress assumptions in order to manipulate the public. We will assume that we, as careful writers, do not share this goal and would not deliberately leave important assumptions unstated. At the same time, we don't want to bore our readers by spelling out unnecessary details. How do we determine what material to include, what to leave out?

George Lakoff and Mark Johnson, in their book *Metaphors We Live By*, point out that meaning is often dependent on context. They offer the following sentence as an example.

We need new sources of energy.

This assertion means one thing to a group of oil executives and quite another to an environmental group. The executives may assume the writer is referring to more offshore drilling, whereas the environmentalists may think the writer is referring to greater development of solar or other alternate sources of energy.

As writers, we must consider our audience carefully and understand the purpose for which we are writing. We make choices about which assumptions must be made explicit according to our knowledge of the reader. Are we writing for an audience predisposed to agree with us or for one that is opposed to our point of view? Are we writing for readers who are knowledgeable about the subject or ignorant? The answers to these questions help us to determine what material to include and what to omit.

EXERCISE 3E

Responding to an Opinion Piece

Choose an opinion piece from one of the following: salon.com, slate.com, huffington post.com, nytimes.com, or a similar website you are familiar with. Reduce it to standard form, supplying any hidden assumptions you may find (put brackets around these), and then write a brief (a paragraph or two) response expressing your reaction to the piece.

SUMMARIES

Standard form is a simplified method of outlining arguments. Another way to explore an argument and reveal the important premises leading to a conclusion is to write a summary.

Educator Mike Rose sees summarizing as an essential writing skill: "I [can't] imagine a more crucial skill than summarizing; we can't manage information, make crisp connections, or rebut arguments without it. The great syntheses and refutations are built on it."

Summaries come in many lengths, from one sentence to several pages, depending on the purpose of the summary and the length of the piece to be summarized. Note, for example, the brief summaries at the conclusion of each chapter in this text.

A good summary is both **complete** and **concise**. To meet these conflicting goals, you must convey the essence of the whole piece without copying whole passages verbatim or emphasizing inappropriate features of the argument. Background information, detailed premise support, and narrative illustrations are usually omitted from summaries. Paraphrases of ideas, rather than direct quotations, are preferred (except for a critically important phrase or two). A summary should also be **objective**, excluding inferences and opinions. These are reserved for argument analysis.

Strategies for Writing a Summary

1. Read the piece you are to summarize carefully to determine the writer's main point or conclusion. Write this conclusion **in your own words.**

2. Write a sentence expressing the most important point in each paragraph **in your own words.**

3. Write a first draft by combining the conclusion with your one-sentence summaries of each paragraph, **making sure the beginning of the summary includes the title and author of the piece.**

4. Edit your draft by eliminating repetition and any details that are not **essential** to the writer's argument. If you decide to include a significant sentence or phrase from the original, use quotation marks.

5. Check this edited draft against the piece being summarized to make sure you haven't overlooked an important idea or included an opinion of your own.

6. Revise for coherence by combining sentences and inserting transitional phrases where necessary. Edit for conciseness by eliminating all "deadwood" from your sentences. Check grammar and spelling.

An Example of a Summary

Following the steps outlined above, we have summarized "Could It Be That Video Games Are Good for Kids?" an editorial included in Chapter 4, page 88.

> Steven Johnson in his editorial "Could It Be That Video Games Are Good for Kids?" argues that children are not negatively affected by playing video games. In fact, he believes high school football encourages more violent thoughts and behavior than video games. As for explicit sexual content, Johnson recommends appropriate ratings.
>
> He contends that children have always played games and most children are not giving up reading the classics to do so. He also maintains that video games are much more challenging than traditional board games. Video games "force kids to learn complex rule systems, master challenging new interfaces, follow dozens of shifting variables in real time and prioritize between multiple objectives," all skills that will prove useful in the workplace. Johnson also points out that teenagers are watching fewer televised sporting events and that playing video games is more demanding than passively watching television.
>
> Violent games are plentiful, but kids today are less violent than in the past, according to the Duke University's Child Well-Being Index—a fact that suggests that these games act as a safety valve. And SAT scores are improving as well. Johnson does concede that children don't get exercise when playing video games and that the rising obesity among children is a serious problem.

In this summary, the 16 paragraphs of the original have been reduced to three paragraphs that reflect the **essence** of the original. If summarizing for note-taking purposes only, you may want to limit yourself to steps 1 and 2 of the summary strategies listed above.

> Summaries should be objective, concise, complete, and coherent, and written in your own words.

WRITING ASSIGNMENT 6

Summarizing an Article

Read the following essay by high school senior Nathan Yan carefully, and write a summary of the article. You may want to compare summaries with classmates.

AP Courses—Mounting Burden, Declining Benefit

NATHAN YAN

For many high school juniors and seniors, this school year has been the year of the   1
AP, a nonstop rush of drills, flash cards and night-before cramming. In every advanced placement class, students devote an immense effort to studying for these

tests; they buy prep books, stay excessive hours after school and spend a disproportionate amount of time on AP over their regular classes.

As one of many AP students, I've experienced the madness myself. Perhaps it is part of our natures, as "top tier" students dedicated to success, but at its core, the work ethic of the majority of AP students represents an unhealthy obsession with the AP test.   2

The AP tests are nationwide standardized tests administered by the private College Board Association. Successfully passing an AP test will count toward college credit and, depending on the college or university, may grant exemptions from certain general education courses. For many high schools it represents the highest class level for students taking a particular course.   3

While preparing for AP tests is not so much of a problem, the issue for almost any AP student is that their focus on passing the test takes precedence over the subject matter of the course. Students spend days and days practicing how to manage their time on the essay prompts, and learning the grading process that AP scorers use, and listening endlessly to the useless "guessing is good if you can eliminate one answer choice" rubbish. Interest in understanding the actual subject takes a backseat, and worst of all, confined by the College Board defined AP curriculum, teachers are stripped of the power to direct the AP crazed students toward actual subject comprehension. School administrators, with their "pass the AP" mandate, are about as inclined to teach the subjects as students are to learn it.   4

All of the time wasted and knowledge lost in studying for the AP test aside, if a student actually needed night time and weekend study sessions, third party prep books and a specialized class *just to pass a test*, one must wonder if passing the AP exam really means anything. Those who have immersed themselves in this AP trap of test drills and endless study are fooling themselves into a false sense of security that a score of 3 or 4 or 5 on some AP test means that they're "smart," that they can get into a University of California campus, that they're ready for the University of California.   5

As for teachers, have they blindly accepted this "pass the AP" mantra as simply part of the job description? Any teacher who has ever taught an AP class knows every hour wasted on explaining how AP graders score essays is an hour that could have been used to educate students on something of real substance. Every AP teacher knows that the AP syllabus, mandating what must be taught, restricts the teachers' freedom in what the class can learn. Despite this, teachers seem willing to approach the standard AP formula as simply another quirk in the education system that must somehow be accommodated.   6

As students, we shouldn't buy into this "failing AP equals Apocalypse" paranoia, this "Oh my God, this AP seems so hard and if I fail I've got no future, I've got to do everything humanly possible to prepare for it!" This is what puts us into a black-or-white, "will this help me on the AP or not?" perspective that distracts us from real education. We don't need AP prep books or daily after-school study sessions, and if any students still feel they do, they need to reassess their ability to handle an AP course.   7

Teachers, similarly, need to realize that they don't need to gear their classes to training for a test; teaching it like any other non-AP class, they will discover that those students who understand the material will be able to pass it, and others will not, simply because they're either lazy or unable to grasp the subject. Both teach-   8 ers and the administration need to realize that a student will never fail an AP test for a lack of test preparation.

Maybe the best solution, then, is to completely drop the college credits and   9 the AP test itself, thereby eliminating all the competitive pressure and failure anxieties of today's AP courses. We would return classroom autonomy to the teachers, and, with a de-emphasis on competition and achieving a good score "on paper," the administration, teachers and, most especially, the students can get back to an environment where we're more concerned with learning about a subject, rather than learning how to pass a test on the subject.

ARGUMENT AND EXPLANATION—DISTINCTIONS

As you elaborate support for premises in written argument, you often rely on explanation—of terminology, of background, of your reasoning—but you must not lose sight of your purpose, which is to persuade your reader of the wisdom of your position.

In **argument**, you present reasons for your conclusion in order to convince someone of your point of view.

In **explanation**, on the other hand, you are clarifying why something has happened. Look at these examples:

> Don't go to that market because it's closed for renovation.

> Don't go to that market because the prices are higher than anywhere else and the checkout lines are slow.

In the first example, we are given an explanation of why the market is closed. In the second, we are given two reasons, two premises, for not shopping at that market—it's too expensive and the checkers are slow. This is an argument.

This distinction between explanation and argument may play a crucial role in your understanding of specific writing assignments and save you wasted effort on a false start. Is the instructor asking for an explanation, information on a particular subject, or is he asking you to write an argument, to take and support a position? The following exercise should help to clarify further this important distinction.

EXERCISE 3F

Distinguishing Arguments from Explanations

The following two pieces both address evolution, the first written by a journalist, Elizabeth Bumiller, the second by a professor and former veterinarian, Lisa Fullam. One presents an argument while the other offers an explanation. Read them both carefully and decide which is which. Keep in mind that the writer of an argument **takes a position** and attempts to persuade the reader of the rightness of that position. Explain your answer with references to specific passages in both pieces. (Note that paragraphs are numbered for easy reference.) You may want to discuss your answer with other students in your class. For more on this issue of intelligent design versus evolution, see "Blinded by Science" in Additional Readings at the end of the text.

Bush Remarks Roil Debate over Teaching of Evolution
ELIZABETH BUMILLER

A sharp debate between scientists and religious conservatives escalated Tuesday over comments by [former] President Bush that the theory of intelligent design should be taught with evolution in the nation's public shcools. 1

In an interview at the White House on Monday with a group of Texas newspaper reporters, Mr. Bush appeared to endorse the push by many of his conservative Christian supporters to give intelligent design equal treatment with the theory of evolution. Recalling his days as Texas governor, Mr. Bush said in the interview, according to a transcript, "I felt like both sides ought to be properly taught." Asked again by a reporter whether he believed that both sides in the debate between evolution and intelligent design should be taught in the schools, Mr. Bush replied that he did, "so people can understand what the debate is about." . . . 2

On Tuesday, the president's conservative Christian supporters and the leading institute advancing intelligent design embraced Mr. Bush's comments while scientists and advocates of the separation of church and state disparaged them. At the White House, where intelligent design has been discussed in a weekly bible study group, Mr. Bush's science adviser, John H. Marburger 3rd, sought to play down the president's remarks as common sense and old news. . . . 3

Intelligent design, advanced by a group of academics and intellectuals and some biblical creationists, disputes the idea that natural selection—the force Charles Darwin suggested drove evolution—fully explains the complexity of life. Instead, intelligent design proponents say that life is so intricate that only a powerful guiding force, or intelligent designer, could have created it. 4

Intelligent design does not identify the designer, but critics say the theory is a thinly disguised argument for God and the divine creation of the universe. Invigorated by a recent push by conservatives, the theory has been gaining support in school districts in 20 states with Kansas in the lead." . . . 5

Of God and the Case for Unintelligent Design
LISA FULLAM

As the theory of intelligent design again hits the news with [former] President Bush's encouragement this week that the theory be taught in schools alongside evolution, I have one question: What about unintelligent design? 1

Take rabbit digestion, for example. As herbivores, rabbits need help from bacteria to break down the cell walls of the plants they eat, so, cleverly enough, they have a large section of intestine where such bacterial fermentation takes place. The catch is, it's at the far end of the small intestine, beyond where efficient absorption of nutrients can happen. A sensible system—as we see in ruminant animals like 2 cattle and deer—ferments before the small intestine, maximizing nutrient absorption. Rabbits, having to make do with an unintelligent system, instead eat some of their own feces after one trip through, sending half-digested food back through the small intestine for re-digestion.

Horses are similarly badly put together: They ferment their food in a large, blind-ended cecum after the small intestine. Unlike rabbits, they don't recycle their feces—they're just inefficient. Moreover, those big sections of hind gut are a frequent location for gut blockages and twists that, absent prompt veterinary intervention, lead to slow and excruciating death for the poor horse. The psalmist writes: "God takes no delight in horses' power." Clearly, if God works in creation according to the simplistic schemes of the intelligent design folks, God not only doesn't delight in horses, but seems positively to have it in for them.   3

Furthermore, why wouldn't an intelligent designer make it possible for animals to digest their natural food without playing host to huge populations of bacteria in the first place: Couldn't mammals have been equipped with their own enzymes to do the job?   4

But that's not all: Consider mammalian testicles. In order to function optimally, they need to be slightly cooler than the rest of the body and so are carried outside the body wall in the scrotum. Why would one carry one's whole genetic potential in such a vulnerable position? Clearly it's not a gonad problem in general—ovaries work just fine at body temperature and are snuggled safely within the pelvic girdle for protection. But for testicles, nope—the scrotum is jerry-rigged to allow for a warm-blooded animal to keep his testicles cool. Surely an intelligent designer could have figured out a way for testicles to work at body temperature, as ovaries do.   5

Here's another: Do you know anyone beyond the age of 20 or so who has not had a backache? Let's face it: The human body is that of a quadruped tipped up on end to walk on only two legs. The delicate and beautiful cantilever curve of the human spine compensates (but not enough) for the odd stresses that result from our unusual posture. Perhaps the God of intelligent design has a special place in his plan for chiropractors? And what about the knee? Between the secure ball-and-socket of the hip and the omnidirectional versatility of the ankle is a simple hinge joint, held together only by ligaments (including the anterior cruciate ligament) whose names are known to athletes and sports fans because they're so easily and frequently injured. Again, unintelligent design.   6

The real problem with intelligent design is that it fails to account for the obvious anatomical and physiological making-do that is evident of so much of the natural world. Evolutionarily minded folks see this as the result of genetic limitations and adaptations accumulated in specialization for certain environments, while the intelligent design folks are left with a designer who clearly cannot have been paying close attention.   7

While there are extremely precise and fine-tuned mechanisms in nature, there is also lots of evidence of organisms just cobbled together. For instance, take marsupials, who give birth to what in other animals are analogous to fetuses, then have to carry them around in what amounts to an exterior uterus until the offspring are ready to face the world.   8

As a theist who sees natural evolution not as a theory but as well-established observation, I take comfort in the catch-as-catch-can of the natural world. I have   9 every confidence that an all-loving creator walks in and with the natural world as it struggles to fruition, cheering on our evolutionary triumphs (let's hear it for the opposable thumb!) and standing in solidarity with the evolutionary misfits and misfires, like rabbit guts and horses generally.

Isn't this how God walks in and with us in our individual lives as well, cheering us on, emboldening us and consoling us in our often misguided attempts to live well and do right, and standing in compassion and solidarity with us when we fail, and loving us into trying again? And isn't this a more compelling vision of God, and truer to the biblical God who comes again and again to offer salvation to erring humankind, than that of a designer who can't quite seem to get things right?

10

SUMMARY

In logic, the word *argument* has a special meaning, referring to rational discourse composed of **premises** and a **conclusion** rather than to a fight. It is useful to be able to recognize premises and conclusions in order to fully understand what an argument is proposing. Expressing arguments in **standard form** is a helpful strategy for understanding arguments.

Arguments are frequently presented with some of the premises or the conclusion implied rather than stated. Sometimes such **hidden assumptions** are obvious, but in other instances they can be misleading and need to be made explicit. Recognizing hidden assumptions in argument is an important part of critical thinking.

Writing a **summary** is a good way to explore an argument and reveal the important premises leading to a conclusion.

The distinction between **argument** and **explanation** may play a role in your understanding of specific writing assignments. In argument, you present reasons for your conclusion in order to convince someone of your point of view. In explanation, you are clarifying why something has happened.

KEY TERMS

Argument   a rational piece of discourse, written or spoken, which attempts to persuade the reader or listener to believe something; composed of at least one premise in support of a conclusion.

Conclusion   the key assertion in an argument, the statement that the other assertions support; the point one hopes to make when presenting an argument.

Explanation   an attempt to clarify why something has happened or why you hold a given opinion.

Hidden assumptions   missing, unstated premises and conclusions in arguments; assertions that are necessary to recognize in order to fully understand an argument.

Joining words   words or phrases that indicate, or signal, the logical relationship between assertions in an argument. "Therefore" and its synonyms signal a conclusion; "because" and its synonyms signal a premise.

Occam's razor   a principle of argument that advocates economy, maintaining that the simplest line of reasoning is usually the best.

Opinion   a provisional judgment or belief, requiring proof or support; a first step in developing an argument.

Premise   a reason that supports the conclusion in an argument.

Standard form   an argument reduced to its essence, its principal premises and conclusion listed in simple outline form, with premises numbered and conclusion stated at the end.

CHAPTER 4

Written Argument

I told him he ought not simply to state what he thinks true, but to give arguments for it, but he said arguments would feel as if he was dirtying a flower with muddy hands. . . . I told him I hadn't the heart to say anything against that, and that he had better acquire a servant to state the arguments.

—BERTRAND RUSSELL

In Chapter 3, we focused on the structure of argument, distinguishing between premises and conclusions and reducing arguments to these two basic components. But how do we flesh out these bare bones to create a complete **written argument**?

FOCUSING YOUR TOPIC

A first critical step is to **focus** and refine the topic. At one time or another, we have all been part of heated political discussions between friends or family members. Dad states that taxes are too high. Cousin Susan points out that corporations do not pay their fair share, while Grandfather shouts that the government funds too many social programs and underfunds social security. These discussions are often discursive and unsatisfying because they are not focused on one clear and precise **question at issue**. Bloggers often think they're presenting an argument, but they are simply offering a one-sided, unfocused rant when they fail to focus on a single question at issue.

For an argument to be successful, one person does not necessarily have to defeat another; one point of view does not have to be proven superior to another. An argument can also be considered successful if it opens a line of communication between people and allows them to consider—with respect—points of view other than their own. But if an argument is to establish such a worthwhile exchange, it must focus first on a single issue and then on a particular question at issue.

The Issue

An **issue** is any topic of concern and controversy. Not all topics are issues, since many topics are not controversial. Pet care, for instance, is a topic but not an issue; it has no **argumentative edge**. Laboratory testing of animals, on the other hand, is an issue.

In the hypothetical family discussion above, three issues are raised: taxes, government-funded social programs, and social security. No wonder such a discussion is fragmented and deteriorates into people shouting unsupported claims at one another.

Where and how do you find appropriate topics for an argument? In your work or personal life you might need to write an argument that has a real-world purpose. Why is product X superior to all other brands, and how will using it turn a customer's business around? Why are you the most qualified applicant for the job? For your classes, you are often assigned topics, but sometimes in a writing class you are asked to select a topic of interest to you. Newspapers, news broadcasts, and websites can suggest issues, as can blogs and podcasts. The Internet has opened up a vast new world of information from which to select a topic. Although it can be useful to choose a subject that you know something about, particularly if you want to take a strong stand right away, don't be afraid of exploring new areas. In a freshman history class some years ago, one of us was handed the unknown name *Leon Trotsky*. That required paper led to a whole new world of knowledge: Russia, the Soviet Union, the Russian Revolution, and communism. Your writing assignments can be a way of opening new worlds.

The Question at Issue

Whether you choose your own issue or are assigned one, the next step is to select one question at issue—a particular aspect of the issue under consideration. **Global warming**, for instance, is an issue that contains many distinct questions at issue:

Does global warming exist?

Should the EPA declare global warming a threat to human health?

Are the effects of global warming as serious as some predict?

Should the federal government increase funding for alternative energy?

Is global warming having an effect on our economy?

Is the melting of the Polar ice cap a catastrophe for polar bears?

A writer who does not focus on one and only one question at issue risks producing a disorganized essay, one that is difficult to follow because the readers will not be sure they understand the point the writer is arguing. Writing on the issue of whether or not global warming will have a significant impact on our economy, one student kept drifting away from that question at issue to whether global warming would affect the weather in her city. Since both her **questions at issue** were part of the **same issue**, global warming, and hence related, she was unaware that her paper was going in two different directions. The result was a disorganized, disjointed essay reflecting muddled thinking.

The following diagram illustrates that a single issue may contain any number of separate and distinct questions at issue. Your task as a writer is to isolate a particular question at issue and stay focused on it.

GLOBAL WARMING

Does global   X   X Is global warming having an
warming exist?   effect on our economy?

Should the EPA declare X   X Should the federal government
global warming a threat   increase funding for alternative
to human health?   energy?

Are the effects of global X   X Is the melting of the polar
warming as serious   ice cap a catastrophe for
as some predict?   polar bears?

> I FIGURE IF WE ARE EXPERIENCING "GLOBAL WARMING," I MIGHT AS WELL MAKE THE MOST OF IT!

The Thesis

The final step in establishing the focus of an essay is determining the **thesis**. Although the issue and question at issue state the subject and focus of the paper, they are neutral statements; they do not reveal the writer's opinion, nor should they. To encourage objective analysis, the question at issue should be expressed in neutral rather than biased or emotionally charged language. The **thesis**, however, states the writer's position, her response to the question at issue, the *conclusion* of her argument, the primary claim she is making. Your thesis takes central stage in both the final paper you write and the thinking you do as you conduct your research and prepare drafts. It controls the evidence you gather and clarifies the stand you take.

Suppose you want to write a paper about global warming and narrow the issue to a more focused question at issue:

Should the government take immediate steps to curb global warming?

You might start with a sentence that states the topic:

The question of global warming has long been debated, but today most are in agreement that global warming, to some degree, is a reality.

Yes, your reader would say. You've chosen a timely topic, but what about the argumentative edge? Where is your opinion? What have you to prove in such a statement? Not much so far. No longer will many people argue with the fact that global warming is a reality. But once you have established a little background on your topic, you need to make a statement about what you want to prove in your paper.

Perhaps you want to convince your reader that it is time for the government to step in with funding.

Although our nation is suffering from deficit spending and budget shortfalls, global warming is too urgent a problem for the government to ignore. Funding is needed immediately.

Or you may want to join those who argue otherwise.

While global warming is a problem, before we start increasing our national debt, we should depend on private initiatives and the individual efforts of us all.

Both of these statements assert a position on a question at issue; both have an argumentative edge. In either case, you need to provide detailed reasoning on the issue and explain why such evidence supports your case. With either thesis statement, you will have pinned down your ideas so that you have a road map to guide you as you search for and sift through the evidence necessary to support your position.

You don't necessarily have to arrive at a completely yes-or-no response to the question at issue. To give another example, if the question at issue is whether or not school administrators should have the right to censor student newspapers, your position may not be unequivocal, but a qualified response:

School administrators should not have the right to censor student newspapers unless an article is libelous or clearly obscene.

> **IN SUMMARY:** You should take the following steps as you prepare to write your argument:
>
> Select an **issue** that is **controversial**.
>
> Narrow that issue to a focused **question at issue**.
>
> Write a **thesis** that makes an assertion about this question at issue; your thesis states your opinion on the question at issue.

Two Kinds of Thesis Statements

Note the two examples of thesis statements that follow. How do they differ? How might the difference affect the paper that follows?

(a) Children's access to the Internet should be controlled in the home and at schools and libraries.

or

(b) Access to the Internet should be controlled, because children need protection from pornography and sexual predators.

We can call (a) an **open thesis**. It states the writer's opinion but not the reasons for her opinion. In contrast, a **complete thesis** (b) includes both the writer's opinion and at least some of the reasons or premises that support this conclusion.

Which thesis statement is preferable? It is a matter of choice—the writer's choice. Some writers fear that the complete thesis will not capture the reader's interest nor arouse curiosity. On the other hand, a writer may prefer the greater clarity of the "complete" thesis, which predicts the content to come.

As a general guideline to assist you in deciding on the most suitable form of your thesis, consider the complexity of the topic, the length of the paper, the needs of your audience, and the purpose of your project. In a long paper on a complex topic, the reader may welcome the clarity of a thesis with stated reasons. But in a short essay on a simple topic, the open thesis may be enough and seem less mechanical.

A thesis is not necessarily restricted to one sentence. In fact, it's not unusual for a thesis to require a paragraph. As your work progresses and new ideas change your thinking, you may need to revise your thesis. You may also find yourself refining the language of your thesis during the final editing process. But a well-thought-out and clearly expressed thesis guides both writer and reader.

EXERCISE 4A

Identifying the Issue, Question at Issue, and Thesis

Complete the following sets by supplying the missing element.

1. *Issue:* _____.

   Question at Issue: Should the government ban the use of handheld electronic devices by drivers?

> **Thesis:** For the safety of all drivers, the government should ban handheld electronic devices by drivers.

2. **Issue:** Fuel economy standards.

   Question at Issue: Should the government have the right to set fuel economy standards for American automakers?

   Thesis: _____.

3. **Issue:** Genetic engineering of crops.

   Question at Issue: _____.

   Thesis: The genetic engineering of crops should continue to have the support of our government and farmers.

4. For the following pair, supply two examples of a thesis: (1) an open thesis (with no stated premises) and (2) a complete thesis (with premises).

   Issue: Evolution in high school biology classes.

   Question at Issue: Should evolution be a required component of high school biology classes?

   Open Thesis: _____.

   Complete Thesis: _____.

SHAPING A WRITTEN ARGUMENT— RHETORICAL STRATEGIES

What do we mean by *rhetorical*? The term **rhetoric** has various shades of meaning, but the following definition from Aristotle provides the most useful approach for our purposes: "The art of using language to good effect, to prove, to convince, to persuade."

And thus to argue. The structure of written argument as we know it today dates back to the orations of the Greeks and Romans. The following features of classical argument, modified by contemporary rhetoric, can serve us well as long as we recognize that they are options, not requisite components. We write to communicate, not to fit a formula or fulfill a set of narrow expectations.

The Introduction

Your introduction may be a single paragraph or run to two or three paragraphs, depending on the strategies you choose and the amount of background required. Usually, you will state your **thesis** somewhere in the introductory paragraphs so that your reader is clear about the purpose of the essay. Some useful strategies:

1. You may begin your essay with a relevant **narrative**, either actual or fictional. For example, if your subject is euthanasia, you may describe a day in the life of

a terminally ill patient. Such a scene captures the reader's interest—not a necessity but sometimes a valuable rhetorical technique.

2. An applicable **quotation** can provide an interesting way into your argument.

3. An **opposing view** allows you to build your argument on a **refutation** of what is often the prevailing wisdom on an issue.

4. Some arguments need an **explanation** of the topic, particularly if it's technical in nature.

For one introductory strategy, examine the introduction to "College Athletes—Special Admissions?" (p. 94). Here the writer provides relevant background on flexibility in college admissions, leading up to the writer's position on special admission standards for college athletes. In "Is Google Making Us Stupid?" (see Additional Readings), Nicholas Carr introduces his essay with a quotation.

The Development of Your Argument

You need to present as many strong **premises** (reasons) in support of your position as necessary. (See Chapter 3.) These in turn have to be explained and defended with as much specific detail as you can provide. You may draw on your own knowledge and personal experience and on research to support your position. Called in classical rhetoric the *confirmation* of your position, this support should be connected explicitly to your thesis. As Plato said in the *Phaedrus*, "What is stated outright will be clearer than what is not."

Sometimes one premise requires a whole paragraph or more. Others may need only a few sentences and can be effectively grouped with additional premises. Here are two examples of paragraphs lifted from the middle of student essays, one that develops a single premise in some detail, another that groups a series of premises together in one paragraph. In both paragraphs, the premises are printed **bold**.

A single-premise paragraph:

Although in 2008 the Supreme Court ruled that the Second Amendment to the Constitution sanctioned the right of Americans to keep loaded handguns in their homes, **the decision should not curtail the right of communities to place constraints on the ownership of guns and their use**. For example, felons must not be authorized to own or use firearms. Communities should still be able to require registration of all guns, including those purchased at gun shows. The ruling leaves open the wise possibility that all guns could be traceable to their source so that law enforcement can keep track of illegal handguns used on the street. It left standing the laws that forbid guns from being carried into most Federal Buildings, public schools, or large public gatherings. The increase of rampages on school grounds since Columbine should be evidence enough that guns must be vigilantly controlled, even if the Constitution protects the right to own them. Although this is a hotly debated issue, ammunition should also be traceable. By analogy, most of us support strict controls over who can drive an automobile, another lethal weapon in the wrong hands, yet a cry goes up when the government threatens to limit the use of guns. While many of these limits are opposed by the NRA, I don't believe that the recent Supreme Court ruling means all restrictions are off the table.

A multipremise paragraph:

Although it is a controversial proposition, legalizing drugs has many advantages. First of all, **it will free the now overburdened legal system to do its job dispensing justice.** Cases will be processed with greater speed because the system won't be overwhelmed with drug cases. With the legalization of drugs, **violent drug-related crimes will decrease.** As a result, prisons will be less crowded, which in turn will allow serious offenders to serve longer terms. **Legalizing drugs will free law enforcement officials to combat other serious crimes more effectively.** With the money saved from law enforcement and legal procedures, a more effective campaign of educating the public on the maladies of drugs can be mounted, and more money will be available for the rehabilitation of drug addicts. Finally, **by legalizing drugs, we can slow down the spread of AIDS among HIV drug users,** who will be able to get clean needles and not have to share with other drug addicts, many of whom are infected with the AIDS virus. The positive results of legalizing drugs definitely outweigh the negative consequences.

How Many Premises Should an Argument Have?

It would seem that the greater the number of premises, the stronger the argument, but weak or questionable premises should not be included just to increase the number of premises. It's possible to have a strong argument with only two or three premises if those premises are convincing and are developed in detail.

The Conclusion

We have no simple rule of thumb here other than to suggest you conclude your essay rather than simply stop. If your paper is long and complex, you need to help your reader by briefly summarizing where you have been and what you propose. If, as a result of your argument, you have definite recommendations for action, your conclusion can carry such suggestions.

You and your readers should feel satisfied at the close of your paper. This does not mean that every paper needs a long and redundant formulaic conclusion. We refer you to the sample essays in Exercise 4E for models.

And so your argument assumes its shape. Commenting on effective rhetoric, Plato summed it up in his *Phaedrus*:

> Every discourse, like a living creature, should be so put together that it has its own body and lacks neither head nor feet, middle nor extremities, all composed in such a way that they suit both each other and the whole.

For further discussion of shaping your essay and developing a thesis, see the website MyCompLab.com.

A DIALECTICAL APPROACH TO ARGUMENT

Effective argument is more than the straightforward presentation of a thesis, premises, and their support. Persuasive argument depends on **dialectical thinking**. What do we mean by dialectical? Dialectic is the art of arriving at the truth by disclosing the views contrary to your own and overcoming them.

The English philosopher John Stuart Mill was trained by his father to argue both sides of every question and was taught that you had no right to a belief unless you understood the arguments for its opposite.

Eleanor Roosevelt advised women in politics to "argue the other side with a friend until you have found the answer to every point which might be brought up against you."

Cognitive psychologist Piaget maintained that one mark of a maturing mind is the ability to take another's point of view and thus be capable of considering two conflicting views on the same issue.

Clearly Lucy is not a dialectical thinker.

Addressing Counterarguments

To take this dialectical approach to argument, you as a writer must pay careful attention to **counterarguments**, to views contrary to your own. But, one might ask, why aid and abet the opposition by calling attention to their arguments? For a number of good reasons.

1. By **anticipating** your opponent's reasoning, you can often disarm the opposition. The "I recognize that . . ." approach can be very effective.

2. You can make your own position stronger when you state and then **refute** opposing premises by demonstrating their weakness or falseness. Writer Louis Menand recognized this point when he wrote, "Every idea or piece of knowledge worth having is, in part, a response to ideas or knowledge less worth having. Refuting a bad argument makes a good argument stronger."

3. By addressing counterarguments to your position, you also appear more **reasonable**. You show yourself to possess the kind of mind that embraces complexity.

4. When you **acknowledge** the possibility of merit in some of your opponents' reasoning, you have taken the ultimate step in establishing yourself as a knowledgeable, generous thinker.

5. You may even **discover weaknesses and contradictions** in your own thinking as you sort through the reasoning of your opponents. It is not easy to abandon cherished beliefs, but clear thinkers sometimes must.

How Much Counterargument?

How much counterargument should writers include in their papers? There is no precise answer. If the writer has strong refutations for every one of the counterarguments, then she may want to address them all. If, on the other hand, a writer thinks her premises are stronger than her refutation, she may want to include only a minimum of counterargument. In any case, a writer cannot ignore the most compelling opposing views, even if they provide the greatest challenge to the writer's own view. For example, for a paper in favor of the medical use of marijuana, the writer would have to deal with the fact that currently marijuana is a federally controlled drug that, like cocaine and heroin, is subject to legal controls.

Refutation and Concession

As you can see from this discussion, there is more than one way to address counterarguments. But address them you must, since to present a contradictory position and then leave it alone would confuse your reader. Here are two possible responses.

Refutation: Present a counterargument and then explain why this position is false, misleading, or irrelevant; discredit it in some well-reasoned way.

From a student essay in support of a law sanctioning active euthanasia:

Some say death and suffering are in keeping with God's universal plan for humanity. The dying process, no matter how long or how agonizing, has both spiritual and moral purpose, functioning to prepare people for the painless eternity of heaven. **To believe this argument though, one must believe there is life after death and many do not. So why can't people live and die in accordance with their own value system? Let both the religious and secular have some control of their own destiny; give those who choose to die that alternative, while honoring the belief of those who do not.**

Concession: Recognize the merit of a counterargument and so concede that point. If, for example, you are arguing in favor of euthanasia and want to refute the counterargument that euthanasia is a form of murder, you might begin this way:

Although I also believe that life is sacred and murder is wrong, I don't think that ending the life of a brain-dead patient is equivalent to murder since in the true sense of the word "life," this patient is not living.

Visually, the relationship between counterargument and refutation and concession looks something like this:

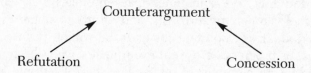

Rogerian Strategy

For a deeper understanding of concession, we turn to the work of Carl R. Rogers (1902–1987), a psychotherapist and communication theorist. Rogers recognized that people establish barriers and grow more rigid in their beliefs when threatened. In order to be heard, we need to develop *empathy*—the ability, in Rogers' words, "**to see the expressed idea and attitude from the other person's point of view**." It is through empathy that we can most successfully understand another's position and so concede appropriate points. The reader will feel less threatened as the writer reduces the gap between them and replaces hostile judgment with "mutual communication."

A British politician turned to Rogerian strategy when Iran and Britain were in a political crisis over the publication of Salmon Rushdie's *The Satanic Verses*, a novel that offended Muslims to such a degree that the Ayatollah Khomeini, then the ruler of Iran, called on Muslims around the world to kill Rushdie, sending the author into hiding for 10 years. The British government, while providing the author with continuous police protection, tried to temper Iran's fury. Britain's foreign secretary, Sir Geoffrey Howe, in a BBC radio broadcast meant to be heard by Iran, delivered the following message:

> We do understand that the book itself has been found deeply offensive
> by people of the Muslim faith. We can understand why it has been criticized.
> It is a book that is offensive in many other ways as well. We are not
> upholding the right of freedom to speak because we agree with the book.
> The book is extremely rude about us. It compares Britain with Hitler's Germany.
> We don't like that any more than people of the Muslim faith like the attacks
> on their faith. . . . [But] nothing in the book could justify a threat to the life
> of the author.

His comments were meant to forge a bond of empathy between the British and the Iranians—both groups, both governments were criticized by Rushdie—so of course, the British understood the anger of the Iranians. Through this mutual understanding, the foreign secretary hoped to persuade Iran to withdraw its demand that Rushdie be assassinated.

In a more recent example, conservative columnist Stephen Hayes, writing in the *Wall Street Journal*, praised Barack Obama's rhetorical style. "When he addresses a contentious issue, Mr. Obama almost always begins his answer with a respectful nod in the direction of the view he is rejecting." Soon after being inaugurated, President Obama held an interview with Hisham Melhem of Dubai-based Al Arabiya TV Network. He **conceded** that "we sometimes make mistakes." He condemned Iran's threats against Israel, support of terrorists, and efforts to obtain nuclear weapons, **"but," he conceded**, "it is important for us to be willing to talk to Iran," to find "potential avenues for progress." He went even further when he reminded his audience that "I have Muslim members of my family. I have lived in a Muslim country." He was meeting the opposition half way. (For additional examples of refutation and concession, see "Blinded by Science" and "Is Google Making You Stupid?" in Additional Readings.)

EXERCISE 4B

Analyzing Counterargument, Concession, and Refutation

1. Note how the writer in the following essay uses counterargument and concession to create a reasoned argument. Then identify, in writing, the writer's position and one example each of counterargument, refutation, and concession.
2. Be prepared to discuss how effectively the author uses all these rhetorical strategies.

Could It Be That Video Games Are Good for Kids?

STEVEN JOHNSON

Dear Sen. Clinton: I'm writing to commend you for calling for a $90-million 1 study on the effects of video games on children, and in particular the courageous stand you have taken in recent weeks against the notorious "Grand Theft Auto" series.

I'd like to draw your attention to another game whose nonstop violence and 2 hostility has captured the attention of millions of kids—a game that instills aggressive thoughts in the minds of its players, some of whom have gone on to commit real-world acts of violence and sexual assault after playing.

I'm talking, of course, about high school football. 3

I know a congressional investigation into football won't play so well with those 4 crucial swing voters, but it makes about as much sense as an investigation into the pressing issue of Xbox and PlayStation2.

Your current concern is over explicit sex in "Grand Theft Auto: San Andreas." 5 Yet there's not much to investigate, is there? It should get rated appropriately, and that's that. But there's more to your proposed study: You want to examine how video games shape children's values and cognitive development.

Kids have always played games. A hundred years ago they were playing stick- 6 ball and kick the can; now they're playing "World of Warcraft," "Halo 2" and "Madden 2005." And parents have to drag their kids away from the games to get them to do their algebra homework, but parents have been dragging kids away from whatever the kids were into since the dawn of civilization.

So any sensible investigation into video games must ask the "compared to what" question. If the alternative to playing "Halo 2" is reading "The Portrait of a Lady," then of course "The Portrait of a Lady" is better for you. But it's not as though kids have been reading Henry James for 100 years and then suddenly dropped him for Pokemon.   7

Another key question: Of all the games that kids play, which ones require the most mental exertion? Parents can play this at home: Try a few rounds of Monopoly or Go Fish with your kids, and see who wins. I suspect most families will find that it's a relatively even match. Then sit down and try to play "Halo 2" with the kids. You'll be lucky if you survive 10 minutes.   8

The great secret of today's video games that has been lost in the moral panic over "Grand Theft Auto" is how difficult the games have become. That difficulty is not merely a question of hand-to-eye coordination; most of today's games force kids to learn complex rule systems, master challenging new interfaces, follow dozens of shifting variables in real time and prioritize between multiple objectives.   9

In short, precisely the sorts of skills that they're going to need in the digital workplace of tomorrow.   10

Consider this one fascinating trend among teenagers: They're spending less time watching professional sports and more time simulating those sports on Xbox or PlayStation. Now, which activity challenges the mind more—sitting around rooting for the Green Bay Packers, or managing an entire football franchise through a season of "Madden 2005": calling plays, setting lineups, trading players and negotiating contracts? Which challenges the mind more—zoning out to the lives of fictional characters on a televised soap opera, or actively managing the lives of dozens of virtual characters in a game such as "The Sims"?   11

On to the issue of aggression, and what causes it in kids, especially teenage boys. Congress should be interested in the facts: The last 10 years have seen the release of many popular violent games, including "Quake" and "Grand Theft Auto"; that period also has seen the most dramatic drop in violent crime in recent memory. According to Duke University's Child Well-Being Index, today's kids are less violent than kids have been at any time since the study began in 1975. Perhaps, Sen. Clinton, your investigation should explore the theory that violent games function as a safety valve, letting children explore their natural aggression without acting it out in the real world.   12

Many juvenile crimes—such as the carjacking that is so central to "Grand Theft Auto"—are conventionally described as "thrill-seeking" crimes. Isn't it possible that kids no longer need real-world environments to get those thrills, now that the games simulate them so vividly? The national carjacking rate has dropped substantially since "Grand Theft Auto" came out. Isn't it conceivable that the would-be carjackers are now getting their thrills on the screen instead of the street?   13

Crime statistics are not the only sign that today's gaming generation is doing much better than the generation raised during that last cultural panic—over rock 'n' roll. Math SAT scores have never been higher; verbal scores have been climbing steadily for the last five years; nearly every indicator in the Department of Education   14 study known as the Nation's Report Card is higher now than when the study was implemented in 1971.

By almost every measure, the kids are all right. 15

Of course, I admit that one charge against video games is a slam dunk. Kids 16 don't get physical exercise when they play a video game, and indeed the rise in obesity among younger people is a serious issue. But, of course, you don't get exercise from doing homework, either.

When There Is No Other Side

What makes an issue worth arguing? While there are no fast rules, issues inappropriate for argument fall into three general categories. Some are so personal or so self-evident that they don't lend themselves to intelligent debate. Take for example the following claims:

Chocolate ice cream is far superior to strawberry.

or

Free, quality education should be provided for all children in America.

Neither proposition lends itself to the kind of exploration we have been discussing in this chapter, in the first instance because it concerns a personal and insignificant preference, and in the second because no one could in all seriousness argue against such a proposition.

A third, and more compelling, category is that in which the issue is simply too offensive to the majority of writers or readers. Arguments advocating racial bigotry or denial of the Holocaust, for example, fall into this category. Sometimes there is no other side worth defending.

Columnist Ellen Goodman illustrates how issues with no defensible other side have affected newspaper reporting.

At the end of the 19th century, when African Americans were strung like "strange fruit" from Southern trees, the *New York Times* required every story about lynching to include a quote from a segregationist justifying the hanging. At some point, the absurdity of that journalistic "evenhandedness" struck home to the editors. Murder is not a story with "another side."

I mention that footnote to my profession's history because I've always found something odd in the notion that "balance" is a seesaw, outfitted with exactly two seats for opponents whose views are carefully and equally weighted. A given story may have 15 sides . . . or one.

When terrorists struck on September 11, there was only one side. No editor demanded a quote from someone saying why it was fine to fly airplanes into buildings. . . .

In their efforts to achieve balance, good journalists try to give equal, or almost equal time to both sides in controversial debates. But as Chris Mooney points out in "Blinded by Science" (See Additional Readings), when the controversy centers on complex scientific issues, journalists need to depend on the opinions of reputable scientists and try to stay close to the facts. In many cases, as Mooney explains, careful research reveals that there is no responsible other side.

LOGICAL CONNECTIONS—COHERENCE

You need to establish a logical sequence of thought in your written argument, both at the sentence level and from paragraph to paragraph.

Joining Words

To incorporate counterargument, refutation, and concession into your written argument, you must signal relationships between ideas. The appropriate choice of conjunctions and transitional phrases can distinguish your position from counterarguments.

In his paper "College Athletes—Special Admissions?" (p. 94), the writer defends special admissions and uses "but" to signal his **refutation** of the counterargument that opens the paragraph, and chooses "while" to offer a **concession** to the opposing view.

> Some would argue that unprepared students admitted on athletic ability alone are at a severe disadvantage with even less time for academic pursuits than those more proficient. **But** most academically competitive schools now have special academic counselors trained to deal with the needs and problems of the student athlete. . . . **While** expensive academic support may not be the norm everywhere, the days of trying to shuffle athletes through the academic system, using them for their athletic skills with no regard for their own well-being, are waning.

It is through the different choices of joining words that writers established their slant on the issue. Let's review these distinctions:

Coordinating Conjunctions	Major Transitions	Subordinating Conjunctions
Counterargument, Refutation	**Counterargument, Refutation**	**Concession**
but yet	however on the other hand	while whereas although though

The degree to which subordinating conjunctions express concession can vary according to the content of the sentence. In some cases you may simply **acknowledge** your opponent's position without really conceding it, as in the following example:

Although smokers correctly defend their constitutional rights, the health of a nonsmoker should come first.

EXERCISE 4C

Making Rhetorical Choices

Take a stance on the issue of general education requirements by combining the first two sentences in number 1, using the appropriate joining word to reflect your position (your argument's **thesis**). Then combine the following pairs of sentences so that the paragraph will be logically "shaped" to support your position and reveal appropriate concessions.

1. Many educators argue for a broad and rigorous series of required general education courses.

   Others claim that students should not have to spend so much time on general courses outside their chosen majors.

2. A general education program often means that students can't graduate in the customary four years and so must delay their careers.

   Graduates with a broad liberal arts background tend to be promoted more consistently than their more narrowly trained competitors.

3. Most students can't afford to prolong their graduation.

   The nation can't afford a workforce of specialists uninformed about the world and unprepared in literacy and thinking skills.

4. Students are not inclined to learn in mandatory classes where they are not interested in the material.

Undergraduates are often unaware of what's available on a college campus or what their interests might be, until they are exposed to a variety of subjects.

More on Coherence

While you can manipulate ideas with joining words to signal relationships between sentences, you also need to develop coherence throughout your paper. The form of your paper can take many shapes, but you want the whole to be held together by an almost invisible glue, the connections clear but not too heavy-handed.

1. Your **thesis** will guide you as you build paragraphs and create a thread that weaves its way from opening sentence to conclusion.

2. Every sentence **should follow** from the sentence before it; each paragraph must follow logically from the one preceding it. As a writer, you take your reader's hand, never letting that reader stray from the flow of your argument. If you were to cut your paper into individual paragraphs, or even sentences, shake them up, and throw them in the air, a stranger should have no difficulty putting your paper together again.

3. Repeat **key words** to keep your reader focused on your train of thought. Pronouns, those words that refer back to nouns, can help relate one sentence to another, as can synonyms for nouns when repetition becomes monotonous.

4. For more on keeping ideas connected within sentences and paragraphs, see Chapter 8, "Parallelism," and our discussion of paragraph coherence on page 207.

EXERCISE 4D

Identifying Coherence Strategies

Once you have completed Writing Assignment 8, ahead in this chapter, or another writing assignment, make a copy and then cut the paper into separate paragraphs. Shuffle the paragraphs and bring the pieces to class. Exchange your paper with a classmate and see if you can reconstruct each other's work in the order the writer intended. If you encounter difficulties, consult with your partner to see what coherence strategies she needs to provide for a better flow of ideas from paragraph to paragraph.

SAMPLE ESSAYS

To help you see some of the rhetorical features of effective written argument in action, we have selected two examples for you to examine closely. The first is by a student, the second by a professional journalist.

EXERCISE 4E

Identifying Rhetorical Features of Argument

In the first essay, we identify the elements of written argument presented in this chapter. In the second, we ask you to do the same.

thesis

premises

counterarguments

refutations

concessions (You'll find that some concessions reflect Rogerian strategy.)

College Athletes—Special Admissions?

There are many different types of students, among them those who do well academically without really trying; those who do well but have to exert a lot of time and energy to do so; those who don't do well but could if given the right opportunity and set of circumstances; and those who don't do well but do excel in other areas. High school students who have excellent academic records will have little trouble meeting rigorous admissions requirements and getting accepted to an academically competitive school. But there are many students who don't necessarily have that choice. Many students with less outstanding academic records must rely on other strengths to allow them an equal chance at a good education. One of the most common strengths a student can have besides academic proficiency is athletic skill. Because each individual, regardless of academic record, has something important to offer a college or university, and because the world isn't clearly divided into "those who are smart" and "those who are not smart," I feel it is crucial for schools to be flexible in their admissions policies. Therefore, although some might argue that it is not fair for academically competitive colleges and universities to continue admitting academically ill-equipped student athletes, I think it is crucial, both for the sake of the student athlete and the school. 1

Many people argue that admitting inferior students simply because they are good athletes is unfair to those students under consideration for their academic records alone, that this practice discriminates against or constitutes unfair treatment of qualified applicants who aren't athletically inclined. But, in fact, as a matter of policy, colleges and universities accept a certain number of academically ineligible students, called "special admits," under several separate programs. Special admits are usually students with outstanding specialized talents (in music, dance, theatre, art, for example), or from overseas, or with unique life experiences, not to mention legacies with family connections, as well as students from disadvantaged backgrounds. So, why not consider those with superior athletic ability? 2

Others complain about the number of student athletes who don't graduate, claiming that schools waste their time and money on these students who never complete a degree. I agree that the statistics are frightening. Overall graduation rates for scholarship athletes are low. But if viewed in context, in comparison to all dropout rates, the picture takes on a different light, as suggested in an article a few years ago in *The Wall Street Journal*. 3

[margin annotations: Thesis–2 premises; Counterargument; Refutation; Counterargument; Concession]

Many people claim that only a small proportion of students who attend college on an athletic scholarship ever obtain a degree; but this is true of all entering freshmen in our colleges, since fewer than half emerge with degrees (McCormick).

Refutation

And in a more recent article in *U.S. News & World Report*, Ben Wildavsky claims that

. . . scholarship athletes at Division 1 schools actually graduate at a rate slightly higher than the overall student population: 58 percent versus 56 percent, according to the NCAA's latest annual report. The athletes' rate is up a bit compared with 1985 but has generally held steady since the NCAA passed controversial new academic requirements known as Proposition 48 in 1986 (2).

Wildavsky cites Duke University's athletic program as an outstanding example of success, with a graduation rate of 90 percent for scholarship athletes versus a 93 percent average for all Duke students (2).

Counterargument

Some would argue that unprepared students admitted on athletic ability alone   4 are at a severe disadvantage with even less time for academic pursuits than those more proficient. But most academically competitive schools now have special academic counselors trained to deal with the needs and problems of the student athlete. Specialized programs like San Francisco State's PLUK (Please Let Us Know) Program are there to see that athletes become better equipped intellectually, strengthening academic skills which may have been neglected in the past due to athletic participation. Bolstering the high academic achievement of its student athletes, Duke recognizes the pressures they face and provides exceptional "access to tutoring and coaching in study skills—particularly time management" (Wildavsky 2). While expensive academic support may not be the norm everywhere, the days of trying to shuffle athletes through the academic system, using them for their athletic skills with no regard for their own well-being, are waning.

Refutation

Concession

I agree that the academic performance of many student athletes remains a chal-   5 lenge. But in the meantime, it would be wrong not to allow these student athletes a chance to mature and gain social and intellectual skills that will help them wherever they go after college. In its "Big Ten Resolution on Intercollegiate Athletics" (representing 10 mid-western universities), the Committee on Institutional Cooperation stated:

. . . Participation in committed athletic training and competition can be deeply rewarding for students as a field of personal excellence, and can foster character through discipline, team membership, and the mutual respect expressed in fair play. Skilled coaches can offer outstanding leadership to college athletes, and exemplify standards of dedication, expertise, and sportsmanship that complement and enrich the academic missions of their campuses (1).

Refutation

Skip Prosser, the men's basketball coach at Wake Forest University, added to this position: "I've seen so many kids [college basketball players], given the opportunity, become great ambassadors for Wake Forest or wherever" (Suggs 4). And reviewing a recent book on the subject, *Reclaiming the Game: College Sports and*

Educational Values, John Thelin comments "one can attribute important educational values to varsity sports participation that are not strictly academic. . . . We cannot assume a sport subculture is necessarily antithetical to the proper values of the college experience" (108–109).

Premise

Allowing schools the option to admit such student athletes might be the only way these students could attend college. Their high school records might be so poor that they wouldn't be accepted anywhere on academics alone. In addition, many such students may not be able to afford tuition and would be excluded from scholarships unless money was available for athletes as well as scholars. In on-going efforts to raise graduation rates for college athletes, the National Collegiate Athletic Association (NCAA) has been recommending more demanding academic requirements. However,   6

> coaches charge that they will knock more black players out of college. "They're legislating against African-American individuals," fulminates Jim Harrick, the men's basketball coach at the University of Georgia. . . . Most of the top basketball players are black, and coaches like Mr. Harrick fear any move could jeopardize their efforts to recruit the best players (Suggs 2).

Besides, college sports programs provide one of the very few avenues available for promising young athletes to fully develop the necessary athletic prowess necessary for attempting to break into professional sports. Since it is often the more academically competitive schools that have the resources to build and support reputable, widely recognized sports programs, these are the schools that young athletes need to attend in order to increase their chances of fulfilling their primary career goal—professional sports. This idea is similar to that of a superior academic student who wants to attend Harvard Business School to increase his or her chances of fulfilling a career goal in business. Those students with superior athletic ability shouldn't be discriminated against and kept out of the good colleges and universities.   7

While it's the student athletes themselves I'm most concerned with—their right to higher education, including preprofessional training—the schools who accept these athletes benefit as well. Recruiting promising high school athletes can add significantly to a college's established sports program and a good sports program can, in turn, be a big factor in attracting desirable applicants, both academic and athletic. Winning teams add to the overall reputation of a school, both inside and outside its immediate geographical area. Schools with winning teams can attract many good applicants as well as casting the deciding vote for a student torn between two otherwise equal schools.   8

Successful sports programs can also greatly affect alumni giving and community support for a school. Sports booster clubs, alumni, and parents of students, past and present, are some of the largest givers of financial support to colleges and universities. Giving to favorite teams can also spill over into donations to other areas of a university with overall giving increasing, especially if it has winning teams.   9

And so, for the good of the school, and more importantly, for the benefit of students who might not otherwise have a chance to realize their dreams or goals, I feel it is of the utmost importance for schools to continue admitting student athletes, even those not academically qualified.   10

Premise *Premise* *Premise* *Conclusion—restates Thesis*

Works Cited

Big Ten Resolution on Intercollegiate Athletics. 2 Nov. 2001. Web. 29 Apr. 2005
  <http://www.math.umd.edu/~jmc/COIA/BigTen.html>.

McCormick, Robert E. "Colleges Get Their Athletes for a Song." *The Wall Street Journal* 20 Aug. 1995. Print.

Suggs, Welch. "Who's Going to Play?" *Chronicle of Higher Education* 48 (26 July 2002). EBSCO*host*. San Francisco State U., J. Paul Leonard Lib. Web. 28 Apr. 2005.

Thelin, John R. "Reclaiming the Game: College Sports and Educational Values." *Journal of Higher Education* 76 (Jan/Feb 2005). EBSCO*host*. San Francisco State U, J. Paul Leonard Lib. Web. 28 Apr. 2005.

Wildavsky, Ben. "Graduation Blues." *USNews.com* 18 Apr. 2002. Web. 29 Apr. 2005.

A Case for Affirmative Action

CYNTHIA TUCKER

Why are many Americans—white Americans, mostly—so upset about college   1
admissions programs that take race into account for a handful of students whose test scores are slightly below standards? Why are programs that boost the chances of black and brown students so controversial, while similar programs that benefit white students go without notice?

For example, the country's premier colleges and universities have long   2
reserved places for the lesser-achieving children of their well-heeled graduates and donors. At the University of Georgia, family connections are one of the dozen or so factors—along with race—used to assess about 20 percent of its applicants who don't quite meet academic standards. In other words, a kid whose test scores and grades are not quite good enough may get into Georgia anyway if his mom or dad is a graduate.

That practice allows weaker students—most of them white—to be admitted at   3
the expense of better students. Yet no one bemoans it as an assault on the vaunted "meritocracy."

College admissions also grant athletic "preferences," a device that happens to   4
benefit many kids—black, white, and brown—who otherwise could not get near their chosen college. For some reason, a black kid with low SATs who can score touchdowns and generate a lot of money for the university is not nearly as offensive as a black kid with low scores who just wants an education.

To be fair, some criticism of college admissions efforts is legitimate. Awarding   5
scholarships based on race makes no sense, since they would often end up giving financial aid to the black upper-middle-class but not to the white poor. Besides that, poorly run affirmative-action programs, such as the contracting set-aside program run by the city of Atlanta, tend to generate resentments that splash over onto better-run and more necessary programs.

But much criticism of affirmative action in college admissions is based on myth,   6
misunderstanding and—how shall I say this?—simple bigotry. Affirmative-action programs exist only in 25 percent to 40 percent of the nation's institutions of higher learning; the other 60 percent to 75 percent accept all applicants. So the controversy centers around the nation's most prestigious institutions.

Admission to those elite colleges is highly competitive, because a diploma from 7
Harvard or Emory nearly guarantees a financially rewarding career. Rejected white
applicants, looking for an explanation for their failure, often believe they were
unfairly supplanted by an unqualified minority student.

Consider, however, an analogy used by Thomas Kane of the Brookings Institu- 8
tion, likening affirmative action in colleges to the handicapped parking space:

> Eliminating the reserved space would have only a minuscule effect on parking
> options for non-disabled drivers. But the sight of the open space will frustrate
> many passing motorists who are looking for a space. Many are likely to be-
> lieve that they would now be parked if the space were not reserved.

Scaling back affirmative action would cripple the prospects for black partici- 9
pation in this nation's economic, political and social elite. William Bowen, former
president of Princeton University, and Derek Bok, former president of Harvard
University, recently conducted a landmark study of affirmative action at 28 elite
institutions, including Atlanta's Emory University. They found that black graduates of those colleges go on to earn advanced degrees—medicine, law, MBAs—at
slightly higher rates than their white counterparts, and also become more active
in civic affairs.

Because America proffers advancement through education, programs to en- 10
hance educational opportunities for students of color remain critical—perhaps
more important than any other form of affirmative action. Since my grandfathers
would not have been admitted to white universities, it does not seem unreasonable
to create a form of "legacy" for their descendants.

A TWO-STEP PROCESS FOR
WRITING A COMPLETE ARGUMENT

The next two writing assignments provide steps in completing a polished argument.

WRITING ASSIGNMENT 7

Arguing Both Sides of an Issue

The Approach

Below is a list of proposals advocating a position on a social issue. Choose **one** and
write two separate arguments, one **defending** and one **refuting** the proposal. For
each argument:

1. Write a short **thesis** at the top of each page.
2. For each position, provide **relevant premises (reasons)** that are, to the best
   of your knowledge, accurate although not fully developed yet.

3. You will have two separate papers with **a paragraph for each premise**. Although each paragraph should be written coherently with fluent sentences, you don't, at this stage, need to provide logical transitions between paragraphs for a coherent whole.

4. You need not provide an introduction or conclusion. All this will come later in Writing Assignment 8.

The Topics

Choose carefully because your topic will be the same for the expanded argument you'll write for Writing Assignment 8.

1. Parents should be permitted to withhold vaccines from their school-age children.

2. The use of electronic devices while a driver is in motion should be prohibited in every state.

"This one's too hard to type on while I'm driving."

3. The military draft should be reinstated.

4. Public service should be required for all people between the ages of 18 and 25.

5. The federal government should provide financial support for stem cell research.

6. Evolution should be a required component of biology classes in high schools.

7. Medical research on animals should be forbidden by law.

8. Athletes who have used performance-enhancing drugs should be permitted to hold the records they have achieved.

9. The SAT should be considered a necessary component of college admission criteria.

10. Restaurants should not be allowed to use trans fats in their food.

11. All restaurants should be required to post the calories of their menu items.

12. Students should be paid to do well on standardized tests.

13. Girls 17 and under should be required to obtain parental permission before having an abortion.

14. Nationwide standardized tests throughout elementary and secondary school have a negative effect on education.

15. Torture is justified when the security of the nation is at stake.

If another issue interests you more, be sure the issue is one worth arguing from both sides and can be expressed as a proposal similar to those above. Consult your instructor before selecting an alternative topic.

Audience

A wide range of your peers: those who might take one side or the other and those who have not, as yet, formed any opinion.

Purpose

To present both sides of a controversial issue so you and your readers are forced to consider opposing views. Here is an example:

In a recent edition, the *Wellness Letter* of the University of California, Berkeley, addressed the question at issue, "Who needs Alzheimer's testing?" Summarizing their findings, they presented arguments for and against in the same format we propose for Assignment 7.

Who Needs Alzheimer's Testing?

Some arguments made for universal screening:

An early diagnosis of Alzheimer's or another type of dementia allows the family and patient to prepare financially and emotionally. While still competent, the patient can make a will and other legal arrangements.   1

As the disease progresses, the patient can be urged to give up driving, cooking, traveling alone, and other potentially dangerous activities.   2

Medications can be administered. There are five FDA-approved drugs. They neither prevent nor cure dementia, but in some people they produce temporary slowing of mental decline.   3

Public awareness would increase, which might lead to an upsurge in research spending.   4

If we develop reliable tests now, we'll be ahead of the curve when we do have good treatments.   5

Screening may uncover dementias with other causes, such as certain thyroid problems, depression, or vitamin B-12 deficiency, which can be treated.   6

On the con side:

Universal screening would include many people with no memory problems at all. Apart from the waste of time and money, testing can lead to worry, depression, and family disruption.   7

There's no sure way to differentiate between mild age-related cognitive impairment, which may never get worse, and early Alzheimer's. If the test tells you that you're okay now but may develop dementia later, what can you do with that information?   8

Diagnostic tests for early dementia are not reliable, especially in people under 70. Misdiagnoses could be devastating. People might lose their jobs, driver's licenses, or even their potential caregivers, and be unable to get medical or life insurance.   9

Alzheimer's medications are expensive, and their benefits are very limited and of short duration. They are prescribed only for people who are already exhibiting clear signs of dementia.   10

Early diagnosis would benefit the drug companies more than the public, according to some critics. And for some researchers and doctors, there's money to be made from devising and administering the tests.   11

WRITING ASSIGNMENT 8

Taking a Stand

In this essay, take a stand on one side of the issue you debated in Writing Assignment 7, constructing as persuasive an argument as possible.

1. Your **thesis** should express your **own position** on the proposition you addressed in the previous assignment.

2. To support **your position**, draw on the **premises** you presented in Assignment 7, discarding reasoning that seems weak or irrelevant, adding reasons where you find gaps in your earlier paper. Strengthen your argument with as much data as you think necessary to make your case for a skeptical audience.

3. Address significant **opposing views**, acknowledging, conceding, and refuting in the manner best suited to your stand on the issue. Do not elaborate the opposing views in the same way you develop your own premises.

4. Include an introduction and a conclusion.

5. Revise your paper for coherence, at both the sentence and paragraph level.

For help in organizing your paper, refer to the sample essays in Exercise 4E.
Important: To complete the assignment, include the following attachment typed out on a separate sheet as an introductory page:

    a. Your **issue, question at issue**, and **thesis**

    b. Your principal argument set out in **standard form** (see Chapter 3)

Audience

A wide range of your peers: those who would agree with you, those who would disagree, and those who have not, as yet, formed any opinion.

Purpose

To present a convincing, balanced argument for your position on a controversial issue in order to persuade your readers to adopt your point of view.

A FINAL CHECKLIST FOR AN EFFECTIVE ARGUMENT

    Choose an issue worth arguing.

    Express your thesis clearly.

    Support your own position as thoroughly as possible.

    Anticipate relevant opposing views (counterarguments).

    Provide appropriate concessions and refutations.

    Develop empathy with your audience.

    Create a coherent flow.

SUMMARY

Convincing arguments usually contain an introduction to the topic, a stated **thesis**, well-supported **premises**, acknowledgment of **opposing views**, and a conclusion. Successful written argument depends on a **dialectical approach** in which writers address both their own position and the views of others.

A well-written argument requires joining sentences for logic and fluency and developing coherent links between paragraphs to express relationships.

KEY TERMS

Concession   a statement that grants the opposing view.

Counterargument   an opposing view in an argument.

Dialectic   a method of argument that systematically weighs contradictory ideas.

Empathy   the ability to see and understand an idea or issue from the other person's point of view.

Issue   any topic of concern and controversy.

Question at issue   a particular aspect of the issue under consideration.

Refutation   an explanation of why a position is false or weak.

Rhetoric   the art of using language to good effect, to prove, to convince, to persuade.

Rogerian strategy   an explicit effort to see ideas from an opponent's point of view; the cultivation of empathy with the opposition; a concept derived from the research of psychologist Carl Rogers.

Thesis   a statement of a writer's position; in argument, a response to the question at issue.

CHAPTER 5

The Language of Argument— Definition

"When I use a word," Humpty Dumpty said in rather a scornful tone, *"it means just what I choose it to mean—neither more nor less."*

—LEWIS CARROLL, *ALICE THROUGH THE LOOKING GLASS*

"If you would argue with me, first define your terms."

—VOLTAIRE

"Every word has its story."

—ANTOINE MEILLET

In Chapter 4, we discuss how to construct written arguments that explore an issue in depth and address opposing views. Now we'd like to concentrate on the precise use of language, on paying close attention to how we choose our words, and thus on how we make our meaning precise and clear to others. It is important that we know the meaning and the power of the words we use, and that when we write, our readers share our understanding of these words. When we cannot assume that our readers share an understanding of our terms, we need to define them.

DEFINITION AND PERCEPTION

Who Controls the Definitions?

Ellen Willis, writing in *Rolling Stone*, admonishes us, "Find out who controls the definitions, and you have a pretty good clue who controls everything else." Toni Morrison, in her novel *Beloved*, illustrates the brutal oppression of slavery with the story of the slave Sixo. When the schoolteacher accused him of stealing the shoat (a piece of pork), Sixo claimed he wasn't *stealing* but *improving his property*. The teacher beat Sixo "to show him that definitions belonged to the definers—not the defined."

Alice responded to Humpty Dumpty's claim in the opening quotation of this chapter with, "The question is, whether you *can* make words mean so many different things." Humpty Dumpty continued, "The question is, which is to be master—that's all."

In her book *Waiting for Daisy*, Peggy Orenstein chronicles her experience with infertility. She learns that 90 percent of women in their late thirties will conceive a child in two years (if their partner has a viable sperm count), but the medical establishment defines infertility as one year of trying but failing to get pregnant. Who benefits from this definition?

Nowhere is the precision of language more important than in politics. Yet nowhere is meaning more likely to be manipulated. Writing in the *New York Times Magazine*, political writer Matt Bai explained how the Republican party controlled the language of debate during the 2004 election. The Republicans chose terms like "tax relief" and "partial-birth abortions" to cast a favorable aura around their policies of low taxes and opposition to abortion.

Defining Ourselves

Through the centuries, people have been defining what they consider themselves to be, using the term *man* in a number of inventive ways.

Plato
First, he put man in the class "biped" and differentiated him from others in the class by describing him as "a featherless biped." When his rival, Diogenes, produced a plucked chicken, Plato had to add "having broad nails" as a further distinguishing characteristic.

Shakespeare
"What a piece of work is a man! How noble in reason! how infinite in faculty! in form, in moving, how express and admirable! in action how like an angel! in apprehension how like a god! the beauty of the world! the paragon of animals! And yet, to me what is this quintessence of dust? Man delights not me; no, nor woman neither." (*Hamlet*)

Ambrose Bierce
"An animal so lost in rapturous contemplation of what he thinks he is as to overlook what he indubitably ought to be. His chief occupation is extermination of other animals and his own species, which, however, multiplies with such insistent rapidity as to infest the whole habitable earth and Canada." (*Devil's Dictionary*)

Our definitions can reveal how we see people—as individuals and collectively. In his book *Days of Obligation*, writer Richard Rodriguez points out that American feminists have appropriated the word *macho* "to name their American antithesis," a man who is "boorish" and "counterdomestic." But Rodriguez tells us that in Mexican

Spanish "*machismo* is more akin to the Latin *gravitas*. The male is serious. The male provides. The Mexican male never abandons those who depend upon him." As this example illustrates, when different cultures share languages, shifts in meaning often occur, reflecting cultural bias. Feminist Gloria Steinem pointed out our culture's sexual bias in its traditional definitions of the following terms, definitions that have played crucial roles in determining how women and men view themselves and others:

> *work:* something men do, go to; as distinguished from housework and childcare, which is what women do
>
> *art:* what white men produce
>
> *crafts:* what women and ethnic minorities do

Shifting Definitions

Fortunately, these definitions are changing. Indeed, we have historical precedent for scientific definitions shifting to conform to new ways of thinking. In the 19th century, alcoholism was defined as criminal behavior. When the term was redefined as an illness after World War I, considerable progress in treatment became possible. Conversely, when the American Psychological Association stopped classifying homosexuality as an illness, the homosexual community was understandably gratified by the revision of a definition unjust and damaging.

In 2005, three astrophysicists surprised the scientific community when they identified what they thought to be a tenth planet, later named *Eris*. But more surprising, the smallest of the nine known planets, *Pluto*, was then determined to be too small to qualify. Heated debate erupted over the definition of what constituted a planet. If it was size, then Pluto had to go. In fact, Pluto and Eris are currently considered "dwarf planets." After 78 years of counting nine planets, we now have only eight, not ten as it seemed for a year or two. One astronomer cast the controversy this way: "Like continents, planets are defined more by how we think of them than by someone's after-the-fact pronouncement." Even in fact-based science, precise definitions can be slippery.

A look at a few familiar words can illustrate how meaning can migrate. For example:

> **elite:** Once a French word carrying an accent over the *é*, it referred to the privileged who had power, taste, and money and were looked up to or envied. Gradually it moved in a less favorable direction, until today the right-wing media use the term "the liberal elite" to denigrate liberals, especially celebrities, journalists, and academics.
>
> **brand:** Formerly the term meant simply the company name for a product. Nike was just the name of an athletic shoe. Today, a website offers instructions to companies on marketing their product and defines *brand* as the "proprietary visual, emotional, rational, and cultural image" associated with a company, a product, or even a person. Soccer player David Beckham is considered a brand. During the 2008 presidential campaign, Frank Rich in the *New York Times* commented, "Obama-branded change is snowballing . . . ," while according to the *San Francisco Chronicle*, McCain was building "his brand." People appeared to be "identifying more with

"Elitist!"

Brand McCain" rather than "Obama's hope brand." "Candidates are brands . . . the key to all branding is to get people to identify with the candidate." **"Selling voters on the brand is crucial to closing the deal,"** claimed the headline. Painter Andy Warhol foresaw this phenomenon, first with his portraits of Campbell's soup cans and then his multiple images of Marilyn Monroe, Jackie Kennedy, and Elizabeth Taylor. The image is the brand; people become objects.

market: Originally, it was a place where one bought and sold agricultural products and food in general. Now anything or even a person can be a *market*, the target for anyone trying to sell anything.

When meaning moves, it can both reflect and influence changes in the culture.

"Spin through and see if anything's targeted at us tonight."

Definition: the Social Sciences and Government

In a study on child abuse and health, which we cite in an exercise in Chapter 7, the researchers first had to define child abuse before they could determine its effect on women's health. They separated child abuse into three categories—emotional, physical, and sexual. Then they defined each category.

emotional abuse: repeated rejection or serious physical threats from parents, tension in the home more than 25 percent of the time, and frequent violent fighting among parents.

physical abuse: strong blows from an adult or forced eating of caustic substances; firm slaps were excluded.

sexual abuse: any nonvoluntary sexual activity with a person at least five years older.

Researchers interviewed 700 women from a private gynecological practice and tabulated their responses according to these categories. Without **clear-cut definitions** to guide them, social scientists would be left with subjective impressions rather than quantifiable results.

In law, definitions often need to be revised to avoid unfair applications as society changes. Such was the case when SUVs slipped though a giant loophole in the tax code inadvertently left gaping. To help small businesses and farmers, the government provided tax credits and accelerated depreciation for small trucks, vehicles defined not by function but by their weight—more than 6,000 pounds. Into this provision slipped the SUV, once rare for personal use but for many years now a popular family vehicle. A variety of professional people could receive a tax break for driving very large, very expensive SUVs to work and around town. To achieve fairness, we need new definitions: "work vehicles" and "passenger vehicles."

Texas politicians and educators understand the role of definition. In 2004 the Texas Board of Education approved new definitions of marriage for the state's high school and middle school textbooks. Where formerly the texts used terms like *married partners*, the board agreed to rewrite the definition of marriage as a "lifelong union between a husband and a wife," thus conforming to Texas law banning gay marriage. (For discussion of another Texas law, see "Blinded by Science" in Additional Readings.)

LANGUAGE: AN ABSTRACT SYSTEM OF SYMBOLS

Abstract words can present particular difficulties when it comes to stipulating precise meaning. But language itself, whether it refers to an **abstraction** (politics) or a **concrete** object (a given politician), is an abstract system of symbols. The word is not the thing itself, but a *symbol* or *signifier* used to represent the thing we refer to, which is the *signified*. For example, the word *cat* is a symbol or signifier for the animal itself, the signified.

"Cat"

THE SYMBOL or SIGNIFIER
(the word)

THE SIGNIFIED
(the thing being referred to)

But meaning is made only when the signified is processed through the mind of someone using or receiving the words. Whenever a speaker, writer, listener, or reader encounters a word, a lifetime of associations renders the word, and thus the image it conjures up, distinct for each individual.

As literary theorist Stanley Fish points out, meaning is dependent not only on the individual but also on the context, situation, and interpretive community. To illustrate this point, let's look at the word *host*. It means one thing if we are at a party, something different if we're discussing parasites with a biologist, and something else entirely if we are at a Christian church. Hence, the context or situation determines our understanding of *host*.

If, however, you are not a member of a religion that practices the ritual of communion or are not conversant with parasitology, then you may understand the meaning of *host* only as the giver of a party. You are not part of the interpretive community, in this case a religious community or a scientific discipline, that understands *host* as a consecrated wafer, a religious symbol, or as an organism on which another lives.

Even when the signified is concrete, individual experience and perception will always deny the word complete stability; the range of possible images will still be vast. Take the word *table*. Nothing of the essence of table is part of the word *table*. Although most words in English (or any modern language) have roots and a history in older languages, the assignation of a particular meaning to a given term remains essentially arbitrary. While all English speakers share a general understanding of the word *table*, each user or receiver of this word, without having considerably more detail, will create a different picture.

If the symbolic representation of a **concrete**, visible object such as a table is as unstable as our discussion suggests, think how much more problematic **abstract** terms must be. Were we to substitute the abstraction *freedom* for the concrete *table*, the range of interpretations would be considerably more diverse and much more challenging to convey to others. This becomes particularly evident when political issues are at stake. For example, some see the war in Iraq as bringing "**freedom**" to Iraqis; others see it as an unlawful "**occupation**" of a foreign country.

Visual pictures, which arise when concrete objects are signaled, don't come to mind as readily when we refer to abstractions, a distinction that led Shakespeare to explain why poets must give "to airy nothing a local habitation and a name."

In the following poem, Thomas Lux explores the instability of language as readers, even when reading the same text, make it uniquely their own.

THE VOICE YOU HEAR WHEN YOU READ SILENTLY

is not silent, it is a speaking
out-loud voice in your head: it is spoken,
a voice is saying it
as you read. It's the writer's words,
of course, in a literary sense
his or her "voice" but the sound
of that voice is the sound of your voice.
Not the sound your friends know
or the sound of a tape played back
but your voice
caught in the dark cathedral
of your skull, your voice heard
by an internal ear informed by internal abstracts
and what you know by feeling,
having felt. It is your voice
saying, for example, the word "barn"
that the writer wrote
but the "barn" you say
is a barn you know or knew. The voice
in your head, speaking as you read,
never says anything neutrally—some people
hated the barn they knew,
some people love the barn they know
so you hear the word loaded
and a sensory constellation
is lit: horse-gnawed stalls,
hayloft, black heat tape wrapping
a water pipe, a slippery
spilled chirrr of oats from a split sack,
the bony, filthy haunches of cows . . .
And "barn" is only a noun—no verb
or subject has entered into the sentence yet!

The voice you hear when you read to yourself
is the clearest voice: you speak it
speaking to you.

EXERCISE 5A

Reading Language

1. In this poem, what is the difference between the voice of the writer and the voice of the reader?
2. What is the significance of the exclamation mark at the end of the following lines?
   And "barn" is only a noun—no verb
   or subject has entered into the sentence yet!
3. What is Lux saying about language and the act of reading?

(For further discussion of the art of reading, see "Is Google Making Us Stupid?" in Additional Readings.)

The Importance of Concrete Examples

Semanticist S. I. Hayakawa discussed the idea of an **abstraction ladder** in which language starts on the ground, so to speak, with an object available to our sense of perception, and moves up to concepts abstracted from, derived from, the concrete source—for example, from a specific cow (Bessie) to cow to livestock to farm assets to asset and finally to wealth. Liberally adapted from Hayakawa, such a ladder would look like this:

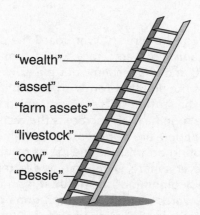

"wealth"
"asset"
"farm assets"
"livestock"
"cow"
"Bessie"

He stressed that our powers of abstraction are indispensable. "The ability to climb to higher and higher levels of abstraction is a distinctively human trait without which none of our philosophical or scientific insights would be possible." But he cautioned against staying at too high a level of abstraction. The kind of "thinking" we must be extremely wary of is that which *never* leaves the higher verbal levels of abstraction, the kind that never points *down* the abstraction ladder to lower levels of abstraction and from there to the extensional world:

> "What do you mean by *democracy*?"
> "Democracy means the preservation of human *rights*."
> "What do you mean by *rights*?"
> "By rights I mean those privileges God grants to all of us—I mean man's inherent privileges."
> "Such as?"
> "Liberty, for example."
> "What do you mean by *liberty*?"
> "Religious and political freedom."
> "And what does that mean?"
> "Religious and political freedom is what we enjoy under a democracy."

The writer never moves down to the essential lower levels on the abstraction ladder, and a discourse consisting only of abstractions, devoid of concrete details and examples, is necessarily vague, often difficult for the reader to understand, and, in this definition of democracy, circular.

To avoid the confusion that abstractions can generate, Hayakawa suggested pointing down "to extensional levels wherever necessary; in writing and speaking, this means giving **specific examples** of what we are talking about," grounding our arguments in the **concrete**.

Compare the empty, circular definition of **democracy** Hayakawa quotes above with the **concrete illustrations** that illuminate E. B. White's celebrated World War II definition of the same term.

> We received a letter from the Writers' War Board the other day asking for a statement on "The Meaning of Democracy." It presumably is our duty to comply with such a request, and it is certainly our pleasure. Surely the Board knows what democracy is. It is the line that forms on the right. It is the don't in don't shove. It is the hole in the stuffed shirt through which the sawdust slowly trickles; it is the dent in the high hat. Democracy is the recurrent suspicion that more than half of the people are right more than half of the time. It is the feeling of privacy in the voting booths, the feeling of communion in the libraries, the feeling of vitality everywhere. Democracy is a letter to the Editor. Democracy is the score at the beginning of the ninth. It is an idea that hasn't been disproved yet, a song the words of which have not gone bad. It's the mustard on the hot dog and the cream in the rationed coffee. Democracy is a request from a War Board, in the middle of a morning in the middle of a war, wanting to know what democracy is.

Such specificity is what writer Annie Dillard values when she says, "This is what life is all about: salamanders, fiddle tunes, you and me and things . . . the fizz into **particulars.**" And what novelist Vladimir Nabokov prizes when he asks us to "Caress the details, the divine **details.**"

EXERCISE 5B

Levels of Specificity

Good writing requires that general concepts or categories be illustrated by specific examples. To practice providing the kind of concrete, specific detail Dillard and Nabokov talk about above, rank the words and phrases in the following lists, giving a *1* to the most general, with higher numbers moving through each level of specificity. You may find more than one item on a given level.

> *Example:*   2   1   4   3   2
>   actors;   performers;   Will Smith;   movie actors;   singers;
>
>   4   4   3
>   Mariah Carey;   Jennifer Aniston;   pop singers

1. painting
   work of art
   Whistler's Mother
   American painting
   painting by Whistler
2. shuffle
   move
   amble
   walk slowly
   travel on foot
   drive
   walk
3. sport
   doubles
   five-card draw
   boxing
   card games
   activity
   poker

   tennis
   bridge
   singles
   welterweight fight
4. negative characteristic
   characteristic
   cheating
   unethical characteristic
   plagiarism
5. novel
   American novel
   reading
   The Grapes of Wrath
   fiction
   literature
   novel by Steinbeck
   modern novel
6. vertebrates
   Alaskan huskies

biped	Jessica Simpson
Chris Rock	man
woman	cat
dogs	Siamese cats
animals	basset hounds
quadruped	

Abstractions and Evasion

Sometimes people use abstractions and evasive language, consciously or unconsciously, to confuse, distort, conceal, or avoid; in short, to manipulate others—a practice Hemingway laments in his war novel, *A Farewell to Arms:*

> I was always embarrassed by the words sacred, glorious, and sacrifice and the expression in vain. We had heard them, sometimes standing in the rain almost out of earshot, so that only the shouted words came through, and had read them, on proclamations that were slapped up by billposters or other proclamations, now for a long time, and I had seen nothing sacred, and the things that were glorious had no glory and the sacrifices were like the stockyards at Chicago if nothing was done with the meat except to bury it. There were many words that you could not stand to hear and finally only the names of places had dignity. Certain numbers were the same way and certain dates and these with the names of the places were all you could say and have them mean anything. Abstract words such as glory, honor, courage, or hallow were obscene beside the concrete names of villages, the numbers of roads, the names of rivers, the numbers of regiments and the dates.

Hemingway eloquently indicates the power of concrete nouns to honor the dead.

Orville Schell, dean of the Graduate School of Journalism at the University of California at Berkeley, refers to the **obfuscation** (to make unclear) surrounding discussion of the Iraq war. "The wanton corruption of the meaning of words in political discourse has reached a perilous point where it is difficult to take the utterance of any public figure at face value. . . . As words have lost their descriptive power, we have suffered a break in the normative order. Our whole process of describing, thinking, discussing and acting has been corrupted at its source."

Today, we use the term *war on terror* without thinking about its precise implications. In Britain, a government spokesman explained why British officials chose to avoid the term because, on careful analysis, they recognized that "we can't win by military means alone, because this isn't us against one organized enemy with a clear identity and a chosen set of objectives." They saw that such an abstract term is "vague and simplistic," acknowledging that the "fight against extremists is not a clash or a war of civilizations."

British writer George Orwell addressed the political significance of language in his celebrated essay "Politics and the English Language," claiming that:

> If thought corrupts language, language can also corrupt thought. To think clearly is a necessary first step towards political regeneration: so that the fight against bad English is not frivolous and is not the exclusive concern of professional writers . . . Political speech and writing are largely the defense of the indefensible. . . . Defenseless villages are bombarded from the air, the inhabitants driven out into the countryside, the cattle machine-gunned, the huts set on fire with incendiary bullets: this is called *pacification*.

Pacification is an example of a **euphemism** that deliberately obscures the concrete reality of war.

Euphemism and Connotation

Euphemisms—indirect, less expressive words or phrases for sensitive ideas—are sometimes justified as a means of sparing feelings: Someone *passed away* rather than *died*, or a fat person is referred to as *big-boned*. But we must be particularly wary of language that **deliberately** camouflages precise meaning. A few years ago, when opposition to building the controversial MX missile grew heated, the proponents began to call the missiles "peacemakers," hoping to deflect public reaction away from the notion of an arms buildup.

" 'Born in conservation,' if you don't mind. 'Captivity' has negative connotations."

As suggested by the elephants' conversation, euphemisms can give a positive connotation to a negative experience. Many words carry both a denotative and a connotative meaning.

Denotation refers to the basic dictionary meaning of a word, separate from its emotional associations.

Connotation means the suggestive or associative implications beyond the literal, explicit sense of a word.

For example, think of the words *bachelor* and *spinster*. Both refer to (denote) an unmarried adult. But now consider the connotation. In our culture, one word carries a positive connotation, the other a negative one. The two words *slender* and *skinny* both mean thin. But one would be a compliment, the other not. On a more serious level, Susan Jacoby, in her book *The Age of American Unreason*, points to politicians and the media, who substitute *troop* for *soldier*, turning "an individual . . . into an anonymous-sounding troop," encouraging "the public to think about war and its casualties in a more abstract way."

EXERCISE 5C

Beware the Euphemism

Below is a list of paired terms or phrases. For each, briefly explain how the language of the second phrase dulls or deflects the meaning of the initial term, and discuss why you think such euphemistic language crept in.

TERM		EUPHEMISM
1) foreign	/	offshore
2) taxes	/	revenue enhancement
3) tax cuts	/	tax relief
4) civilian losses	/	collateral damage
5) cloning	/	"somatic cell nuclear transfer"
6) shot by a fellow soldier	/	friendly fire
7) face wrinkles	/	laugh lines
8) torture	/	alternative set of procedures
9) waterboarding	/	enhanced interrogation
10) timber industry legislation allowing forest exploitation	/	Healthy Forests Restoration Act

DEFINITION IN WRITTEN ARGUMENT

Appositives—A Strategy for Defining Terms Within the Sentence

As we have illustrated in this chapter, abstract terms need illustration with specific, concrete examples, and words that might be obscure to a general audience need defining so that our readers understand what we mean. How does a writer define terms without derailing the organization and flow of the paper or paragraph? Often, the answer is to use **appositives—noun phrases (or pronouns) placed beside other nouns to elaborate on their meaning within the sentence.** We illustrate this relationship in the examples below with **an arrow pointing from the appositive to the noun it modifies**.

Appositives usually follow the nouns they modify:

> The next topic will be <u>muscular dystrophy</u>, *a chronic disease* in which patients suffer from a wasting of the muscles.

To understand the topic, students need a definition of the technical term *muscular dystrophy*.

> Writer Susan Jacoby is deeply concerned about <u>debased speech</u>, *"a kind of low-level toxin"* she sees as coarsening our discourse and reflecting fuzzy thinking.

Jacoby explains what she means by debased speech in order to continue with an extended argument on the subject.

> The <u>Sacramento River</u>, *the main source of surface water in California*, has its headwaters in the far northern ranges of Siskiyou County.

By placing important detail in an appositive, writer Joan Didion describes a California river and identifies its origins, all in one fluent sentence. But writers may also introduce a sentence with an appositive:

> *An expression of frustrated rage*, <u>rap</u> tries to be outrageous in order to provoke strong reactions.

The phrase *an expression of frustrated rage* modifies *rap*. Such additions allow a writer to include essential information or background details that may not warrant separate sentences.

EXERCISE 5D

Recognizing Appositives

In the three passages that follow, identify the appositives and the nouns they modify by underlining the appositives and drawing an arrow pointing to the nouns or pronouns they modify.

1. Definition

> As Baranczak points out, Nobel Prize–winning poet Milosz rejects symbols in favor of metonymy and synecdoche, those figures of speech which represent a whole by a thing allied to it or by a part of it.

—HELEN VENDLER IN *THE NEW YORKER*

2. Identification

Cotton Mather was an exception, one who so fully accepted and magnified the outlook of his locality that he has entered folklore as the archetypal Puritan, not only a villainous figure in the pages of Hawthorne, William Carlos Williams and Robert Lowell, but an object of parody even to his fellow townsmen in 18th-century Boston.

—Larzer Ziff, *The New York Times Book Review*

3. A descriptive passage with examples

The Evertons are introduced to a second national peculiarity, one they will soon recognize on the streets of Ibarra and in towns and cities beyond. It is something they will see everywhere—a disregard for danger, a companionship with death. By the end of a year they will know it well: the antic bravado, the fatal games, the coffin shop beside the cantina, the sugar skulls on the frosted cake.

—Harriet Doerr, *Stones for Ibarra*

Appositives and Argument

Appositives in arguments are useful, allowing you to define terms, expand and emphasize ideas, and show opposing points of view in the same sentence, as illustrated in the following example:

A <u>unilateral attack</u> on a foreign enemy, *a policy that was considered difficult and dangerous by many, but one that was vigorously promoted by a number of hardline strategists*, means the US would strike without the support of other nations.

Two views on American foreign policy are juxtaposed in one strong sentence.

You will also find appositives helpful when identifying sources within the text of your paper:

S. I. Hayakawa, *a noted semanticist*, points out that advertising and poetry are alike.

Punctuation of Appositives

Punctuation choices are simple and logical. In most cases, the appositive phrase is set off from the noun it modifies with commas, as we illustrate above. If you want greater emphasis, you can do as Harriet Doerr did and use a dash: "It is something they will see everywhere—*a disregard for danger, a companionship with death.*"

Occasionally, when an appositive ends a sentence, a colon is appropriate for even sharper emphasis. This is a good choice when you're concluding a sentence with a list.

The stimulus package contained many components: *funds to banks, to small businesses, to schools, for tax relief, for homeowners' relief, to cite a few examples.*

EXERCISE 5E

Creating Appositives

Most of you already use appositives to some extent in your writing whether you recognize them or not. But a little conscious practice may expand your use of this handy device.

A. Combine the following sets of sentences by reducing one or more sentences to appositives. You may find more than one way to combine them.

> **Example:**
>
> A unilateral attack on a foreign enemy was considered difficult and dangerous by many. It means the US would strike without the support of other nations.
>
> becomes
>
> A unilateral attack on a foreign enemy means the US would strike without the support of other nations, *a policy that was considered difficult and dangerous by many.*
>
> or
>
> A unilateral attack on a foreign enemy, *a policy that means the US would strike without the support of other nations,* was considered difficult and dangerous by many.

1. New York has long been the destination of America's adventurous young. It is a city of danger and opportunity.

2. Punk was a return to the roots of rock 'n' roll. It was a revolt against the predictability of disco.

3. People have very different ideas about the meaning of poverty. It is a condition that to some suggests insufficient income, to others laziness, and to still others a state of unwarranted discomfort.

4. Writing ability can have far-reaching effects on a college graduate's future accomplishments. Writing ability is the capacity to generate and organize relevant ideas, compose coherent sentences, choose precise diction, control mechanics.

5. According to the lieutenant's testimony during his court-martial, he was simply following orders as any military man is trained to do. These orders came from his commanding officers.

6. When the Soviets sent troops into Vilnius, Vytautas Landsbergis isolated himself and members of his government in a fortified parliament building.

Vilnius is the capital of Lithuania, and Landsbergis was the Lithuanian president.

7. Over time, psychiatrists have expanded the definition of the term *addiction*. It is a word whose meaning has undergone revision to cover a broader range of compulsive behaviors. These compulsions now include sex, television viewing, designer clothes, shopping, computers. These extend to a whole spectrum of dependencies.

8. Concrete has spread over wider and wider areas of the American landscape. It has covered not just the weed patches, deserted lots, and infertile acres but whole pastures, hillsides, and portions of the sea and sky.

B. Write a sentence about your major, your job, or another interest, being sure to include a related technical term. Then add an appositive that defines or illustrates the term.

C. In your next essay or in a revision of a previous assignment, write and identify at least four appositives.

Extended Definition

An appositive is a valuable device for defining a word or a person, but sometimes an entire argument rests on a definition. Before you take a position on abortion for instance, you need to define when you think life begins. Before mounting an argument on gun control, you need to define what you think the wording of the Second Amendment means and stipulate the particular firearms you're considering. You must also consider your audience, what terminology might be unfamiliar to them.

Note how student Nathan Yan (see Chapter 3) defines the high school AP test early in his essay. If he were writing this piece for an AP class, he would not need to define "advanced placement," but writing for a newspaper, he knows many readers will be unfamiliar with such tests and thus, without clarification, will not continue reading his argument. Note how smoothly he has integrated his definition into the flow of his paper:

> The AP tests are nationwide standardized tests administered by the private College Board Association. Successfully passing an AP test will count toward college credit and, depending on the college or university, may grant exemptions from certain general education courses. For many high schools it represents the highest class level for students taking a particular course.

Andrew Sullivan, a writer at *The Atlantic*, and William Bennett, former secretary of education, clarify their opposing positions on gay marriage in the essays that follow. Both provide their own carefully defined understanding of the term *marriage* to mount their very different arguments.

Let Gays Marry
ANDREW SULLIVAN

"A state cannot deem a class of persons a stranger to its laws," declared the   1
Supreme Court last week. It was a monumental statement. Gay men and lesbians, the conservative court said, are no longer strangers in America. They are
citizens, entitled, like everyone else, to equal protection—no special rights, but
simple equality.

For the first time in Supreme Court history, gay men and women were seen not   2
as some powerful lobby trying to subvert America, but as the people we truly are—
the sons and daughters of countless mothers and fathers, with all the weaknesses
and strengths and hopes of everybody else. And what we seek is not some special
place in America but merely to be a full and equal part of America, to give back to
our society without being forced to lie or hide or live as second-class citizens.

That is why marriage is so central to our hopes. People ask us why we want the   3
right to marry, but the answer is obvious. It's the same reason anyone wants
the right to marry. At some point in our lives, some of us are lucky enough to meet
the person we truly love. And we want to commit to that person in front of our family and country for the rest of our lives. It's the most simple, the most natural, the
most human instinct in the world. How could anyone seek to oppose that?

Yes, at first blush, it seems like a radical proposal, but, when you think about it   4
some more, it's actually the opposite. Throughout American history, to be sure,
marriage has been between a man and a woman, and in many ways our society is
built upon that institution. But none of that need change in the slightest. After all,
no one is seeking to take away anybody's right to marry, and no one is seeking to
force any church to change any doctrine in any way. Particular religious arguments
against same-sex marriage are rightly debated within the churches and faiths
themselves. That is not the issue here: there is a separation between church and
state in this country. We are only asking that when the government gives out civil
marriage licenses, those of us who are gay should be treated like anybody else.

Of course, some argue that marriage is by definition between a man and a   5
woman. But for centuries, marriage was by definition a contract in which the wife
was her husband's legal property. And we changed that. For centuries marriage
was by definition between two people of the same race. And we changed that. We
changed these things because we recognized that human dignity is the same
whether you are a man or a woman, black or white. And no one has any more of a
choice to be gay than to be black or white or male or female.

Some say that marriage is only about raising children, but we let childless het-   6
erosexual couples be married (Bob and Elizabeth Dole, Pat and Shelley Buchanan,
for instance). Why should gay couples be treated differently? Others fear that
there is no logical difference between allowing same-sex marriage and sanctioning polygamy and other horrors. But the issue of whether to sanction multiple
spouses (gay or straight) is completely separate from whether, in the existing

institution between two unrelated adults, the government should discriminate between its citizens.

This is, in fact, if only Bill Bennett could see it, a deeply conservative cause. 7 It seeks to change no one else's rights or marriages in any way. It seeks merely to promote monogamy, fidelity and the disciplines of family life among people who have long been cast to the margins of society. And what could be a more conservative project than that? Why indeed would any conservative seek to oppose those very family values for gay people that he or she supports for everybody else? Except of course, to make gay men and lesbians strangers in their own country, to forbid them ever to come home.

Leave Marriage Alone
WILLIAM BENNETT

There are at least two key issues that divide proponents and opponents of same-sex 1 marriage. The first is whether legally recognizing same-sex unions would strengthen or weaken the institution. The second has to do with the basic understanding of marriage itself.

The advocates of same-sex marriage say that they seek to strengthen and celebrate 2 marriage. That may be what some intend. But I am certain that it will not be the reality. Consider: the legal union of same-sex couples would shatter the conventional definition of marriage, change the rules which govern behavior, endorse practices which are completely antithetical to the tenets of all of the world's major religions, send conflicting signals about marriage and sexuality, particularly to the young, and obscure marriage's enormously consequential function—procreation and child rearing.

Broadening the definition of marriage to include same-sex unions would stretch it 3 almost beyond recognition—and new attempts to expand the definition still further would surely follow. On what principled ground can Andrew Sullivan exclude others who most desperately want what he wants, legal recognition and social acceptance? Why on earth would Sullivan exclude from marriage a bisexual who wants to marry two other people? After all, exclusion would be a denial of that person's sexuality. The same holds true of a father and daughter who want to marry. Or two sisters. Or men who want (consensual) polygamous arrangements. Sullivan may think some of these arrangements are unwise. But having employed sexual relativism in his own defense, he has effectively lost the capacity to draw any lines and make moral distinctions.

Forsaking all others is an essential component of marriage. Obviously it is not 4 always honored in practice. But it is the ideal to which we rightly aspire, and in most marriages the ideal is in fact the norm. Many advocates of same-sex marriage simply do not share this ideal; promiscuity among homosexual males is well known. Sullivan himself has written that gay male relationships are served by the "openness of the contract" and the homosexuals should resist allowing their "varied and complicated lives" to be flattened into a "single, moralistic model." But that "single, moralistic model" has served society exceedingly well. The burden of proof ought to be on those who propose untested arrangements for our most important institution.

A second key difference I have with Sullivan goes to the very heart of mar-   5
riage itself. I believe that marriage is not an arbitrary construct which can be
redefined simply by those who lay claim to it. It is an honorable estate, insti-
tuted of God and built on moral, religious, sexual and human realities. Marriage
is based on a natural teleology, on the different, complementary nature of men
and women and how they refine, support, encourage and complete one
another. It is the institution through which we propagate, nurture, educate and
sustain our species.

That we have to engage in this debate at all is an indication of how steep   6
our moral slide has been. Worse, those who defend the traditional understanding of marriage are routinely referred to (though not to my knowledge
by Sullivan) as "homophobes," "gay-bashers," "intolerant" and "bigoted."
Can one defend an honorable, 4,000-year-old tradition and not be called
these names?

This is a large, tolerant, diverse country. In America people are free to do as   7
they wish, within broad parameters. It is also a country in sore need of shoring up
some of its most crucial institutions: marriage and the family, schools, neighbor-
hoods, communities. But marriage and family are the greatest of these. That is why
they are elevated and revered. We should keep them so.

EXERCISE 5F

Defining Marriage

1. William Bennett believes that "broadening the definition of marriage to
   include same-sex unions would stretch it almost beyond recognition—and
   [that] new attempts to expand the definition still further would surely follow."
   Among these "new attempts" he suggests group marriages, polygamy, and
   incest. How does Sullivan address these charges?
2. What concession does Sullivan grant to forces opposed to same-sex marriage?
   (See "Refutation and Concession" in Chapter 4.)
3. How does Sullivan refute the traditional definition?
4. Why does Sullivan see same-sex marriage as "a deeply conservative cause"?

WRITING ASSIGNMENT 9

Determining Your State's Position on Gay Marriage

Write a paper in which you explore the position on gay marriage taken in your state
and discuss your reaction to this position. If your state hasn't yet taken action on the
subject, you may select another state.

Audience

The instructor, other members of the class, and possibly members of your state
legislature.

Purpose

To explain your state's position on a controversial issue and present your opinion.

WRITING ASSIGNMENT 10

Composing an Argument Based on a Definition

> *"Words usually have something to hide—you have to shake them until the top pops off and some revelation tumbles out. . . ."*
>
> —GEOFFREY NUNBERG

Step 1

Choose a word from the list of abstract terms below, think about its implications for a few minutes, and then start writing a definition that captures its meaning and significance for you. Using a freewriting approach (see Chapter 1), keep going for about twenty minutes. If time and your instructor permit, do this in class; you will find the combination of spontaneity and structure imposed by writing during class to be an aid to composing. You can't get up to make a phone call or make a sandwich. Volunteers can enlighten (and entertain) the class by reading these drafts aloud.

addiction	heroism
alcoholism	identity
ambition	law
art	leader
business	maturity
cool	political correctness
courage	politician
cult	pornography
defeat	progress
depression	sexual harassment
education	spin
elite	terrorism
gossip	violence

Step 2

With more time for reflection and revision, take the spontaneous draft you have written and expand and edit your definition. In the process of defining your term, arrive at a significant point and support your position as Sullivan and Bennett do.

You need to argue your point, to use the term you are defining as a springboard for a complete written argument. As the discussion in this chapter has emphasized, you must include specific detail to animate your abstraction.

Here are some possible strategies for writing an extended definition; do not feel compelled to use them all.

- Stipulate your precise meaning, but don't begin with a dictionary definition unless you plan to use it or disagree with it.
- Provide examples of the term.
- Explain the function or purpose of the term.
- Explore etymology (origin and history of a word). The most fruitful source for such explorations is the *Oxford English Dictionary*, a multivolume work available online and in most college libraries and a dictionary well worth your acquaintance. Use the history of a term to help make a point.
- Examine the connotations of the term.
- Discuss what it is not (use this sparingly).
- Draw analogies. Here you will want to be precise; be sure the analogy really fits. (See references to analogy in Chapters 1 and 6 and examples of analogies in "When Human Rights Extend to Humans" in Additional Readings.)

Audience

The instructor and other members of the class.

Purpose

To make the definition of a term the focal point of an argument.

An Alternative

According to your instructor's preference, you may choose to write a shorter version of your definition in the manner of the two student examples and one professional column by Maureen Dowd below.

Different Approaches to the Same Term

Radical [1]

The word "radical" has been defined in the *Oxford English Dictionary* as "going to   1
the root or origin, touching or acting upon what is essential and fundamental."
Thus, a radical reform is said to be a fundamental, "thorough reform." In a political
sense, an advocate of "radical reform" was described as "one who holds the most
advanced views of political reform on democratic lines, and thus belongs to the
extreme section of the Liberal party." While this may have been a commonly
accepted usage of the term in England at the time, the word "radical" has drifted
away from its original specific meaning to a rather vague term for anyone who
appears to be trying to disrupt the status quo.

In the late 1800s and early 1900s, socialists, Communists, and anarchists alike   2
were popularly categorized by the general American public with the term "radical."
With the controversy surrounding the political goals of these different activists, "a
radical" was at the very least a controversial figure. More often than not, the word
"radical" brought to mind some sort of disruptive character, a nonspecific image of
an extremist, most probably from the far left. On the political spectrum the "radical" is still viewed as an individual on the extreme left, opposite the "right" or
"conservative" parties. "Conservatives" holding radically different views and goals
are not normally termed "radicals"; they are merely part of the "ultraright."

The term "radical" today is used less as a description of political intent and   3
more as a critique of overall manner and appearance. While many of the "radicals"
in the 1960s did indeed advocate numerous political reforms, the general public
was more impressed by their personal character and style of advocacy. It is not surprising that when asked to define "a radical," most individuals conjure up a vague
image of some young person wearing ragged clothes and long hair. It is a pity that
in this society, where progressive change is so essential, the term "radical" has
been imbued with so much negativity, so many connotations that really have nothing to do with political reform.

Radical [2]

A radical is an algebraic symbol that tells a person to carry out a certain mathematical operation. The end result of this operation will tell a person the root or origin of a number or problem.

Recently, while in Los Angeles, I overheard someone describe a car as radical. I immediately thought to myself, something is wrong here. Radicals do not have engines. They may contain a number, like 32, underneath their top line, but never a stock Chevy 302 engine. It simply would not fit. When I asked this person why he called the car a radical, he replied, "Because the car is different and unusual." Once again, I thought to myself, he has made a mistake. Radicals are quite common. In fact, they are an essential part of most algebraic theories. I had to infer that this man knew nothing about algebra. If he did, he would have realized that radicals are not different or unusual at all, and would not have called the car one.

While I was in New York this past summer, I happened to see a group of people carrying signs of protest in front of the United Nations Building. As I watched them, a man came over to me, pointed at the group and muttered, "Radicals." I thought to myself, man are you ever wrong. Radicals do not carry signs saying, "Feed the Poor." They may carry a number, like 2, in their top right hand corner, but this number only means to find the root of a problem. It does not mean, "Feed the Poor."

These two events show that there is a great deal of misunderstanding throughout the country in regard to what a radical is. At their simplest level, radicals tell us to find the root of a problem. At their most complex level, they tell us the same thing.

Slut

MAUREEN DOWD

After eons of being a summary judgment that a woman is damaged goods, the word slut has shifted into more ambiguous territory. It can still be an insult, especially since there is no pejorative equivalent to suggest that a man has sullied himself with too many sexual partners. Men are players, women are sluts, just the way men are tough and women are bitchy.

Republicans denigrated the prim law professor Anita Hill by painting her, in David Brock's memorable phrase, as "a little bit nutty and a little bit slutty." Clinton defenders demonized Monica Lewinsky the same way.

But as women express themselves more, sexually and professionally, and no longer need to "use their virginity as a meal ticket," as the anthropologist Helen Fisher puts it, the slur may have lost some sting. *The Times*'s Stephanie Rosenbloom writes that the word has morphed into a term of endearment and teasing, with teenage girls greeting each other with "Hi slut!"—the way "queer" and "pimp" took on different coloration, and the way "girl" went from an insult in early feminist days to a word embraced by young women. The gangsta rap characterizations of women that some found offensive are now being embraced by many young women.

"Slut" is a faddish appellation for everything from lip balm to cocktails, and 4
applies to voracious behavior of all kinds; *Cosmopolitan* recently ran a quiz on how
to tell if you're an "attention slut."

"It's just a really fun word to say," explains my classy 26-year-old girl-friend. 5
"Usually women only call someone a slut if she's not slutty, but if you do call a
slutty friend a slut, you can get away with it because, oh, it was just a *joke*, even
when it's not. So, yet another way for mean girls to flourish."

It was probably inevitable, once women began discovering their inner slut 6
with microminis and other provocative outfits, and with high school and
college girls reporting a much more blasé attitude about performing oral sex, that
they'd turn the word itself inside-out. But, semantics aside, have attitudes really
changed much?

Studies show that superiors, men and women, may penalize female executives 7
who dress in too sexy a manner—proving that it's not always safe to strut as a slut.
And Don Reisinger, a student in Albany, told Ms. Rosenbloom, "When I think of the
word slut, I think of a woman who has been around the block more times than my
dad's Chevy. I might date a slut, but I certainly wouldn't marry one."

That men are counting those spins around the block is a fact that's not lost on 8
women. The late-night comic Craig Ferguson dryly observed that women often
get back with their exes because they don't want their total number to go up.

One 24-year-old Washington reporter agreed that "redos" of previous partners 9
can keep your number below the slut threshold, defined by two of her male friends
as "less than 20." She thinks she is "chaste" with a number of six, but admits she
sometimes subtracts one or two when telling a guy her romantic history. She said
she kept dating Mr. Six after she'd lost interest simply because she didn't want to
up the number to Mr. Seven.

One 25-year-old writer in D.C. said his ideal girl's number is one or two 10
fewer than his. When he had "the numbers talk" with one date, she gave him
an answer that he found both satisfactory and sexy: "Enough to know what
I'm doing."

INVENTING A NEW WORD TO FILL A NEED

Alice Walker, author of the *The Color Purple*, sought to rectify some of the linguistic imbalance in gender representation when she coined the term *womanist* for her collection of nonfiction, *In Search of Our Mothers' Gardens: Womanist Prose*. Why, we might ask, did she need to invent such a word? We can assume that she experienced a condition for which there was no term, so she created one. Her word stuck, turning up in a 2008 book review: "Amy Richards serves on the boards . . . of such blue-chip **'womanist'** organizations as *Ms. Magazine* . . . and Planned Parenthood." A student came up with *strugglesome*, a term we're often tempted to use ourselves. Writer and performer Rich Hall created the word *sniglet* for "any word that doesn't appear in the dictionary, but should." Two examples from his collection:

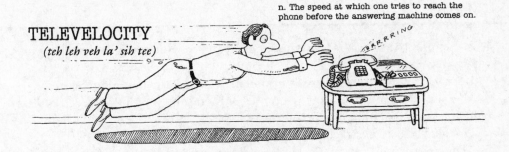

TELEVELOCITY
(teh leh veh la' sih tee)

n. The speed at which one tries to reach the phone before the answering machine comes on.

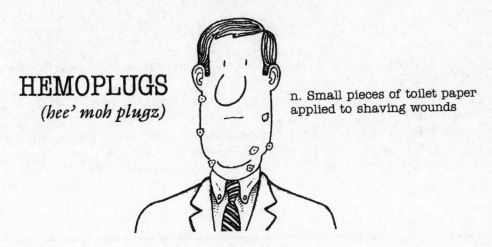

HEMOPLUGS
(hee' moh plugz)

n. Small pieces of toilet paper applied to shaving wounds

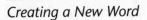

WRITING ASSIGNMENT 11

Creating a New Word

Now it's your turn to create a new word. Give the word an extended definition so that those in your class can see how to use it and why our culture needs such an addition to the language. Here you have an opportunity to develop an argument while using your imagination. Your new word will serve as a springboard.

Audience

The instructor and other members of the class.

Purpose

To identify a meaning in need of a name.

SUMMARY

It is important that our readers understand the meaning of the words we use when we write.

Controlling the **definitions** is important, particularly in politics.

Definitions can affect how people view themselves and others, *alcoholism* being one example of many such terms.

Language is an abstract system of symbols.

The assignation of a particular meaning to a given term remains essentially arbitrary.

Meaning is dependent to a large degree on the individual, the context, and the interpretive community.

Political systems and advertising often manipulate abstract language for their own purposes.

The power to abstract is what makes us human. **Concrete, specific details** are what flesh out our ideas so our readers can grasp, visualize, and retain meaning.

We must beware of evasive language and euphemisms.

Appositives help define terms at the sentence level.

KEY TERMS

Appositives   noun phrases placed beside nouns to elaborate on their meaning, useful for defining, identifying, explaining, and describing terms within the sentence.

Connotation   the suggestive or associative implications beyond the literal, explicit sense of a word.

Denotation   the basic dictionary meaning of a word, separate from its emotional associations.

Euphemism   an indirect, less expressive word or phrase, for a sensitive or controversial idea.

CHAPTER 6

Fallacious Arguments

Her reasoning is full of tricks
And butterfly suggestions,
I know no point to which she sticks;
She begs the simplest questions,
And, when her premises are strong
She always draws her inference wrong.

—*Upon Lebia Arguing* by Alfred Cochrane (1865–?)

WHAT IS A FALLACIOUS ARGUMENT?

To answer this question, we ask you to look carefully at two short arguments:

> Short people do not make good presidents.
> The Democratic candidate is short.
> Therefore, the Democratic candidate will not be a good president.

> Senator Smith was expelled from college for cheating on an exam.
> His wife divorced him because of his numerous affairs.
> Therefore, he is a man without honor, a politician who cannot be
>   trusted, and we should not support his National Health Bill.

Which of these two arguments is more persuasive? Technically, the line of reasoning in the first argument is logical because the two premises lead inescapably to the conclusion. There is nothing fallacious in the *form* of this argument. The difficulty lies in the first premise; it is an absurd claim and an unacceptable premise. This argument is not persuasive and would convince no one. (Look ahead to Chapter 7, "Deductive and Inductive Argument," for a detailed explanation of form and acceptability of premises.)

But what about the second argument? Would you be in favor of a National Health Bill created by such a man? Some might find it persuasive, believing that he could not propose worthwhile legislation. But because nothing in the premises indicates flaws in the bill—only flaws in the man—the conclusion is not logically supported. The bill may be worthwhile despite the nature of the man who proposes it. This then is a **fallacious argument,** an argument that is persuasive but does not logically support its conclusion.

Because fallacious arguments are both appealing and abundant, we as critical readers and writers must guard against them. The first step in this defense is to familiarize ourselves with the most common fallacies. Fallacious reasoning may be intentional, as is sometimes the case with unscrupulous merchandisers and politicians, or it may be an innocent mistake resulting from fuzzy thinking or unexamined bias. In any case, if we are familiar with fallacies we can avoid them in our own thinking and writing. We can also spot them in the arguments of others, a skill that makes us wiser consumers and citizens.

There are many fallacies, a number of which tend to overlap. In one sense, the Latin term **non sequitur—it does not follow**—covers most fallacies. Our intention here is not to overwhelm you with an exhaustive list of fallacies and a complex classification scheme. Instead, we offer a list of the more common fallacies, presented in alphabetical order for easy reference.

Appeal to Authority

The opinion of an authority can support an argument only when it reflects his special area of expertise; the authority must be an expert on the subject being argued, as is the case in the following examples:

> The surgeon general warns that smoking is injurious to health.
> Vladimir Horowitz, the internationally acclaimed pianist, preferred the
>   Steinway piano.
> Studies conducted by the *Washington Post,* the *Los Angeles Times,* and CNN
>   suggest that increasing numbers of parents object to video game violence.

But if the appeal is to an authority that is not appropriate, the appeal is fallacious, as is the case in the following example:

> Abortion to save the life of a mother is an irrelevant issue because a former surgeon general, a well-known pediatric surgeon, claimed that in all his years of surgical practice he had never seen a case in which such a dilemma had arisen.

The problem here is that a pediatric surgeon is not an appropriate authority on an issue involving obstetrics, a different medical specialty.

Fallacious appeals to authority are bountiful in advertising, which employs well-known actors and athletes to sell us everything from banking services to automobiles to coffee. Since many of these celebrities have no specialized knowledge—no authority—on the particular service or product they are promoting, they are not credible sources. For example, George Foreman, a boxer, gave his name to an appliance, the George Foreman Grill, though he has never been a chef or worked in the food industry.

Appeals to authority also appear in the form of **snob appeal** or **appeal to the authority of the select few**. The following advertisement for a resort hotel illustrates this fallacy, which appeals to people's desire for prestige and exclusivity:

> Palmilla's not for everyone. The best never is.

Keep in mind that fallacious appeals to authority should not cause us to doubt all authorities but rather should encourage us to distinguish between reliable and unreliable sources. In constructing your own arguments, be prepared to cite, explain, and, if necessary, defend your sources when relying on authority.

Appeal to Fear

An appeal to fear attempts to convince by implicitly threatening the audience. Its efforts to persuade are based on emotion rather than reason. An ad for a business college uses this approach:

> Will there be a *job* waiting when *you* leave college?

The ad attempts to frighten students by implying that unless they attend this business college, they will be unable to get a job after attending a four-year traditional college.

Former senator Jesse Helms of North Carolina raised millions in campaign funds by sending voters a letter that contained the following warning:

> Your tax dollars are being used to pay for grade school classes that teach our children that CANNIBALISM, WIFE-SWAPPING and the MURDER of infants and the elderly are acceptable behavior.

Appeal to Pity

An appeal to pity attempts to win our sympathy in order to convince us of the conclusion. Like an appeal to fear, it appeals to our emotions rather than our intellect. Some students use this approach when arguing for a particular grade.

> Professor Hall, I must get an A in your course. If you don't give me an A, I won't be able to go to law school.

As we know, a student's work in a course—papers, exams, participation—determines the final grade. The consequences of a grade, no matter how dire they may be, should have no effect in determining that grade.

Emotion may play a part in argument, but its role must be secondary, a backdrop to logical reasoning. In fact, effective arguments often begin with frightening statistics— "If nothing is done about global warming, the earth's temperature will increase 10 degrees by the year 2015 with disastrous consequences for our environment." Or they may begin with an emotional illustration. For example, an argument for mandatory fencing around all private swimming pools may open with a description of a mother caring for a child who is brain damaged as a result of almost drowning in a private pool. Either of these introductions will capture the emotions and interest of the audience, but they should be followed by facts, appropriate appeals to authority, and logical reasoning.

Begging the Question

When a person **begs the question**, he offers no actual support for his conclusion while appearing to do so. Instead, he may argue in a circle, just restating, as a premise, his conclusion in different words.

> "The reason he's so strong is because of his strength." (a TV commentator at an NCAA basketball tournament)

The writer is simply stating that the basketball player is strong because he's strong. He does not offer reasons for the player's strength. He begs the question. Or, take a couple of classics:

> Parallel lines will never meet because they are parallel.

> . . . your noble son is mad.
> Mad call I it, for to define true madness,
> What is't but to be nothing else but mad?
> —POLONIUS TO QUEEN GERTRUDE IN *HAMLET*, II.II

[We can discern something of Polonius's character from the manner of his argument.]

> Money is better than poverty, if only for financial reasons.
> —WOODY ALLEN

Even a president can be guilty of circular reasoning:

> The reason I keep insisting that there was a relationship between Iraq and al Qaeda [is] because there was a relationship between Iraq and al Qaeda.
> —FORMER PRESIDENT GEORGE W. BUSH

Some such fallacious arguments beg the question not by restating the conclusion but by supporting the conclusion with assumptions (stated or hidden) that are as much in need of proof as is the conclusion. For example, those opposed to rent control argue that rent control should be removed in order to boost construction and thus increase the number of affordable rental units. A letter to the editor points out the weakness:

> Editor: In your editorial concerning the housing crisis, you rely on one of the oldest rhetorical tricks of accepting as a given that which you could not possibly

"You know what I like about power? It's so damn empowering."

prove, that is, "There can be little question that removal of rent controls would result in a boom in apartment house construction . . . ." If rent control is such an important factor, construction should have been booming in the '80s before rent control laws existed in our state. It wasn't. . . .

Before we can accept the conclusion, the "truth" of the premise—that construction of new housing will increase if rent control laws are abolished—must be established.

We can also encounter question begging (avoiding the issue) in the form of an actual question, a **loaded question**. An example:

Have you started paying your fair share of taxes yet?

First, the questioner would have to establish what he means by "fair share" and then establish that the person to whom he addressed the question had not been paying it.

In some arguments, just a single word—*reactionary*, *negligent*, *warmonger*, *deadbeat*—can beg the question. Be on the alert for such prejudicial language.

Double Standard

When an argument contains the fallacy of **double standard** (sometimes referred to as special pleading), it judges and labels the same act differently, depending on the person or group who performs the act.

Shannon Faulkner, the first woman ever admitted to the Citadel, a military college in South Carolina, dropped out in her first year. The other cadets cheered as she departed the campus, and the media covered her departure in great detail. What the jeering male cadets and the media ignored were the 34 other first-year students, all men, who also dropped out. Shannon Faulkner and her classmates made the same decision, but she was subjected to ridicule and close media scrutiny while her 34 male classmates were not; a double standard was applied.

Editorialist Cynthia Tucker accuses our government of having a double standard in its dealings with China and Cuba:

> If diplomatic relations and free trade are a sound policy toward China, which restricts religious freedoms, limits free speech, builds nuclear weapons, and poses a threat to its neighbors, doesn't the same apply to Cuba, which restricts religious freedoms, limits free speech, and has no nuclear weapons and poses no threat to its neighbors?

Sometimes a double standard can be applied subtly through the manipulative use of language. A well-known defense lawyer, while discussing legal strategies on television, stated that he "prepares" his witnesses while the prosecution "coaches" theirs. "Prepares" suggests professional legal preparation for the courtroom, whereas "coaches" suggests that a witness is encouraged to say what the lawyer tells her to whether it is true or not. Both lawyers are working with their clients before trial, but the defense lawyer's subtle use of language casts a negative slant on opposing counsel.

Equivocation

Equivocation is the shifting of the meaning of a given term within a single argument. This fallacy stems from the often ambiguous nature of language. A term may be ambiguous because it has more than one meaning; for instance, the word *affair* may mean a party, a controversial incident, or an extramarital relationship. Look at this example:

> We are told by the government that to discriminate against a person in employment or housing is wrong and punishable by law. But we must discriminate when

we hire an individual (Does he have the necessary experience?) or when we rent an apartment (Does he have sufficient income?). Discrimination is a necessary part of making such decisions.

The word *discriminate* is the culprit. In the first sentence, "discriminate" refers to prejudice, to denying an individual employment or housing because of his or her race, sex, or religion. In the second sentence, "discriminate" refers to making careful distinctions between applicants on the basis of relevant issues.

In writing our own arguments, we can avoid equivocation by defining all ambiguous terms and being consistent in our use of them. (See Chapter 5.)

False Analogy

One creative way to mount an argument can be through analogy. An argument by analogy compares two or more things, alike in certain respects, and suggests that since they share certain characteristics, they probably share other characteristics as well. By comparing the brain to the heart, a doctor argues effectively for drug therapy over psychotherapy as the best treatment for schizophrenia or severe depression. "The brain is an organ, like the heart, and like that organ, can malfunction as a result of biochemical imbalances."

But in a **false analogy,** one compares two things in which the key features are different. A mountain climber offers this analogy to minimize the danger of his sport:

> I don't want to die falling off a rock. . . . But you can kill yourself falling in the bathtub, too.
>
> —JOHN BACHAR

He is comparing two extremely dissimilar acts: climbing a mountain and taking a bath, one a sport, the other a daily routine. And while it is possible to kill oneself slipping in the bathtub, if we were to compare the number of deaths in proportion to the number of bathers and the number of mountain climbers, we would surely find a higher incidence of deaths resulting from mountain climbing than from bathing. To construct a more convincing analogy, the mountain climber should compare the risk in mountain climbing with that in another high-risk sport such as race car driving.

A *Dear Abby* reader writes in response to Abby's recommendation that young people use contraceptives for premarital sex: "We know that premarital sex is wrong, just as we know shoplifting is wrong." Dear Abby's reply points out the fallaciousness of this comparison.

> One of the most powerful urges inborn in the human animal is the sex drive. Nature intended it to ensure perpetuation of our species. It is not comparable with the temptation to swipe a candy bar or a T-shirt.

Writer Alice Walker compares the genital mutilation of female children in some parts of Africa to the plastic surgery performed on women in the West. But is this an accurate analogy? Young girls have no say in the surgery performed on them, while adult women choose to have surgery to enhance their appearance.

The following letter to *Miss Manners* argues on the basis of analogy, an analogy that in her reply Miss Manners shows to be false:

> Dear Miss Manners:
>   If I were to entertain someone at dinner whom I knew to be a vegetarian, I would make certain there would be plenty of things on the menu that a vegetarian could eat. Besides my lamb chop, there would be plenty of vegetables, breads, salads, etc. I would not feel compelled to become a vegetarian myself for the occasion.
>   Were I to dine at the home of vegetarians, I would expect of them a similar accommodation, so that in addition to their usual fare, they might serve me a small steak, perhaps, though of course they wouldn't need to partake of it themselves.

Miss Manners replies:

> Gentle Reader:
>   You lose the argument. Here is the problem: Serving vegetables to guests does not violate your principles, nor does it make you a vegetarian. However, expecting your vegetarian friends to serve you something that they exclude from their households would require their violating their principles.

Reasoning by analogy is appealing because it is vivid and accessible and thus can be an effective argument strategy. But we must not accept analogies without careful examination. We must ask if the two things being compared are similar in ways that are significant to the point being made. (For more examples of analogies, see "When Human Rights Extend to Nonhumans" in Additional Readings.)

False Cause

The fallacy of **false cause** is also called **post hoc reasoning,** from the Latin *post hoc, ergo propter hoc*, which means "after this, therefore because of this." As this translation indicates, the fallacy of false cause assumes a cause–effect relationship between two events because one precedes another. It claims a causal relationship solely on the basis of a chronological relationship. Mark Twain uses this relationship for humorous effect:

> I joined the Confederacy for two weeks. Then I deserted. The Confederacy fell.

We know, as Twain did, that his desertion did nothing to end the Civil War, but this fallacy is not always so obvious. Look at the following example:

> Governor Robinson took office in 2006.
> In 2008, the state suffered a severe recession.
> Therefore, Governor Robinson should not be reelected.
> (Hidden assumption: The governor caused the recession.)

Elected officials are often credited with the success or blamed for the failure of the economy. But in fact, anything as complex as the economy is affected by numerous factors such as inflation, environmental changes, and fluctuations in the stock market. Elected officials may indeed affect the economy but are unlikely to be the sole cause of its success or failure.

In another example of post hoc reasoning, an author attributes his nephew's autism to a vaccination. A doctor criticizes the writer's conclusion in a letter to the *New York Times Book Review*:

> To the Editor:
>   There will always be people who are convinced that because the signs of mental retardation or a seizure disorder or autism first became evident after an immunization, then certainly the immunization caused their problems; millions of dollars have been awarded in damages because some such people served on juries.
>   For those people of reason who remember that **post hoc, ergo propter hoc** is a logical fallacy and not a standard of proof, let me state categorically that careful review of the literature confirms that a DPT shot might result in a fever or a sore leg or an irritable child. But it will not cause retardation, it will not precipitate epilepsy, and it never has and never will lead to autism.
>
>   DIANE LIND FENSTER, M.D.
>   GREEN BAY, WIS.

Some have argued that the atomic bombs we dropped on Hiroshima and Nagasaki caused Japan to surrender at the end of World War II. Others argue that this is a case of post hoc reasoning, that other factors such as Russia's threat to enter the war against Japan caused Japan to surrender, so that the killing of 110,000 Japanese, many of them women and children, was unnecessary.

Determining the cause of all but the simplest events is extremely difficult. Post hoc reasoning is appealing because it offers simple explanations for complex events.

False Dilemma

A **false dilemma** presents two and only two alternatives for consideration when other possibilities exist. For this reason, a false dilemma is often referred to as **either/or reasoning**.

In his essay "Love One, Hate the Other," movie critic Mick LaSalle rails against what he calls "false polarities." He offers the following examples: Lennon *or* McCartney, Monroe *or* Bardot, Hemingway *or* Fitzgerald, Freud *or* Jung. He calls them false "because, in each case, two elements are arbitrarily set apart as opposites when they are not opposite at all, and the idea is that we must choose between the two when there's no legitimate need to do that."

Narrowing to two choices is a strategy designed to forestall clear thinking and force a quick decision. This kind of reasoning can be seductive because it reduces the often difficult decisions and judgments we must make by narrowing complex problems and issues to two simple options.

"Damn it, Eddie! If you don't believe in nuclear war and you don't believe in conventional war, what the hell kind of war <u>do</u> you believe in?"

What alternative has the speaker completely overlooked?

Columnist Ellen Goodman offers an example of one young critical thinker who refused to accept the limits of either/or thinking.

Remember the story of Heinz, the man whose wife was dying for lack of medicine or the funds to buy it? Children are asked to decide whether it's OK for Heinz to steal the drugs. On the one hand it's wrong to break the law, on the other, it's wrong to let the woman die.

What I remember most about the Heinz dilemma is the response of an 11-year-old little girl named Amy, as described in Carol Gilligan's book, *In a Different Voice*. Amy didn't think that Heinz should steal the drugs because if he did he might end up in jail—and what would happen next time his wife needed the pills? Nor did Amy think she should die.

This 11-year-old refused to choose from column A or column B. She thought they should "talk it out," get a loan, or find another way out of the dilemma. Traditional moralists thought Amy was "illogical." But the truth was that she took the long, wide moral view—six steps down the road, up a side road, and back to the main road. Amy stepped outside the multiple-choice questionnaire.

Hasty Generalization

A **hasty generalization** is a conclusion based on a sample that is too small or in some other way unrepresentative of the larger population.

> Students in Professor Hall's eight o'clock freshman composition class are often late. There's no doubt that people are right when they claim today's college students are irresponsible and unreliable.

In this case the sample is both unrepresentative and too small; unrepresentative because we would expect an eight o'clock class to have more late students than classes offered later in the day, and too small because one section can't represent an entire freshman class.

In Chapter 7, we ask students to collect hasty generalizations. Here are some of our favorites:

> Jocks can't type.
> Women in bridal departments are airheads.
> Anyone who listens to heavy metal is not intelligent.
> Older guests always arrive early.
> Everyone in the South is gun crazy.
> Everyone in Germany dances by themselves.
> Women who work full time have unsuccessful marriages.

It is impossible to avoid making generalizations, nor should we try. But we must examine the basis for our generalizations to determine their reliability (see Chapter 7).

One way to avoid this fallacy is to qualify your generalizations with words such as *many* or *some*. Most of us would accept the claim that "some women are bad drivers" but would reject and be offended by the claim that "women are bad drivers."

Personal Attack

Often called by its Latin name, **_ad hominem_** ("against the man"), the fallacy of personal attack substitutes for a reasoned evaluation of an argument an attack against the person presenting the argument. The person is discredited, not the argument.

When Rachel Carson's *Silent Spring*, a seminal work on the health hazards of insecticides and pesticides, was published in 1962, a leading scientist (male) questioned her concern for future generations because she was a spinster who had no children. He attacked her personally, not her argument that certain commonly used chemicals caused cancer.

As a newspaper columnist, writer Jon Carroll often receives mail from readers who disagree with him. One such reader called him a "bunny hugger" for his protect-the-environment point of view. Carroll's response:

> . . . here's a little rule: If you hurl ad hominems at people, you are forcing them to shut their ears. You could be Albert Bloody Einstein, and if you start your note with "Dear Idiot," your message will not come through.

Those given to Latin names like to label a particular kind of personal attack as *tu quoque*—"you also." In this instance, a person and thus his arguments are discredited because his own behavior does not strictly conform to the position he holds. We've all heard about the parent who drinks too much but admonishes his child about the dangers of drinking.

Anti-gun-control groups were delighted when Carl Rowan, a prominent Washington columnist and a staunch advocate of gun control, used an unregistered pistol to wound a young man who broke into his backyard. But Rowan's failure to follow his own beliefs does not necessarily make his argument for gun control a weak one.

Poisoning the Well

A person **poisons the well** when he makes an assertion that precludes or discourages an open discussion of the issue. This assertion will intimidate the listener, who fears that any resistance on his part will lead to a personal disagreement rather than a critical discussion.

> Every patriotic American supports legislation condemning the desecration of the flag.

The listener must now prove his patriotism rather than express his doubts about the legislation, and the speaker avoids having to defend his conclusion with relevant premises.

Red Herring

The term **red herring** comes to us from fox hunting. The strong-smelling fish, red after being smoked, was used to throw hunting dogs off the trail of the fox. Mystery writers often throw red herrings in their readers' path, leading them away from the real culprit by making them suspect other characters. In argument, a red herring is a distraction from the issue under discussion; a different, irrelevant topic. For example:

While the hospital bond issue has merit, there are too many bond issues on this ballot.

Attention is being diverted from the merits of a particular bond issue to another topic—the number of bond issues on the ballot.

Don't confuse red herring with *straw man* on the next page. Straw man is a distortion of an opponent's argument, while red herring introduces a completely different topic in order to divert attention from the topic under discussion.

Slippery Slope

We know the **slippery slope** fallacy by other names too: the **domino theory**, the ripple effect, the snowball effect, the doomsday scenario, or opening the floodgates. One thing leads to another. People often claim that an action should be avoided because it will inevitably lead to a series of extremely undesirable consequences. Sometimes such a chain reaction is possible, but often it can be exaggerated for effect.

Writer Wendy Kaminer, reviewing *Under Fire: The NRA and the Battle for Gun Control*, presents one group's position on gun control:

What seems like reasonable restrictions on guns with no legitimate civilian purpose (assault rifles, for example) will lead inevitably to total prohibition of gun ownership that ends in virtual slavery at the hands of a totalitarian regime.

The argument here is that if we allow the government to take one step—the banning of assault weapons—the next step will be the banning of all guns, and the final step, loss of all freedom for all citizens. In this argument, the downward slope is more precipitous than the evidence warrants, leading to an erroneous conclusion.

Linguist Geoffrey Nunberg notes that slippery slope is a "convenient way of warning of the dire effects of some course of action without actually having to criticize the action itself, which is what makes it a favorite ploy of hypocrites: 'Not that there's anything wrong with A, mind you, but A will lead to B and then C, and before you know it we'll be up to our armpits in Z.'" Nunberg also notes that this fallacy is used to protect the status quo, the existing state of affairs. English legal scholar Glanville Williams would agree, calling slippery slope "the trump card of the traditionalist, because no proposal for reform is immune to [it]."

Columnist William Safire points out that "Logicians are very cautious about *slippery slope* arguments because it is impossible to know beforehand, with absolute deductive certainty, that an 'if-then' statement is true." Careful reasoning helps us distinguish between probable and outrageous claims.

Straw Man

In a **straw man** argument, a person creates and then attacks a distorted version of the opposition's argument:

> The candidate wants the federal government to house everyone, feed everyone, care for everyone's children, and provide medical care for everyone. And he's going to take 50 percent of every dime you make to do it.

This argument overlooks the candidate's proposal to reduce defense spending to meet his goals. Hence, this is an unfair presentation of the opposing view, but one that could be extremely effective in discouraging votes for the candidate. This is the purpose of a straw man argument: to frighten supporters away from the opponent's camp and into one's own. Columnist Ellen Goodman comments on this strategy in an essay titled "The Straw Feminist":

> The straw man has been a useful creature throughout history. Whenever people argued, he could be pulled together quickly out of the nearest available haystack, and set up as an opponent. The beauty of the straw man was that he was easily defeated. The straw man was also useful as a scarecrow. The arguments attributed to him were not only flimsy, they were frightening.
>
> So I wasn't surprised when the straw feminist was sighted burning her bra at a "Miss America" pageant. The fact that there never was a bra-burning was irrelevant. Feminists became bra-burners. Not to mention man-haters.
>
> The straw feminist wanted to drive all women out of their happy homes and into the workforce. The straw feminist had an abortion as casually as she had a tooth pulled. The straw feminist was hostile to family life and wanted children warehoused in government-run day and night care. At times, the straw feminist was painted slightly pinko by the anticommunists or rather lavender by the antilesbians. But it was generally agreed upon that she was a castrating—well, you fill in the blank.
>
> This creature was most helpful for discrediting real feminists but also handy for scaring supporters away.

A caution: German philosopher Arthur Schopenhauer [1788–1860] pointed out that "it would be a very good thing if every trick could receive some short and obviously appropriate name, so that when a man used this or that particular trick, he could at once be reproved for it." Fallacies provide us with those short and appropriate names for tricks or errors in reasoning, but we must not assume that all such errors can be labeled. Whenever we find fault with a particular line of reasoning, we should not hesitate to articulate that fault, whether or not we have a label for it. On the other hand, we must be careful not to see fallacies everywhere, perhaps even where they don't exist.

EXERCISE 6A

Identifying Fallacies

Identify by name the fallacies in each of the following arguments and justify your responses. You may want to turn to the end of the chapter for a chart of the fallacies.

> **Competition and collaboration:** An interesting approach to this exercise combines competition and cooperation. The class is divided into two teams who compete in identifying the fallacies, with team members cooperating on responses as an option.

 1.

SIPRESS

"It could go badly, or it could go well, depending on whether it goes badly or well."

2. "A group of self-appointed 'life-style police' are pushing to control many aspects of our daily lives. If they succeed, we lose our basic right to free choice. Today they're targeting smoking. What's next? Red meat? Leather? Coffee? If fifty million smokers can lose their rights anyone can." (From an ad for the National Smokers Alliance)

3. America: Love it or leave it.

4. You can't expect insight and credibility from the recent book *The Feminist Challenge* because its author David Bouchier is, obviously, a man.

5. Politicians can't be trusted because they lack integrity.

6. "We would not tolerate a proposal that states that because teenage drug use is a given we should make drugs more easily available." (Archbishop John

R. Quinn in response to a National Research Council's recommendation that contraceptives and abortion be made readily available to teenagers)

7. How long must we allow our courts to go on coddling criminals?

8. "I'm firm. You are stubborn. He's pig-headed." (Philosopher Bertrand Russell)

9. Anyone who truly cares about preserving the American way of life will vote Republican this fall.

10. "Why is it okay for people to choose the best house, the best schools, the best surgeon, the best car, but not try to have the best baby possible?" (A father's defense of the Nobel Prize winners' sperm bank)

11. Socrates, during his trial in 399 B.C.: "My friend, I am a man, and like other men, a creature of flesh and blood, and not of wood or stone, as Homer says; and I have a family, yes, and sons, O Athenians, three in number, one almost a man, and two others who are still young; and yet I will not bring any of them hither in order to petition you for an acquittal." (Plato, *The Apology*)

12. "All Latins are volatile people." (Former senator Jesse Helms, on Mexican protests against Senate Foreign Affairs subcommittee hearings on corruption south of the border)

13. Mark R. Hughes, owner of Herbalife International, was questioned by a Senate subcommittee about the safety of the controversial diet products marketed by his company. Referring to a panel of three nutrition and weight-control authorities, Hughes asked: "If they're such experts, then why are they fat?"

14. The Black Panthers—Were they criminals or freedom fighters? (From a television ad promoting a documentary on the 1960s radical group)

15. When the Supreme Court ruled that school officials need not obtain search warrants or find "probable cause" while conducting reasonable searches of students, they violated freedoms guaranteed under the Bill of Rights. If you allow a teacher to look for a knife or drugs, you'll soon have strip searches and next, torture.

16. Since I walked under that ladder yesterday, I've lost my wallet and received a speeding ticket.

17. Sometimes, the *best* is not for everyone. (An ad for a "Parisian boutique")

18. "I'm being denied the right to own a semiautomatic firearm simply because someone doesn't like the way it looks. If you look at all the different automobiles out there, the majority of them travel on regular roads. So how do you explain the dune buggies or off-road vehicles? They're different, but you don't hear anybody saying, 'Why does anyone need to have a dune buggy or an off-road vehicle? What's wrong with your regular run-of-the-mill traditional automobile?' It's all a matter of personal preference." (Marion Hammer, president of the National Rifle Association)

19. We are going to have to ease up on environmental protection legislation or see the costs overwhelm us.

20. Any rational person will accept that a fetus is a human being.

21. A tax loophole is something that benefits the other guy. If it benefits you, it is tax reform.

22. Heat Wave Blamed for Record Temperatures Across U.S. (A Grass Valley *Union* headline)

23. The erosion of traditional male leadership has led to an increase in divorce because men no longer possess leadership roles.

24. "Just as instructors could prune sentences for poor grammar, so the principal was entitled to find certain articles inappropriate for publication—in this situation because they might reveal the identity of pregnant students and because references to sexual activity were deemed improper for young students to see."

25.

26. Now, all young men, a warning take, And shun the poisoned bowl; [alcohol] 'Twill lead you down to hell's dark gate, And ruin your own soul. (Anonymous, from Carl Sandburg, ed., *The American Songbag*)

27. While our diplomats in France were gathering intelligence, their diplomats in Washington were practicing espionage.

28. I recently read about a homeless man with a burst appendix who was turned away from a hospital emergency room to die in the street. It's obvious that hospitals don't care about people, only money.

29. Do the vastly inflated salaries paid to professional athletes lead them into drug abuse?

30. The Nuclear Freeze movement was misguided and dangerous from the beginning, dependent as it was on "unilateral" disarmament. (This is a common argument of the movement's opponents. Those supporting the Nuclear Freeze movement actually proposed "bilateral" disarmament.)

31. *Haemon:* So, father, pause, and put aside your anger. I think, for what my young opinion's worth, that, good as it is to have infallible wisdom, since this is rarely found, the next best thing is to be willing to listen to wise advice. *Creon:* Indeed! Am I to take lessons at my time of life from a fellow of his age? (Sophocles, *Antigone*)

32. S & W vegetables are the best because they use only premium quality.

33. In the presidential election of 2000, Al Gore challenged George W. Bush's victory on grounds of voter fraud in Florida. The electoral college votes, deciding the winner, hung in the balance, even though Gore held the lead in the popular vote. Some asserted that Gore should concede, just as Nixon did when John F. Kennedy won in 1960. In that election, votes for Kennedy in Illinois were said to have been fraudulently earned, although without the Illinois electoral votes, Kennedy still held his lead as he also held the lead in the popular vote.

34. Reading test scores in public schools have declined dramatically. This decline was caused by the radical changes in teaching strategies introduced in the 1960s.

35. Howard Dean, as head of the Democratic National Committee, claimed that the Republican party consisted of white Christians.

36. "I give so much pleasure to so many people. Why can't I get some pleasure for myself?" (Comedian John Belushi to his doctor in justification of his drug use)

37. "Editor: Now that it has been definitely established that nonsmokers have the right to tell smokers not to pollute their air, it follows that people who don't own cars have the right to tell car owners not to drive. Right?" (Jim Hodge, *San Francisco Chronicle*)

38. We must either give up some of our constitutional liberties to ensure that the government can protect us against terrorism or we will again fall prey to terrorists.

39. "Students should not be allowed any grace whatsoever on late assignments. Before you know it, they will no longer complete their work at all. If they don't do their assignments, they will be ignorant. If the students who are being educated are ignorant, then all of America will become more ignorant." (Thanks to a former student)

40. I think there is great merit in making the requirements stricter for graduate students. I recommend that you support it, too. After all, we are in a budget crisis and we do not want our salaries affected.

41. Potential customer to cosmetics saleswoman : "What is the difference between the daytime moisturizer and the nighttime moisturizer?"

   Saleswoman: "You put the daytime moisturizer on in the daytime and the nighttime moisturizer on at nighttime."

42.

43.

EXERCISE 6B

Analyzing a Short Argument

The following letter is not a genuine letter to the editor but a critical thinking test devised by educators. Test yourself by writing a critique of this deliberately flawed argument. It contains at least seven errors in reasoning, some of them fallacies that you have studied in this chapter, some of them weaknesses that can be identified and described but not labeled.

230 Sycamore Street
Moorburg
April 10

Dear Editor:

Overnight parking on all streets in Moorburg should be eliminated. To achieve this goal, parking should be prohibited from 2 a.m. to 6 a.m. There are a number of reasons why an intelligent citizen should agree.

For one thing, to park overnight is to have a garage in the streets. Now it is illegal for anyone to have a garage in the city streets. Clearly then it should be against the law to park overnight in the streets.

Three important streets, Lincoln Avenue, Marquand Avenue, and West Main Street, are very narrow. With cars parked on the streets, there really isn't room for the heavy traffic that passes over them in the afternoon rush hour. When driving home in the afternoon after work, it takes me thirty-five minutes to make a trip that takes ten minutes during the uncrowded time. If there were no cars parked on the side of these streets, they could handle considerably more traffic.

Traffic on some streets is also bad in the morning when factory workers are on their way to the 6 a.m. shift. If there were no cars parked on these streets between 2 a.m. and 6 a.m., then there would be more room for this traffic.

Furthermore there can be no doubt that, in general, overnight parking on the streets is undesirable. It is definitely bad and should be opposed.

If parking is prohibited from 2 a.m. to 6 a.m., then accidents between parked and moving vehicles will be nearly eliminated during this period. All intelligent citizens would regard the near elimination of accidents in any period as highly desirable. So we should be in favor of prohibiting parking from 2 a.m. to 6 a.m.

Last month the Chief of Police, Burgess Jones, ran an experiment which proves that parking should be prohibited from 2 a.m. to 6 a.m. On one of our busiest streets, Marquand Avenue, he placed experimental signs for one day. The signs prohibited parking from 2 a.m. to 6 a.m. During the four-hour period there was *not one accident* on Marquand. Everyone knows, of course, that there have been over four hundred accidents on Marquand during the past year.

The opponents of my suggestions have said that conditions are safe enough now. These people don't know what "safe" really means. *Conditions are not safe if there's even the slightest possible chance for an accident.* That's what "safe" means. So conditions are not safe the way they are now.

Finally let me point out that the director of the National Traffic Safety Council, Kenneth O. Taylor, has strongly recommended that overnight street parking be prevented on busy streets in cities the size of Moorburg. The National Association of Police Chiefs has made the same recommendation. Both suggest that prohibiting parking from 2 a.m. to 6 a.m. is the best way to prevent overnight parking.

I invite those who disagree as well as those who agree with me to react to my letter through the editor of this paper. Let's get this issue out in the open.

Sincerely,

Robert R. Raywift

WRITING ASSIGNMENT 12

Analyzing an Extended Argument

Choose one of the two following editorials (or find one in a newspaper or periodical) on which to write an essay evaluating the argument.

The Approach

1. Analyze each paragraph of your chosen editorial in order. Compose a list of the fallacies you find in each paragraph—give names of fallacies or identify weaknesses in reasoning (not all weaknesses can be precisely named) and illustrate with specific examples from the editorial. Avoid the trap of being too picky; you won't necessarily find significant fallacies in every paragraph.

2. During this paragraph-by-paragraph analysis, keep the argument's conclusion in mind and ask yourself if the author provides adequate support for it.

3. Next, review your paragraph-by-paragraph analysis to determine the two or three major problems in the argument. Then group and condense your list of faults or fallacies and, in a coherently written essay organized around these two or three principal categories, present your evaluation of the argument. For example, if you find more than one instance of personal attack, devote one of your paragraphs to this fallacy and cite all the examples you find to support your claim. Follow the same procedure for other weaknesses. Identify each specific example you cite either by paraphrase or direct quotation, imagining as you write that the reader is not familiar with the editorial you are critiquing. In your introduction, briefly discuss the issue of the editorial you've chosen, possibly supplying background information not covered in the editorial itself.

Audience

College-age readers who have not read the editorial and who are not familiar with all of the fallacies listed in the text.

Purpose

To illustrate to a less critical reader that published arguments written by established professionals are not necessarily free of fallacious reasoning.

On Date Rape

CAMILLE PAGLIA

Humanities professor and cultural critic, *San Francisco Examiner*

Dating is a very recent phenomenon in world history. Throughout history, women 1
have been chaperoned. As late as 1964, when I arrived in college, we had strict rules.
We had to be in the dorm under lock and key by 11 o'clock. My generation was the
one that broke these rules. We said, "We want freedom—no more double standard!"
When I went to stay at a male friend's apartment in New York, my aunts flew into a
frenzy: "You can't do that, it's dangerous!" But I said, "No, we're not going to be like
that anymore." Still, we understood in the '60s that we were taking a risk.

Today these young women want the freedoms that we won, but they don't 2
want to acknowledge the risk. That's the problem. The minute you go out with a
man, the minute you go to a bar to have a drink, there is a risk. You have to accept
the fact that part of the sizzle of sex comes from the danger of sex. You can be
overpowered.

So it is women's personal responsibility to be aware of the dangers of the 3
world. But these young feminists today are deluded. They come from a protected,
white, middle-class world, and they expect everything to be safe. Notice it's not
black or Hispanic women who are making a fuss about this—they come from cultures that are fully sexual and they are fully realistic about sex. But these other
women are sexually repressed girls, coming out of pampered homes, and when
they arrive at these colleges and suddenly hit male lust, they go, "Oh, no!"

These girls say, "Well, I should be able to get drunk at a fraternity party and go 4
upstairs to a guy's room without anything happening." And I say, "Oh, really? And
when you drive your car to New York City, do you leave your keys on the hood?"
My point is that if your car is stolen after you do something like that, yes, the police
should pursue the thief and he should be punished. But at the same time,
the police—and I—have the right to say to you, "You stupid idiot, what the hell
were you thinking?"

I mean, wake up to reality. This is male sex. Guess what, it's hot. Male sex is 5
hot. There's an attraction between the sexes that we're not totally in control of.
The idea that we can regulate it by passing campus grievance committee rules is
madness. My kind of feminism stresses personal responsibility. I've never been
raped, but I've been very vigilant—I'm constantly reading the signals. If I ever got
into a dating situation where I was overpowered and raped, I would say, "Oh well,
I misread the signals." But I don't think I would ever press charges.

Boxing, Doctors—Round Two

LOWELL COHN

Sportswriter, *San Francisco Chronicle*

Before I went on vacation a few weeks ago, I wrote a column criticizing the Ameri- 1
can Medical Association for its call to abolish boxing. As you might have expected,
I have received letters from doctors telling me I'm misinformed and scientifically

naive. One doctor even said I must have had terrible experiences with doctors to have written what I wrote.

That just shows how arrogant doctors are. It never would occur to them that I might have a defensible position. If I disagree with them, it's because I'm ignorant. 2

Doctors are used to being right. We come into their offices sick and generally not knowing what's wrong with us. We are in awe of their expertise and afraid for our well-being. We have a tendency to act like children in front of them. "If you can only make me well, Doc, I will love you for life." Doctors, who start out as regular human beings, come to expect us to worship them. They thrive on the power that comes from having knowledge about life and death. 3

Which brings us to their misguided stand against boxing. Doctors are offended by injuries in boxing, although they don't seem as mortified by the people who die skiing or bike riding or swimming every year. You rarely hear a peep out of them about the many injuries football players sustain—that includes kids in the peewee leagues and high school. Why the outrage over boxing? 4

Because many doctors are social snobs. They see people from ethnic minorities punching each other in a ring and they reach the conclusion that these poor, dumb blacks and Latinos must be protected from themselves because they don't know any better. The AMA is acting like a glorified SPCA, arrogantly trying to prevent cruelty to animals. They would never dare preach this way to football players, because most of them went to college. Nor would they come out against skiing, because many doctors love to ski. 5

Boxers know the risks of taking a right cross to the jaw better than doctors, and they take up the sport with a full understanding of its risks. A man should have the right to take a risk. Doctors may want to save us from adventure, but there still is honor in freely choosing to put yourself on the line. Risk is why race-car drivers speed around treacherous tracks. Danger is why mountain climbers continue to explore the mystery of Mount Everest. Yet doctors do not come out against auto racing or mountain climbing. 6

One physician wrote a letter to the Sporting Green saying the AMA's position against boxing is based on medical evidence. As I read the letter's twisted logic, I wondered if the AMA causes brain damage in doctors. "Skiing, bicycle riding and swimming kill more people each year (than boxing)," he writes. "Obviously, far more people engage in those activities than enter a boxing ring." 7

Does his position make sense to you? We should eliminate boxing, the sport with fewer negative consequences, but allow the real killer sports to survive. Amazing. If this doctor were really concerned with medical evidence, as he claims, he would attack all dangerous sports, not just boxing. 8

But he doesn't. The truth is, boxing offends the delicate sensibilities of doctors. They don't like the idea that two men *intentionally* try to hurt each other. They feel more comfortable when injuries are a byproduct of a sport—although ask any batter who has been beaned by a fastball if his broken skull was an innocent byproduct. 9

In other words, doctors are making a moral judgment, not a medical judgment, about which sports are acceptable. Every joker is entitled to ethical opinions, but doctors have no more expertise than you or I when it comes to right and wrong. If preaching excites them, let them become priests. 10

What if the AMA is successful in getting boxing banned? Will the sport disap-   11
pear? No way. As long as man is man, he will want to see two guys of equal
weight and ability solve their elemental little problem in a ring. If the sport
becomes illegal, it will drift off to barges and back alleys, where men will fight in
secret without proper supervision. And then you will see deaths and maiming like
you never saw before.

Whom will the AMA blame then?   12

KEY TERMS

Term	Description	Example
Appeal to authority (2 forms)	1. Appeals to an authority who is not an expert on the issue under discussion.	Abortion to save the mother is irrelevant because a pediatric surgeon has never seen a case in which such a dilemma has risen.
Snob appeal	2. Appeals to people's desire for prestige and exclusivity.	Pamilla's not for everyone. The best never is.
Appeal to fear	Implicitly threatens the audience.	Will there be a *job* waiting when *you* leave college?
Appeal to pity	Attempts to win sympathy.	Professor Hall, I must get an A in your course. If you don't give me an A, I won't be able to go to law school.
Begging the question	1. Offers no actual support; may restate as a premise the conclusion in different words.	The reason he is so strong is because of his strength.
Loaded question	2. Asks a question that contains an assumption that must be proven.	Have you started to pay your fair share of taxes yet?
Question-begging epithet	3. Uses a single word to assert a claim that must be proven.	Reactionary, negligent, warmonger, deadbeat.
Double standard	Judges and labels the same act differently depending on the person or group who performs the act.	China and Cuba both restrict religious freedoms and limit free speech. China has favored-nation status whereas Cuba is not recognized by the United States.

Term	Description	Example
Equivocation	Shifts the meaning of a term within a single argument.	We are told that to discriminate in employment or housing is punishable by law. But we must discriminate when we hire an individual or rent an apartment.
Fallacious argument	Persuasive but does not logically support its conclusion.	Senator Smith was expelled from college for cheating on an exam. His wife divorced him because of his numerous affairs. Therefore, he is a man without honor, a politician who cannot be trusted, and we should not support his National Health Bill.
False analogy	Compares two or more things that are not in essence similar and suggests that since they share certain characteristics, they share others as well.	I don't want to die falling off a rock. But you can kill yourself falling in the bathtub too.
False cause [Latin name: *post hoc, ergo propter hoc*]	Claims a causal relationship between events solely on the basis of a chronological relationship.	I joined the Confederacy for two weeks. Then I deserted. The Confederacy fell.
False dilemma	Presents two and only two alternatives for consideration when other possibilities exist.	Lennon *or* McCartney, Monroe *or* Bardot, Hemingway *or* Fitzgerald, Freud *or* Jung.
Hasty generalization	Generalizes from a sample that is too small or in some other way unrepresentative of the target population.	Students in Professor Hall's eight o'clock freshman composition class are often late. Today's college students are irresponsible and unreliable.
Personal attack [Latin name: *ad hominem*]	1. Attacks the person representing the argument rather than the argument itself.	Because Rachel Carson has no children, she cannot have concern for the effect of insecticides and

Term	Description	Example
		pesticides on future generations.
Tu quoque ("you also")	2. Discredits an argument because the behavior of the person proposing it does not conform to the position he's supporting.	A teenager to his father: Don't tell me not to drink. You drink all the time.
Poisoning the well	Makes an assertion that will intimidate the audience and therefore discourage an open discussion.	Every patriotic American supports legislation condemning the desecration of the flag.
Red herring	Shifts the discussion from the issue to a different topic.	While the hospital bond issue has merit, there are too many bond issues on this ballot.
Slippery slope	Claims that an action should be avoided because it will lead to a series of extremely undesirable consequences.	What seems like reasonable restrictions on guns with no legitimate civilian purpose will lead inevitably to total prohibition of gun ownership that ends in virtual slavery at the hands of a totalitarian regime.
Straw man	Creates and then attacks a distorted version of the opposition's argument.	The Democratic candidate wants the federal government to house everyone, feed everyone, care for everyone's children, and provide medical care for everyone. And he's going to take 50 percent of every dime you make to do it.

CHAPTER 7

Deductive and Inductive Argument

There is a tradition of opposition between adherents of induction and deduction. In my view, it would be just as sensible for the two ends of a worm to quarrel.
—ALFRED NORTH WHITEHEAD

Sometimes arguments are classified as deductive or inductive. Deduction and induction are modes of reasoning, particular ways of arriving at an inference. Different logicians tend to make different distinctions between deductive and inductive reasoning, with some going so far as to declare, as Whitehead did, that such a distinction is spurious. But classifications, if carefully made, help us to understand abstract concepts, and scientists and humanists alike often refer to patterns of reasoning as deductive or inductive. This classification also helps us to distinguish between conclusions we must accept and those we should question, a valuable skill for both reading critically and writing logically.

KEY DISTINCTIONS

The key distinctions between deduction and induction are generally seen as falling into two categories.

(1) Necessity Versus Probability

In a **deductive argument**, the conclusion will follow by *necessity* from the premises if the method of reasoning is valid, as in this familiar bit of classical wisdom:

1. All men are mortal.
2. Socrates is a man.
∴ Socrates is mortal.

In an **inductive argument**, the conclusion can follow only with some degree of *probability* (from the unlikely to the highly probable). British philosopher Bertrand Russell made the point implicitly but emphatically in *The Problems of Philosophy*: "The man who has fed the chicken every day throughout its life at last wrings its neck instead." The chicken reasons thus:

1. He has fed me today.
2. He has fed me this next day.

3. He has fed me this day too.

4. He has fed me yet another day, etc.

∴ He will feed me tomorrow.

The poor chicken has made a prediction, and a reasonable one, based on its past experience.

A related distinction here becomes clear. The premises of a deductive argument contain all the information needed for the conclusion, whereas the conclusion of an inductive argument goes beyond the premises. For this reason, some prefer the certainty of deduction to the probability of induction.

Ambroise Paré, an Italian Renaissance physician, revealed his distrust of induction when he defined inductive diagnosis as "the rapid means to the wrong conclusion." One assumes that he would have argued for the value of a few well-learned principles behind one's observations. In contrast, 19th-century Harvard professor and scientist Louis Agassiz urged his students to practice induction, to observe before making generalizations, believing that: "[A] physical fact is as sacred as a moral principle."

(2) From General to Specific, Specific to General

In a *deductive* argument, the inference usually moves from a generalization to a particular, specific instance or example that fits that generalization. Two examples:

1. All students who complete this course successfully will fulfill the critical thinking requirement.

2. Jane has completed this course successfully.

∴ Jane has fulfilled the critical thinking requirement.

1. Children born on a Saturday will "work hard for a living."

2. Nick was born on a Saturday.

∴ Nick will work hard for his living.

You may not believe this folk wisdom, especially if you were born on a Saturday, but the line of reasoning is still deductive.

In an *inductive* argument, the inference usually moves from a series of specific instances to a generalization.

1. Droughts have been more frequent in some areas.

2. Skin cancers related to ultraviolet rays have been increasing.

3. The tree line is moving north about 40 meters a year.

4. Polar ice has been melting more rapidly than in the past.

5. Oceans have been rising at measurable annual rates around the globe.

∴ Clearly, global warming is upon us.

*"Gentlemen, it's time we gave some serious thought
to the effects of global warming."*

Sometimes in inductive reasoning, we begin with a **hypothesis, an unproved theory or proposition**, and gather the data to support it. For instance, when Jonas Salk thought his vaccine would cure polio, he first had to test it inductively by administering it to a broad sample before concluding that the vaccine prevented polio.

THE RELATIONSHIP
BETWEEN INDUCTION AND DEDUCTION

In Exercise 7B we ask you to distinguish between inductive and deductive reasoning, but in reality the two are inextricable. Consider the source for the generalizations upon which deductions are based. In some cases they seem to be the laws of nature, but more often than not we arrive at these generalizations by means of repeated observations. Throughout history, people have observed their own mortality, so we can now take that generalization—all people are mortal—as a given from which we can deduce conclusions about individual people. Induction has, in this case, led to a trusted generalization that in turn allows us a "necessary," or deductive, inference.

Humorists have sometimes turned these concepts on their heads. Here's Woody Allen reflecting on deduction: "All men are Socrates." And Lewis Carroll, in "The Hunting of the Snark," on induction: "What I tell you three times is true." While studying logic in college, Steve Martin was inspired by Lewis Carroll's wacky arguments. One example:

1. Babies are illogical.
2. Nobody is despised who can manage a crocodile.
3. Illogical persons are despised.

Therefore babies cannot manage crocodiles.

Martin began closing his show by announcing: "I'm not going home tonight. I'm going to Bananaland, a place where only two things are true, only two things: one, all chairs are green; and, two, no chairs are green."

In a more serious approach, Robert Pirsig, in his philosophical novel *Zen and the Art of Motorcycle Maintenance*, attempts to explain deduction, induction, and the relationships between them in language we can all understand. These terms were never intended to be the exclusive domain of academics but, rather, descriptive of the ways in which we all think every day.

Note how the following excerpt from Pirsig's novel explains both the differences between induction and deduction and their dependence on one another.

Mechanics' Logic

Two kinds of logic are used (in motorcycle maintenance), inductive and deductive. 1 Inductive inferences start with observations of the machine and arrive at general conclusions. For example, if the cycle goes over a bump and the engine misfires, and then goes over another bump and the engine misfires, and then goes over another bump and the engine misfires, and then goes over a long smooth stretch of road and there is no misfiring, and then goes over a fourth bump and the engine misfires again, one can logically conclude that the misfiring is caused by the bumps. That is induction: reasoning from particular experiences to general truths.

Deductive inferences do the reverse. They start with general knowledge and 2 predict a specific observation. For example, if, from reading the hierarchy of facts about the machine, the mechanic knows the horn of the cycle is powered exclusively by electricity from the battery, then he can logically infer that if the battery is dead the horn will not work. That is deduction.

Solution of problems too complicated for common sense to solve is achieved by 3 long strings of mixed inductive and deductive inferences that weave back and forth between the observed machine and the mental hierarchy of the machine found in the manuals. The correct program for this interweaving is formalized as scientific method.

Actually I've never seen a cycle-maintenance problem complex enough really 4 to require full-scale formal scientific method. Repair problems are not that hard. When I think of formal scientific method an image sometimes comes to mind of an enormous juggernaut, a huge bulldozer—slow, tedious, lumbering, laborious, but invincible. It takes twice as long, five times as long, maybe a dozen times as long as informal mechanic's techniques, but you know in the end you're going to *get* it. There's no fault isolation problem in motorcycle maintenance that can stand up to it. When you've hit a really tough one, tried everything, racked your brain and nothing works, and you know that this time Nature has really decided to be difficult, you say, "Okay, Nature, that's the end of the *nice* guy," and you crank up the formal scientific method.

For this you keep a lab notebook. Everything gets written down, formally, so   5
that you know at all times where you are, where you've been, where you're going and where you want to get. In scientific work and electronics technology this is necessary because otherwise the problems get so complex you get lost in them and confused and forget what you know and what you don't know and have to give up. In cycle maintenance things are not that involved, but when confusion starts it's a good idea to hold it down by making everything formal and exact. Sometimes just the act of writing down the problems straightens out your head as to what they really are.

The logical statements entered into the notebook are broken down into six cat-   6
egories: (1) statement of the problem, (2) hypotheses as to the cause of the problem, (3) experiments designed to test each hypothesis, (4) predicted results of the experiments, (5) observed results of the experiments and (6) conclusions from the results of the experiments. This is not different from the formal arrangement of many college and high-school lab notebooks but the purpose here is no longer just busy-work. The purpose now is precise guidance of thoughts that will fail if they are not accurate.

The real purpose of scientific method is to make sure Nature hasn't misled you   7
into thinking you know something you don't actually know. There's not a mechanic or scientist or technician alive who hasn't suffered from that one so much that he's not instinctively on guard. That's the main reason why so much scientific and mechanical information sounds so dull and so cautious. If you get careless or go romanticizing scientific information, giving it a flourish here and there, Nature will soon make a complete fool out of you. It does it often enough anyway even when you don't give it opportunities. One must be extremely careful and rigidly logical when dealing with Nature: one logical slip and an entire scientific edifice comes tumbling down. One false deduction about the machine and you can get hung up indefinitely.

In Part One of formal scientific method, which is the statement of the problem,   8
the main skill is in stating absolutely no more than you are positive you know. It is much better to enter a statement "Solve Problem: Why doesn't cycle work?" which sounds dumb but is correct, than it is to enter a statement "Solve Problem: What is wrong with the electrical system?" when you don't absolutely *know* the trouble is *in* the electrical system. What you should state is "Solve Problem: What is wrong with cycle?" and *then* state as the first entry of Part Two: "Hypothesis Number One: The trouble is in the electrical system." You think of as many hypotheses as you can, then you design experiments to test them to see which are true and which are false.

This careful approach to the beginning questions keeps you from taking   9
a major wrong turn which might cause you weeks of extra work or can even

hang you up completely. Scientific questions often have a surface appearance of dumbness for this reason. They are asked in order to prevent dumb mistakes later on.

Part Three, that part of formal scientific method called experimentation, is 10 sometimes thought of by romantics as all of science itself because that's the only part with much visual surface. They see lots of test tubes and bizarre equipment and people running around making discoveries. They do not see the experiment as part of a larger intellectual process and so they often confuse experiments with demonstrations, which look the same. A man conducting a gee-whiz science show with fifty thousand dollars' worth of Frankenstein equipment is not doing anything scientific if he knows beforehand what the results of his efforts are going to be. A motorcycle mechanic, on the other hand, who honks the horn to see if the battery works is informally conducting a true scientific experiment. He is testing a hypothesis by putting the question to Nature. The TV scientist who mutters sadly, "The experiment is a failure; we have failed to achieve what we had hoped for," is suffering mainly from a bad scriptwriter. An experiment is never a failure solely because it fails to achieve predicted results. An experiment is a failure only when it also fails adequately to test the hypothesis in question, when the data it produces don't prove anything one way or another.

Skill at this point consists of using experiments that test only the hypothesis 11 in question, nothing less, nothing more. If the horn honks, and the mechanic concludes that the whole electrical system is working, he is in deep trouble. He has reached an illogical conclusion. The honking horn only tells him that the battery and horn are working. To design an experiment properly he has to think very rigidly in terms of what directly causes what. This you know from the hierarchy. The horn doesn't make the cycle go. Neither does the battery, except in a very indirect way. The point at which the electrical system *directly* causes the engine to fire is at the spark plugs, and if you don't test here, at the output of the electrical system, you will never really know whether the failure is electrical or not.

To test properly the mechanic removes the plug and lays it against the engine 12 so that the base around the plug is electrically grounded, kicks the starter lever and watches the spark-plug gap for a blue spark. If there isn't any he can conclude one of two things: (a) there is an electrical failure or (b) his experiment is sloppy. If he is experienced he will try it a few more times, checking connections, trying every way he can think of to get that plug to fire. Then, if he can't get it to fire, he finally concludes that *a* is correct, there's an electrical failure, and the experiment is over. He has proved that his hypothesis is correct.

In the final category, conclusions, skill comes in stating no more than the 13 experiment has proved. It hasn't proved that when he fixes the electrical system the motorcycle will start. There may be other things wrong. But he does know that the motorcycle isn't going to run until the electrical system is working and he sets up the next formal question: "Solve Problem: What is wrong with the electrical system?"

He then sets up hypotheses for these and tests them. By asking the right questions and choosing the right tests and drawing the right conclusions the mechanic 14 works his way down the echelons of the motorcycle hierarchy until he has found the exact specific cause or causes of the engine failure, and then he changes them so that they no longer cause the failure.

An untrained observer will see only physical labor and often get the idea that   15
physical labor is mainly what the mechanic does. Actually the physical labor is the smallest and easiest part of what the mechanic does. By far the greatest part of his work is careful observation and precise thinking. That is why mechanics sometimes seem so taciturn and withdrawn when performing tests. They don't like it when you talk to them because they are concentrating on mental images, hierarchies, and not really looking at you or the physical motorcycle at all. They are using the experiment as part of the program to expand their hierarchy of knowledge of the faulty motorcycle and compare it to the correct hierarchy in their mind. They are looking at underlying form.

EXERCISE 7A

Analyzing Pirsig

1. According to Pirsig, what is the most important part of the mechanic's work?
2. How does Pirsig define induction and deduction?
3. Which method of reasoning—induction or deduction—does the scientific method rely on?
4. Return to the statement by mathematician and philosopher Alfred North Whitehead (1861–1947), which begins this chapter, and explain its meaning.

EXERCISE 7B

Distinguishing Inductive from Deductive Reasoning

Read the following passages carefully to determine which are based on inductive reasoning and which on deductive. Briefly explain your answers.

1. Only 18-year-old citizens can vote, and Felix is not a citizen, so he can't vote in the upcoming presidential election.
2. The United States Supreme Court nominee received excellent grades throughout his school career and made law review at Harvard Law School. Add to these excellent credentials the fact that everyone who has ever known him says that he is kind and fair. I think he will make an excellent Supreme Court justice.
3. Marie must be out of town. She hasn't answered her phone in a week, nor has she returned the messages that I have left on her answering machine. When I drove by her house last night, I noted that the lights inside and out were off.

4. Cat lovers do not care for dogs, and since Colette had numerous cats all of her life, I assume she did not care for dogs.

5. According to polls taken prior to the national convention, the candidate I support held a substantial lead in the presidential race. I am now confident that he will win in November.

6. Every Frenchman is devoted to his glass of *vin rouge*. Philippe is a Frenchman, so he too must be devoted to that glass of red wine.

7. George W. Bush lied to the American people about weapons of mass destruction in Iraq. Bill Clinton lied about his relationship with a White House intern. Richard Nixon lied about Watergate. Lyndon Johnson lied about the Gulf of Tonkin and the Vietnam War. I'll let you draw your own conclusions.

8. As an expert testified on the *NewsHour* following the *Challenger* space shuttle disaster, the solid rocket booster had proved safe in more than 200 successful launchings of both space shuttles and Titan missiles. It was reasonable to conclude that the same rocket booster would function properly on the *Challenger* mission.

9. Over time the only investment to keep pace with inflation is an investment in the stock market. So despite the current economic crisis, responsible retirement fund managers should continue to buy stocks.

10. When people are confident and cheerful, they are generally inclined to spend more freely. With this in mind, we have designed these ads to project a feeling of cheerful confidence that should encourage viewers to spend more freely on your product. (Ad agency pitch to a potential client)

DEDUCTIVE REASONING

Class Logic

Having established the differences between deductive and inductive reasoning, we can now examine each in greater detail. Underlying both forms of reasoning is an understanding of class logic. In fact, good reasoning in general often depends on seeing relationships between classes. **A class in logic is all of the individual things—persons, objects, events, ideas—that share a determinate property, a common feature**. What is that determinate property? Anything under the sun. A class may consist of any quality or combination of qualities that the classifier assigns to it. A class may be vast, such as a class containing everything in the universe, or it may be small, containing only one member, such as Nick's last girlfriend. Making classes and assigning members to those classes is an essential part of everyday reasoning—it's how we order our experience. Indeed, each word in the language serves as a class by which we categorize and communicate experience. We can then take these words in any combination to create the categories or classes that serve our purpose.

A recent article in the *Journal of the American Medical Association*, for example, features a piece titled "Risk of Sexually Transmitted Diseases Among Adolescent Crack Users in Oakland and San Francisco." This title, which identifies one class (and the subject of the article), was created by combining seven classes: the class of things involving risk, the class of things that are sexually transmitted, the class of disease, the class of adolescents, the class of crack users, the class of persons living in Oakland, and the class of persons living in San Francisco.

Relationships Between Classes

There are three possible relationships between classes: **inclusion**, **exclusion**, and **overlap**.

INCLUSION   One class is included in another if every member of one class is a member of the other class. Using letters, we can symbolize this relationship as all As are Bs. Using circle diagrams, also called Euler diagrams after Leonhard Euler, an eighteenth-century mathematician, we can illustrate a relationship of inclusion this way:

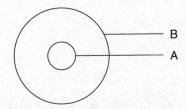

For example, the class of professional basketball players is included in the class of professional athletes because all professional basketball players are also professional athletes. The following diagram illustrates this relationship:

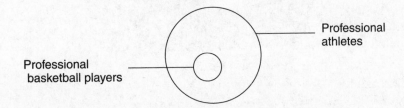

EXCLUSION   One class excludes another if they share no members, that is, if no As are Bs. Such a relationship exists between handguns and rifles:

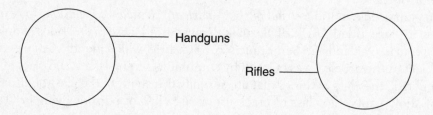

OVERLAP   One class overlaps with another if both have at least one member in common—if at least one A is also a B—for example, students at this university and students who like classical music:

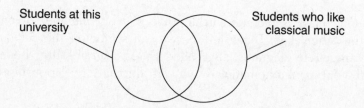

Cartoonists Roz Chast and Hilary B. Price have fun with the relationship of overlap between classes:

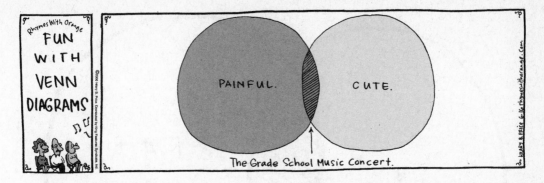

The way our public institutions classify relationships between groups of people can have a significant impact on their lives. The federal Department of Housing and Urban Development (HUD) is authorized to allocate housing funds to individuals with disabilities. People with AIDS argued that they were entitled to such funds, but HUD, until recently, had denied them any such subsidy. Clearly, HUD saw the relationship between disabilities and AIDS as one of exclusion, whereas those with AIDS saw their relationship to those with disabilities as one of inclusion, a relationship they were, over time, able to convince HUD of. (For another look at classifications, see "When Human Rights Extend to Nonhumans" in Additional Readings.)

EXERCISE 7C

Identifying Relationships Between Classes

Using circle diagrams, illustrate the relationships between the following pairs of classes:

1. witches and women
2. cantaloupes and watermelons
3. judges and lawyers
4. Saabs and convertibles
5. mollusks and amphibians
6. cosmetics and hairspray
7. the homeless and the mentally ill
8. euthanasia and suicide
9. concession and Rogerian strategy (see Chapter 4)
10. What is the meaning of the following diagram, which appeared on the *New York Times*'s editorial page?

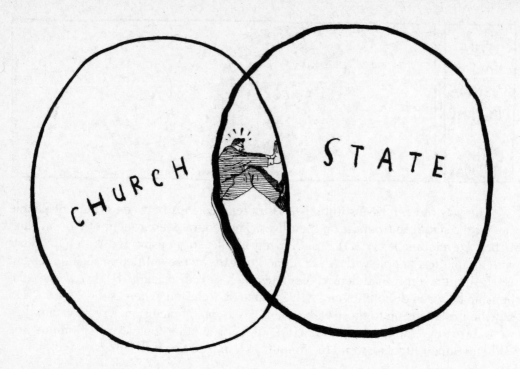

Now create your own classes:

1. Identify two classes, one of which is inclusive of the other.
2. Identify two classes that are exclusive of one another.
3. Identify two classes that overlap one another.

Class Logic and the Syllogism

Both inductive and deductive reasoning often depend on supporting a conclusion on the basis of relationships between classes. Let's look first at deduction. Deductive arguments usually involve more than two classes; in fact, the simplest form of deductive argument involves three classes. Remember this famous argument?

All men are mortal.

Socrates is a man.

∴ Socrates is mortal.

The three classes are *men*, *mortality*, and *Socrates*. We can use circle diagrams to illustrate the relationship between these three classes. The first premise asserts that the class of men is included in the class of mortality. The second premise asserts that the class of Socrates is included in the class of men; and thus the conclusion can claim that Socrates is included in the class of mortality.

This type of argument is called a **categorical syllogism**—a deductive argument composed of three classes; such an argument has two premises and one conclusion derived from the two premises.

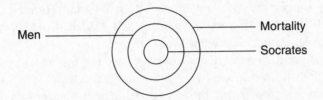

THE SUBJECT AND THE PREDICATE   To help identify the three classes of a categorical syllogism, you may want to identify the subject and predicate of each premise. Categorical propositions, and indeed all English sentences, can be broken down into two parts—the subject and predicate. These terms are shared by both grammar and logic and mean the same thing in both disciplines. The subject is that part of the sentence about which something is being asserted, and the predicate includes everything being asserted about the subject. In the first premise above, *all men* is the subject and *are mortal* is the predicate; in the second premise, *Socrates* is the subject and *is a man* is the predicate. The subject identifies one class; the predicate, the other.

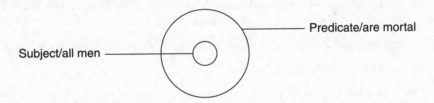

Note: If the premise stated *men are mortal* rather than *all men are mortal*, the meaning would be the same because, if a class is not quantified in some way—*some, many, few, one*—it is assumed that the assertion refers to the entire class.

TRUTH, VALIDITY, AND SOUNDNESS   If the conclusion follows of necessity, inescapably, from the premises, as it does in the syllogism about Socrates, then it is a **valid** argument.

We frequently use the term *valid* in everyday language. For example, we say, "That's a valid point." But in logic, **validity** has this very precise meaning: The conclusion follows of necessity from the premises, the form of the argument is correct, the line of reasoning conforms to the rules of logic. When we learn to evaluate the validity of a deductive argument, we can see what it means for a conclusion to follow inescapably from the premises.

Validity, however, is not the only requirement for a successful deductive argument; the premises must also be **true** or **acceptable**. Logicians use the term *true*, appropriate when a proposition can be evaluated by absolute or mathematical standards. But proof must often fall short of what can be claimed as true, an absolute term too imposing, even intimidating, for many assertions that we would nonetheless be inclined to accept. In most of our arguments, we must settle for what is **reasonable to believe**, what has been adequately supported and explained. Oliver Wendell Holmes, Supreme Court Justice (1841–1935), skirted the issue when he said, "What is true is what I can't help believing." We prefer the term *acceptable* to *true*.

An important point here is that to evaluate an argument successfully, we must begin by evaluating the premises, one by one, rather than moving in on the conclusion first. The conclusion will only be as acceptable as the sum of its premises.

To summarize, **two requirements must be met for us to accept the conclusion of a deductive argument**:

1. The structure of the argument must be valid—that is, the conclusion must follow of necessity from the premises.

2. The premises must be *acceptable* (true).

A deductive argument whose premises are acceptable and whose structure is valid is a **sound** argument—**a successful deductive argument**. Put another way, if the argument is valid and the premises are acceptable, then the conclusion cannot be false. Keep in mind that the terms *validity* and *soundness* can refer only to the argument as a whole. In contrast, individual statements can only be described as acceptable or unacceptable (true or false). In logic, we don't describe an argument as being true or a premise as valid.

Some examples of sound and unsound arguments:

1. A sound argument—the premises are acceptable and the structure valid.

   Drift-net fishing kills dolphins.

   Mermaid Tuna uses drift nets.

   ∴ Mermaid Tuna kills dolphins.

2. An unsound argument—one of the premises (in this example the first one) is false or not acceptable, even though the structure is valid.

   All Greeks are volatile.

   Athena is a Greek.

   ∴ Athena is volatile.

3. An unsound argument—the premises are acceptable but the structure is invalid.

   All athletes are people.

   All football players are people.

   ∴ All football players are athletes.

Note that in example 3, all the statements are acceptable, both the premises and the conclusion, but because the structure of the argument is invalid—the premises do not lead inescapably to the conclusion—the argument is unsound. Sketch this argument with circle diagrams to illustrate the principle.

Unreliable syllogisms turn up as accident and as humorous intent in a variety of places. Writer and critic Donald Newlove once claimed that, because he fell asleep while reading Harold Brodkey's *Runaway Soul*, which he also did his first time through literary classics *Moby Dick* and *Ulysses, Runaway Soul* must also be a great work of literature. Writer Ian Frazier found the following graffiti on a library table at Columbia University:

Bono is supreme.

God is supreme.

∴ Bono is God.

GUILT BY ASSOCIATION   Let's look at another example of an invalid argument with acceptable premises.

Members of the Mafia often have dinner at Joe's Place in Little Italy.

My neighbor frequently dines there.

∴ My neighbor is a member of the Mafia.

Most of us would reject this argument, but this pattern of reasoning, erroneous as it is, is fairly common. One famous example took place in 1950 when communism was referred to as the "red menace," and Senator Joseph McCarthy and the House Un-American Activities Committee were beginning their witch hunt against anyone who had ever had an association, no matter how slight or distant, with communism. It was in this climate of national paranoia that Republican Richard Nixon, running against Democrat Helen Gahagen Douglas for a California senate seat, presented the following argument, allowing the voters to draw their own conclusions:

Communists favor measures x, y, and z.

My opponent, Helen Gahagen Douglas, favors these same measures.

∴ [Helen Gahagen Douglas is a Communist.]

This kind of reasoning, based on guilt by association, is faulty (but often effective—Douglas lost the election) because it assumes that if two classes share one quality, they share all qualities. Such reasoning is a source of much sexism and racism; it assumes that if two people are of the same sex or race, they share not only that characteristic but an entire set of characteristics as well. Simple diagrams can illustrate where the logic fails:

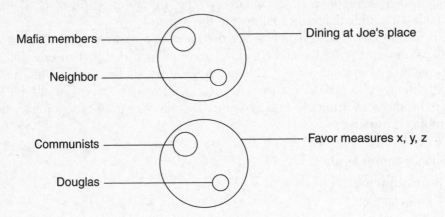

Faulty as this logic is, it was used in the recent presidential race. Those against Obama publicized the fact that he and Bill Ayers, a former 60s radical involved in terrorist activities, sat on the same board, implying that Obama was also a radical and a terrorist. This time the guilt by association strategy ultimately failed. Barack Obama was elected. But many voters believed that Obama was tainted by his association with Ayers even though the president was eight years old when Ayers was engaged in radical activities.

MORE ON SYLLOGISMS   Before you examine some syllogisms on your own, we need to look once again at exclusion, overlap, and inclusion. Examine the following example and use circle diagrams to illustrate the relationship between each of the classes to determine the validity of the reasoning.

All Alice's friends are business majors.

Deborah is not a business major.

∴ Deborah is not a friend of Alice.

Were you able to illustrate by exclusion that this is a valid argument? Can you do the same for this one?

None of Alice's friends are business majors.

Deborah is not a friend of Alice.

∴ Deborah is not a business major.

Can you illustrate why this reasoning is not reliable, why the argument is invalid?

So far we have been dealing with what we call a **universal proposition**, an assertion that refers to all members of a designated class. What happens when we qualify a premise with *some* and then have what logicians call a **particular proposition**? Let's look at an example:

> All gamblers are optimists.
> Some of my friends are gamblers.
> ∴ Some of my friends are optimists.

A diagram illustrates that because the conclusion is qualified, it can follow from one qualified, or *particular*, premise. Although it's possible for some friends to fall outside the class of gamblers and thus, perhaps, outside the class of optimists, the second premise guarantees that some (at least two) of my friends are included in the class of gamblers.

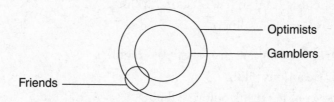

Five steps to determine the soundness of a categorical syllogism:

1. **Identify three classes:** subject and predicate in the first premise, subject in the second premise.

2. Represent the relationship between the three classes by drawing **circle diagrams**.

3. **Compare** the circle diagram to the conclusion. If they match, the structure of the argument is valid. If not, the structure is invalid.

4. Determine the **acceptability** of the premises.

5. If the structure is valid and the premises acceptable, the argument is **sound**. If both criteria are not met, the argument is **unsound**.

EXERCISE 7D

Determining the Soundness of Categorical Syllogisms

First use Euler diagrams to determine the validity of the following categorical syllogisms. Then determine if the premises are acceptable or not. If the structure of the argument is valid and the premises acceptable, the argument is sound.

Example

1. Stealing is a criminal act.

   Shoplifting is stealing.

   ∴ Shoplifting is a criminal act.

VALID inclusion and the premises are acceptable, so argument is SOUND

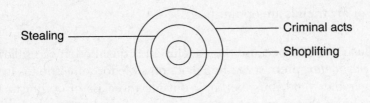

1. Liberals want to ban offshore drilling.

   Conservationists want to ban offshore drilling.

   ∴ Conservationists are liberals.

2. A cautious pilot wouldn't drink before a flight.

   Maxine is a cautious pilot.

   ∴ Maxine wouldn't drink before a flight.

3. All Jose's parrots understand Spanish.

   Pepe is his favorite parrot.

   ∴ Pepe understands Spanish.

4. Gauguin's paintings of Tahiti have brilliant and unrealistic colors.

   Starry Night has brilliant and unrealistic colors.

   ∴ *Starry Night* is a Gauguin painting of Tahiti.

5. Young men with shaven heads and swastikas tattooed on their arms are racists.

   John is a young man who doesn't shave his head or have a swastika tattooed on his arm.

   ∴ John is not a racist.

6. Nations that do not respect their citizens' civil liberties shouldn't receive favored nation status.

   China's censorship of the Internet demonstrates China's lack of respect for the civil liberties of its citizens.

   ∴ China doesn't deserve its favored nation status.

7. Every pediatrician knows that each child develops at his own rate.
   Dr. Haskell knows that each child develops at his own rate.
   ∴ Dr. Haskell is a pediatrician.

8. Some artists are completely self-absorbed.
   Frida Kahlo was an artist.
   ∴ Frida Kahlo was completely self-absorbed.

9. Members of the Christian Coalition believe in family values.
   Carlos and Maria believe in family values.
   ∴ Carlos and Maria are members of the Christian Coalition.

10. Killing the innocent is morally wrong.
    Modern warfare always involves killing the innocent.
    ∴ Modern warfare is always morally wrong.

Create three categorical syllogisms of your own—one valid but unsound, one invalid, and one sound.

EXERCISE 7E

Evaluating Deductive Arguments in Everyday Language

Determine whether the following arguments are sound or unsound. For each argument, follow these steps: First, reduce each argument to a categorical syllogism (supplying any unstated premises or conclusions—see "Hidden Assumptions in Argument" in Chapter 3); then use circle diagrams to determine validity; and finally, discuss the truth or acceptability of each premise.

1. Plagiarism is wrong, and paraphrasing the words of others without proper acknowledgment is the same as plagiarism, so paraphrasing the words of others without proper acknowledgment is wrong.

2. Mafia member Joe Bonano was guilty of criminal activities because he claimed the Fifth Amendment in the course of his trial. The Fifth Amendment, you will recall, is the privilege of a witness not to testify on the grounds that the evidence called for might be incriminating. One may choose not to testify against oneself, but there is a risk attached to this privilege. For we cannot avoid the fact that people who take the Fifth Amendment have something to hide—their guilt. In the case of Joe Bonano, that something to hide was his criminal activities.

HYPOTHETICAL ARGUMENTS

Another common type of deductive argument is the hypothetical or conditional argument which, unlike the categorical syllogism, is concerned not with classes but with conditions. For example:

> If Maria drops that glass, it will break.

A condition is established that, if met, will lead to a a specified consequence. The condition is called the **antecedent**; the consequence or result is called, appropriately enough, the **consequent**. The second premise, or minor premise, establishes whether or not that condition has been met.

> Maria dropped the glass.

In this case, the antecedent has been affirmed. The conclusion then follows of necessity: The glass broke. The argument pattern looks like this:

> If A, then B.
>
> A.
>
> ∴ B.

The Valid Hypothetical Argument

This argument pattern *affirms the antecedent* (logicians refer to this argument pattern as *modus ponens*), and any argument that conforms to this pattern is valid; though of course, whether or not the argument is sound, whether or not we accept the conclusion, depends on the acceptability of the premises as well as the validity of the argument.

Another valid argument pattern is one in which the minor premise *denies the consequent*. Logicians refer to this argument pattern as *modus tollens*.

> If Maria drops that glass, it will break.
>
> It did not break.
>
> ∴ Maria did not drop it.

It follows that if the glass didn't break, Maria didn't drop it. Here's the form of this argument.

> If A, then B.
>
> Not B.
>
> ∴ Not A.

The rule governing the validity of a hypothetical argument is really quite simple: *The minor premise must either affirm the antecedent or deny the consequent.*

The Invalid Hypothetical Argument

Conversely, to deny the antecedent or affirm the consequent leads to invalidity.
For example:

If Maria drops the glass, it will break.	[If A, then B.
Maria did not drop the glass.	Not A.
∴ The glass did not break.	Not B.]

It does not follow that if Maria does not drop it, it won't break, since there are many other ways for the glass to break: Jack may drop it or someone may pour very hot liquid into it, just to name two possibilities.
To affirm the consequent will also produce an invalid argument.

If Maria drops the glass, it will break.	[If A, then B.
It broke.	B.
∴ Maria dropped it.	A.]

If the glass did break, it doesn't necessarily follow that Maria was the cause, since, once again, there are many ways for a glass to meet such a fate.

To summarize: These two hypothetical argument patterns are valid.

If A, then B.	If A, then B.
A.	Not B.
∴ B.	∴ Not A.

These two hypothetical argument patterns are invalid.

If A, then B.	If A, then B.
Not A.	B.
Not B.	∴ A.

Determining the validity of hypothetical reasoning reminds us that many conditions or causes can lead to the same result; we can't assume only one specific condition for a particular consequence unless we are told that this is the case.

Necessary and Sufficient Conditions

When there is a condition essential for a particular consequence or result, that condition is called a **necessary condition**—a condition without which something cannot happen. Fire, for example, cannot occur without oxygen; oxygen then is a necessary condition of fire. But oxygen alone cannot start a fire—there must be matter to burn as well as something to ignite it—so oxygen is not a **sufficient condition**. While it is necessary, it is not enough.

Logicians sometimes express a necessary cause as "if and only if." If, and only if, oxygen is present can fire start. Or, as writer Tobias Wolff (in *This Boy's Life*) remembers his mother warning him: "She said I could have the rifle if, and only if, I promised never to take it out or even touch it"—a necessary condition he failed to honor, unfortunately.

"He is physically able to wag his tail—given sufficient cause."

Hypothetical Chains

Hypothetical arguments may also consist of entire chains of conditions, as in the following example.

> If gun control advocates mount a very strong, well-funded campaign, then Congress will pass a law banning handguns.
>
> If Congress passes a law banning handguns, then fewer people will be able to purchase them.
>
> If fewer people are able to purchase them, then there will be fewer guns.

If there are fewer guns, then there will be less violence in our society.

∴ If gun control advocates mount a very strong, well-funded campaign in the fall, then there will be less violence in our society.

The pattern is apparent:

If A, then B.
If B, then C.
If C, then D.
If D, then E.
∴ If A, then E.

If, in such a chain, the first condition is affirmed, the other conditional claims, like falling dominoes, lead us inescapably to the conclusion—providing, of course, that we accept the truth of the claims.

Hypothetical Claims and Everyday Reasoning

As you prepare to do the following exercise on hypothetical arguments, keep in mind that such reasoning is not limited to logic texts. Hypothetical relationships also play a central role when computer programmers design software, and hypothetical reasoning is, in fact, a common feature of the thinking we do every day. For example:

If I miss that review session, I won't be prepared for the midterm.

If I don't stop at the grocery store on my way home, I won't have anything to eat for dinner.

As these examples indicate, we continually make conditional claims and decisions based on these claims and the outcome we desire. In the examples above, if the "I" of the sentences fails to affirm the antecedent, he must be prepared to accept the less-than-desirable consequences.

EXERCISE 7F

Determining the Validity of Hypothetical Arguments

Use argument patterns to determine the validity of the following hypothetical arguments. [Keep in mind that you are not evaluating the acceptability of each premise, so even the valid arguments could be unsound according to the principles of reasoning discussed earlier in this chapter.]

1. If the burglar came in through the window, it would be unlocked. We found the window unlocked. We all agreed that the burglar must have come in through the window.

2. If most nations view ethnic cleansing in Darfur as a crime against humanity, then military action against the aggressors should be stepped up. Indeed, most nations do view ethnic cleansing as a crime against humanity, so military action against the aggressors should be increased.

3. Doctors claim that if you eat barbecued meats on a regular basis, you increase your risk of developing cancer. Fortunately, Calvin is a vegetarian and thus doesn't eat barbecued meats, so he is not at increased risk for cancer.

4. If the burglar came in through the window, it would be unlocked. We found the window locked, leading us to believe that the burglar couldn't have come in through the window.

5. If you respected my opinion, you would seek my advice. You don't seek my advice, so I can only conclude that you don't respect my opinion.

6. If the government doesn't balance the budget, the deficit will increase. The facts speak for themselves: the deficit is increasing. Clearly, the government is not balancing the budget.

7. If the governor makes a strong speech on the necessity of conserving water, he will be able to convince people to do so. Fortunately, he has scheduled a press conference for that purpose, so people will conserve water.

8. All the sportswriters agreed that if the Patriots didn't play well against the Giants, the Patriots were destined to lose the all-important game. As we all remember, they lost in the closing minutes, leaving me with the unhappy knowledge that they didn't play well that day.

9. If the paint is oil-based, the paintbrush cannot be cleaned with water, but the brush is being cleaned with water, so the paint must not be oil-based.

10. If oil supplies from the Persian Gulf are reduced, the price of oil will rise in the United States. If the price of oil in the United States rises, manufacturing costs will rise, and if this happens, an economic recession could develop. So if an economic recession does develop, we can certainly attribute it to reduced oil supplies from the Persian Gulf.

EXERCISE 7G

Analyzing a Timeless Argument

Reduce the following poem by Andrew Marvell (1621–1678) to a hypothetical argument containing two premises and a conclusion, and determine its validity. Hint: The first two stanzas contain the first and second premises, respectively, and the last contains the conclusion.

TO HIS COY MISTRESS

Had we but world enough, and time,
This coyness, Lady, were no crime.
We would sit down, and think which way
To walk, and pass our long love's day.
Thou by the Indian Ganges' side
Shouldst rubies find; I by the tide
Of Humber would complain. I would
Love you ten years before the Flood,
And you should, if you please, refuse
Till the Conversion of the Jews.
My vegetable love should grow
Vaster than empires and more slow;
An hundred years should go to praise
Thine eyes, and on thy forehead gaze;
An age at least to every part,
And the last age should show your heart.
For, Lady, you deserve this *state*,   (dignity)
Nor would I love at lower rate.

But at my back I always hear
Time's winged chariot hurrying near;
And yonder all before us lie
Deserts of vast eternity.
Thy beauty shall no more be found,
Nor, in thy marble vault, shall sound
My echoing song; then worms shall try
That long-preserved virginity,
And your *quaint* honor turn to dust,   (proud)
And into ashes all my lust:

The grave's a fine and private place,
But none, I think, do there embrace.

Now therefore, while the youthful hue
Sits on thy skin like morning dew,
And while thy willing soul *transpires*   (breathes out)
At every pore with instant fires,
Now let us sport us while we may
And now, like amorous birds of prey,

Rather at once our time devour
Than languish in his slow-*chapped* power.   (jawed)
Let us roll all our strength and all
Our sweetness up into one ball,
And tear our pleasures with rough strife
Through the iron gates of life;
Thus, though we cannot make our sun
Stand still, yet we will make him run.

EXERCISE 7H

Evaluating an Argument for Peace

Using your own words, reduce this poem by Wilfred Owen (1893–1918)to a hypothetical argument and determine its validity. Hint: The first premise is stated in the
last stanza, but the minor premise and the conclusion are implicit.

DULCE ET DECORUM EST

Bent double, like old beggars under sacks,
Knock-kneed, coughing like hags, we cursed through sludge,
Till on the haunting flares we turned our backs

And towards our distant rest began to trudge.
Men marched asleep. Many had lost their boots
But limped on, blood-shod. All went lame; all blind;
Drunk with fatigue; deaf even to the hoots
Of tired, outstripped Five Nines that dropped behind.

Gas! Gas! Quick, boys!—An ecstasy of fumbling,
Fitting the clumsy helmets just in time;
But someone still was yelling out and stumbling
And flound'ring like a man in fire or lime . . .
Dim, through the misty panes and thick green light,
As under a green sea, I saw him drowning.

In all my dreams, before my helpless sight,
He plunges at me, guttering, choking, drowning.

If in some smothering dreams you too could pace
Behind the wagon that we flung him in,
And watch the white eyes writhing in his face,
His hanging face, like a devil's sick of sin;
If you could hear, at every jolt, the blood
Come gargling from the froth-corrupted lungs,

Obscene as cancer, bitter as the cud
Of vile, incurable sores on innocent tongues,—
My friend, you would not tell with such high zest
The old Lie: *Dulce et decorum est*
Pro patria mori.*

INDUCTIVE REASONING

The fundamental distinction between deductive and inductive reasoning lies in the relative certainty with which we can accept a conclusion. The certainty guaranteed when a deductive argument is validly reasoned from acceptable premises cannot be assumed in an inductive argument, no matter how carefully one supports the inference. The terms most appropriate for inductive arguments then are **strong** and **weak**, **reliable** or **unreliable**, rather than valid and invalid.

Some logicians prefer the categories *deductive* and *nondeductive* to *deductive* and *inductive*, given the varied forms arguments can take when they don't conform to the rigorous rules of inference required for deduction.

Generalization

Determining cause and effect, formulating hypotheses, drawing analogies, and arriving at statistical generalizations are examples of nondeductive reasoning, or, as we have chosen to call it, inductive reasoning. In this section, we concentrate on the statistical generalization. **Statistical generalizations** are best characterized as predictions, as claims about the distribution of a **projected property** in a given group or population, the **target population**. From the distribution of such a property in *part* of the target population, the **sample**, we infer a proposition, a conclusion that is either strong or weak depending on how carefully we conduct our survey. We make a prediction, an inference, about the unknown on the basis of the known; on the basis of our observations of the sample, we make a generalization about all of the population, including that part we have not observed closely.

Suppose we want to determine whether New York taxpayers will support a tax designated specifically for building shelters for the homeless. Here **the projected property would be the willingness to support this particular tax (what we want to find out). The target population would be New York taxpayers. The sample would be that portion of New York taxpayers polled. From their answers, we would draw a conclusion, make a generalization about New York taxpayers in general:** unanimous support, strong support, marginal support, little support, no support—whatever their answers warrant. But no matter how precise the numbers from the sample, we cannot predict

---

*"It is sweet and fitting to die for one's country." From the Latin poet Horace.

Biographical note: This poem is especially poignant because its author, Wilfred Owen, died on the battlefield in the last week of the First World War at the age of 25.

with absolute certainty what the entire population of New York taxpayers will actually do. When we make an inference from some to all, the conclusion always remains logically doubtful to some degree.

Let's look at another example.

For several years now, scientists and health officials have alerted the public to the increased risk of skin cancer as the thinning of the ozone layer allows more of the harmful ultraviolet rays to penetrate the atmosphere. Imagine that the student health center at your school wanted to find out if students were aware of this danger and were protecting themselves from it. In this case, **the projected property would be taking preventive measures to protect oneself from the sun. The target population would be all the students attending your school, and the sample would be the number of students polled.** Once again, any conclusions reached by the health center on the basis of its survey would be tentative rather than certain, with the certainty increasing in proportion to the size of the sample—the greater the number of students polled, the more reliable is the conclusion, assuming the sample is representative as well.

The Direction of Inductive Reasoning

The direction of inductive reasoning can vary. We may start by noting specific instances and from them make general inferences, or we may begin with a general idea and seek specific examples or data to support it. The following example moves from specific cases to a generalization:

Observing a sudden increase in the number of measles cases in several communities, public health officials inferred that too many infants were going unvaccinated.

You may notice that our ability to think both deductively and inductively has a way of intertwining the two modes of thought, but the structure of this argument is still inductive, the conclusion being probable rather than guaranteed.

Often we start with a tentative generalization, a possible conclusion called a **hypothesis, an assertion we are interested in proving**.

Rousel Uclaf, the French manufacturers of a revolutionary new pill to prevent pregnancy and avoid abortion, hoped to prove that it was both effective and safe. To do so, they had to conduct elaborate studies with varied groups of women over time. Until they had gathered such statistical support in a sample population, their claim that it was effective and safe was only a hypothesis, not a reliable conclusion. But once they had tested their product, RU-486, on 40,000 women in several European countries and found only two "incidents" of pregnancies and no apparent harm, they were ready to claim that RU-486 is reasonably safe and statistically effective.

Even here, the conclusion remains inductive—it is a highly probable conclusion but not a necessary one as it would be in deduction. Unfortunately, there are examples of such inductive reasoning leading to false (and disastrous) conclusions.

Approved for use in Europe, the drug thalidomide, given to pregnant women for nausea in the 1960s, caused many children to be born with grave deformities. And the Dalkon Shield, an intrauterine birth control device of the 1970s, although tested before being made available, caused sterility in many of its users.

Given the degree of uncertainty inherent in any conclusion based on a sample, the Japanese take no chances when it comes to their nation's beef supply. According to the *New York Times*, "Japan tests all the cows it slaughters each year, 1.2 million," while the United States Department of Agriculture relies on a sample, testing approximately one hundred cows a year.

Testing Inductive Generalizations

With inductive arguments, we accept a conclusion with varying degrees of probability and must be willing to live with at least a fraction of uncertainty. But the question always remains, how much uncertainty is acceptable?

CRITERIA FOR EVALUATING STATISTICAL GENERALIZATIONS   *How* we infer our conclusions, the way in which we conduct our surveys, is crucial to determining the strength of an inductive argument. Whether we are constructing our own arguments or evaluating those of others, we need to be discriminating. Many of our decisions on political, economic, sociological, even personal issues depend on inductive reasoning. Scarcely a day goes by without an inductive study or poll reaching newspapers, television news, and the Internet: Surveys show the president's popularity is rising or falling, Americans favor socialized medicine, girls are doing as well as boys in math. A few principles for evaluating such generalizations can help us all examine the conclusions with the critical perspective necessary for our self-defense.

In order to accept a conclusion as warranted or reliable, we need to control or interpret the conditions of the supporting survey.

Two features of the sample are essential:

1. The **size** must be adequate. The proportion of those in the sample must be sufficient to reflect the total size of the target population. Statisticians have developed complex formulas for determining adequate size proportionate to a given population, but for our general purposes common sense and a little well-reasoned practice will serve. The Gallup Organization polls 2,500 to 3,000 people to determine how 80 million will vote in a presidential election and allows for only a 3 percent margin of error. This suggests that the size of a survey can often be smaller than we might initially assume.

2. The sample must be **representative**. It must represent the target population in at least two different ways.

   a. The sample must be selected **randomly** from the target population.

   b. It must also be **spread** across the population so that all significant differences within the population are represented. Such a contrived approach might seem contradictory to a random sample, but some conscious manipulation is often necessary to ensure a sample that is genuinely typical of the target population.

Examine the following diagram to see these principles illustrated:

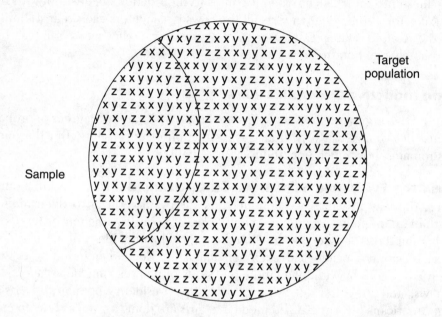

As you can see, we are back to classes (see "Class Logic" on page 168). The sample is a subclass included in the larger class of the target population. As we make inferences, we move from a conclusion about the smaller class, the sample, to a conclusion about the larger class, the target population.

> *If they remove all the fools from Congress, it wouldn't be a representative Congress.*
>
> —POLITICAL COMMENTATOR MOLLY IVINS

Let's evaluate the reasoning in the following argument:

A visitor of modest means from a midwestern city comes to San Francisco for five days and is instructed by her friends to assess the prices of San Francisco's restaurants; some of them are considering a trip there in the near future. Our tourist, let's call her Kate, picks up a guidebook and takes the first five restaurants listed in the book: Aqua, Boulevard, Campton Place, Postrio, and the Ritz Carlton, all of which are located downtown. Verging on bankruptcy, poor Kate returns home with the report that restaurants in San Francisco are staggeringly expensive. For a resident of San Francisco, the error in her conclusion and the flaw in the reasoning that led to her false conclusion are easy to spot—she has inadvertently chosen five of the most expensive restaurants in the city. Before selecting her restaurants, she should have examined her guidebook carefully to be sure that her survey of restaurants was, to some degree, representative. The book clearly began with a list of the major splurges, and that was as far as Kate went.

With only five days, she was necessarily limited when it came to the *size* of her sample, and thus she would have to place a strong qualifier on any conclusions she drew. But, with a little care, she could have aimed for a more *random* sample by investigating different sections of her guidebook, referring to more than one guide, and visiting various geographical areas of San Francisco. Such a sampling would also have helped her arrive at examples spread more effectively over different types of cuisines. A visitor intent on savoring the best fare regardless of cost would have done well following Kate's approach, but one interested in the prices was doomed to a distorted picture.

Can you identify the projected property, the target population, the sample, and the conclusion for this inductive argument?

HASTY GENERALIZATIONS   When, like Kate, we leap to an unwarranted conclusion, we commit the common logical fallacy of hasty generalization. If, for example, after one semester at a university as a student having had two professors who failed to return work, often missed class, or arrived late, you concluded that the university had a rotten faculty, you would be guilty of hasty generalization. The sample is clearly too small to warrant such a conclusion. Newspaper columnist Jon Carroll "remember[s] one [East Coast] writer who came to California, stayed in the Beverly Hills Hotel for three days and concluded that all Californians were stupid, narcissistic and in the movie business." To discredit this hasty generalization, all one would have to do is find a **counterexample**, one Californian who wasn't stupid, narcissistic, and in the movie business. What mistake did the East Coast writer make with his sample? For further discussion of this familiar fallacy, see Chapter 6.

COUNTEREXAMPLES

With any generalization supported by specific examples, one counterexample can discredit, or "embarrass," the conclusion. Warranted conclusions must be consistent with the data used in their support, and where necessary, qualified appropriately—*most, some, usually, occasionally, in most cases.*

Garfield ®   by Jim Davis

Garfield doubts his conclusion when he finds three counterexamples.

Thinking Critically About Surveys and Statistics

Because surveys and statistics suggest an authority they may not warrant, we must read them critically rather than accept them without question. Statistics should contribute to reasoning, not serve as a substitute for it.

Time magazine ran a cover story on the high cost of a college degree titled "How Colleges Are Gouging You," by Erik Larson. In his article, Larson accused colleges of protecting their endowment funds while charging whatever the traffic will bear for tuition. The piece elicited this angry response:

> To generalize the situation at the University of Pennsylvania and other Ivy League schools and apply it to major universities across the board is like using the cost of a Lexus to discuss the price of an average family van. In the real world of most institutions, faculty members do not average earnings of $140,000 a year. And they are teaching larger classes with fewer resources and support staff and reduced budgets for essential expenses. Unfortunately, Larson's diatribe will probably be used by state legislatures as justification to cut budgets of many public institutions.
>
> —JOHN BRUNCH, ASSISTANT PROFESSOR, DEPARTMENT OF MANAGEMENT, KANSAS STATE UNIVERSITY, MANHATTAN, KANSAS

This professor from a public university is rightfully concerned that a generalization based on a study of private universities will be applied to public universities (which often do not have endowment funds), with the consequence of fewer resources for him and his students.

In 1948 Alfred C. Kinsey published *The Kinsey Report*, one of the first surveys on the sexual mores of Americans. Kinsey concluded among other things that 10 percent of the population was homosexual. James H. Jones, who wrote a biography of Kinsey, points out that the sample on which this conclusion was based was not representative of all Americans.

Kinsey did a great deal of interviewing in prisons, where the incidence of homosexuality was higher than in the general population. More damaging still to the
reliability of his sample was his practice of seeking out individuals on the basis of
their sexual tastes and behavior. In compiling his sample of the American population, Kinsey targeted gay people, becoming the first scientist to study in depth the
nascent gay communities in large urban areas and elsewhere. In city after city
he tapped into gay networks, using the contacts he made with gay subjects to
generate introductions to their partners, lovers and friends. This practice enabled
Kinsey to collect a large number of gay histories, but, in conjunction with his
prison interviews, it also skewed his data in the direction of overestimating the
percentage of gay people in the American population.

Bad science is made worse by the media's often reporting of all surveys in abbre-
viated and often sensational ways, frequently giving subtle slants in emphasis to statistics. For example, in the same issue of a major daily newspaper, the summary caption
on page one stated that "A new poll finds that 1 in 5 Californians still resent Japan for
the attack on Pearl Harbor," while the inside story was headed, "50 years after attack
on Pearl Harbor, only 1 in 5 is still resentful, poll shows." What are the different
implications of these two captions?

Mistaking Correlation for Causation

Even when a study is carefully done by a reputable institution, the press will often
reduce the results to the most attention-getting headline. The media reported that
heavy coffee drinkers had two to three times the risk of heart disease on the basis of
a study done at Johns Hopkins University using many subjects over several years.
But a careful reading of the study from beginning to end revealed that its authors
didn't ask participants about their diet, smoking habits, and exercise levels, mitigating factors in any study of heart disease. The report concluded that there was "a
need for further investigation" into the dangers of caffeine, a conclusion the media
failed to report. All that one could safely conclude from the Johns Hopkins study is a
correlation between heavy caffeine use and heart disease, not ***causation***. The distinction between correlation and causation is an important one. There is a correlation
between home ownership and car accidents. If you are a home owner, you're more
likely to own a car, so you're more likely to be in a car accident, but that doesn't mean
that home ownership causes car accidents.

To determine causation, researchers must conduct randomized, controlled
studies; such studies are difficult to design and complete. Large numbers of people
are assigned by chance to different groups. In tests of medications, for example,
neither the scientists in charge of the study nor its participants know whether the
subjects being studied have been taking a particular drug or a placebo (an unmed-
icated substance) until the study is completed and the results analyzed.

Observational studies, on the other hand, begin with a hypothesis such as a belief
that a low-fat diet protects against heart disease. Researchers then gather relevant

patient data and plug this data into computers, which then identify correlations between diet and disease. But mathematical correlations do not necessarily mean causation, a point to remember whenever we see the results of a new study in the headlines or leading the five o'clock news.

Epidemiology

Epidemiology is a branch of medical research devoted to determining the incidence, distribution, and possible control of disease. Since the 1950s it has focused on the causes of chronic diseases, in particular heart disease and cancer. When it comes to the relationship between diet, lifestyle factors, and chronic disease, epidemiologists face special challenges when conducting surveys.

One of these challenges, according to Michael Pollan, author of *In Defense of Food*, is the fact that people lie when answering questions about their diet. "How do we know this? Deduction. Consider: When the study began, the average participant weighed in at 170 pounds and claimed to be eating 1,800 calories a day. It would take an unusual metabolism to maintain that weight on so little food."

Another challenge: the mitigating factor of wealth. The Nurses' Health Study run by Harvard Medical School and Harvard School of Public Health attempted to eliminate this factor by having all the women in the study in the same profession; but what about the husbands of these nurses? What was their income? How many children did each woman have? Did a nurse's income support one person or five?

And the biggest challenge of all is the fact that participants in studies are often healthier than the general population. For example, it's difficult to determine the impact of vitamin supplements on the people who take them. They tend to be educated people who take an active interest in their health and therefore exercise, watch what they eat, and see their doctor on a regular basis. If they are healthier than most, is that because of the vitamin supplements?

AN INTERNET JOKE:

Here's the final word on nutrition.

The Japanese eat very little fat and suffer fewer heart attacks than the British or Americans.

The French eat a lot of fat and also suffer fewer heart attacks than the British or Americans.

The Japanese drink very little red wine and suffer fewer heart attacks than the British or Americans.

The Italians drink excessive amounts of red wine and also suffer fewer heart attacks than the British or Americans.

Conclusion: Eat and drink what you like. Speaking English is apparently what kills you.

RESULTS OF THE

Tropical Fish Sex Survey

Tropical fish who claim to mate two or three times a day.

Tropical fish who, for some strange reason, are under the impression that they never mate.

Tropical fish who would have us believe that they mate two or three times a week.

Tropical fish who think, apparently, that they mate two or three times a year.

Tropical fish who, in their words, mate two or three times a month.

17%

19%

15%

22%

27%

R. Chast

Considering the Source

When evaluating a survey and its conclusions, we must consider the source of the survey—who conducted the survey and who paid for it—to determine if there is a **conflict of interest** or a **hidden agenda**. A study of silicone breast implants concluded that there was no link between ruptured implants and connective tissue disease. Lawyer and consumer advocate Mary Alexander criticizes this study, not only for the limited size of its sample and its failure to allow for the 8.5 years of latency between implantation and silicone disease, but also because two of its authors "admitted on the threat of perjury that they were paid consultants of breast implant manufacturers." Furthermore, Dow Corning, the world's largest silicone breast implant manufacturer, had donated $5 million to one of the hospitals involved in the study. Such a study is riddled with conflict of interest. It is not in the best interest of those who benefit directly from Dow Corning to find fault with the company's product.

Class action lawyers filed an $800 million suit against Motorola, claiming cell phones cause brain cancer. This suit motivated cell phone manufacturers to fund studies of their own. These studies, none of which lasted more than three years, concluded that cell phone use did not cause brain cancer. Both the length of these studies and their sponsors cause us to question their conclusions.

The difficulty lies in the reality that sometimes even the most reliable journals and research organizations lead us astray. One of the most respected medical publications, the *New England Journal of Medicine*, has been found guilty of violating its conflict-of-interest policy. In 1996, the journal ran an editorial claiming that the benefits of diet drugs outweighed the risks but failed to note that the two authors had been paid consultants for firms that made or marketed one of the diet drugs under discussion. And in 1997, the journal featured a negative review of a book connecting environmental chemicals and various cancers, a review written by the medical director of a large chemical company.

Another respected medical journal, *JAMA (Journal of the American Medical Association)*, has also been careless about determining conflict of interest. In 2005 *JAMA* published a study that concluded that fetuses younger than seven months probably did not feel pain. One of the two authors was a former abortion-rights attorney; the other ran an abortion clinic. (For more on evaluation of surveys and their sources see "Blinded by Science" in Additional Readings.)

CRITICAL READING OF SURVEYS

1. Is the sample representative of the target population? Is it large enough? How long did the study last? Was the study random and controlled or was it observational?

2. Does the media's report on the survey seem fair and reasonable?

3. Does the survey establish causation or correlation?

4. Who wrote or published or called your attention to the survey? Are they impartial or do they have a hidden agenda or conflict of interest? Is the survey cited in advertising or in another context in which the motive is to sell you something?

EXERCISE 71

Evaluating Inductive Reasoning

In the following studies, identify the **conclusion**, the **projected property**, the **target population**, and the **sample**. Then, drawing on the principles of reliable inductive generalizations, **evaluate their reliability**.

1. The quality control inspector at Sweet and Sour Yogurt removes and tests one container out of approximately every thousand (about one every 15 minutes) and finds it safe for consumption. She then guarantees as safe all the containers filled that day.

2. On November 1, to consolidate his frequent flier miles, businessman Eric Nichols decided to select one domestic airline from his two favorites. He planned to base his decision on each airline's reliability. From November through April he made 20 evenly spaced trips on United, experiencing two cancellations, nine delayed departures, and eight late arrivals. From May through October, he flew American Airlines 22 times, but improved his record with only one cancellation, seven delays, and five late arrivals. Without further consideration, he chose American as the more reliable of the two.

3. Setting out to document her theory on the prevalence of racism on television, a sociologist examines 40 episodes from the new fall prime-time situation comedies and finds that 36 of them contain racist stereotypes. She concludes that 90 percent of television drama is racist.

4. In her book *Women and Love*, Shere Hite claims that a large percentage of American women are unhappy in their marriages and feel that men don't listen to them. She felt confident in her conclusions after mailing out 100,000 questionnaires to women's political, professional, and religious organizations and having 4 percent of the questionnaires returned.

5. The French Ministry of Social Affairs reported that three well-known research physicians at the Laennec Hospital in Paris had observed "dramatic biological improvements" in a group of patients with AIDS. The physicians reported a "dramatic" slowing of acquired immune deficiency syndrome in one of the six patients and a complete halt in the disease's progress in another after only five days of treatment with a compound called cyclosporine. (Hint: The conclusion is implicit.)

6. A study by the University of Medicine and Dentistry of New Jersey concluded that "women who were abused [physically, emotionally, or sexually] as children have more health problems and require more hospital care than women who were not abused." Seven hundred women from a private gynecological practice were interviewed. Mostly white, middle class with college degrees, they ranged in age from 16 to 76.

7. A study published in *Science* concluded that women did not talk more than men, a contradiction of the commonly held belief that women talk more than men. This study was based on audio clips taken from 200 university students, 100 men and 100 women, who agreed to be recorded for several days sometime between 1998 and 2004. The recording devices would turn on automatically for 30 seconds every 12.5 minutes without the subjects' knowledge. Researchers transcribed and counted these words to estimate how many words each person used in a day.

EXERCISE 7J

Distinguishing Between Correlation and Causation

Read the following essay by Dr. Susan Love, a professor of surgery at UCLA School of Medicine, and answer the questions that follow.

Preventive Medicine, Properly Practiced

There are at least 6 million women in this country who are asking themselves, "What happened?" Over the last several years they have read books and magazine articles, listened to TV pundits and talked to doctors and friends—all of whom assured them that taking hormone replacement therapy for the rest of their lives would keep them healthy. Then one bright summer day, their world shifted. Their little daily pill carried not the promise of health but the risk of disease. How could this be?   1

What happened is that medical practice, as it so often does, got ahead of medical science. We made observations and developed hypotheses—and then forgot to prove them. We start with observational studies, in which researchers look at groups of people to see if we can find any clues about disease. But all this observation can do is find associations: it can't prove cause and effect.   2

With hormone replacement therapy, we did many observational studies. We found that women who were on hormone therapy had a lower incidence of heart disease, stroke, colon cancer and bone fracture. And we accepted these findings before we did the definitive research, overlooking the fact that these women were also more likely to see a doctor (which is how they were put on hormone therapy in the first place), and probably more likely to exercise and to eat a healthful diet, than women who were not taking the drug. It wasn't clear whether hormones made women healthy or whether healthy women took hormones.   3

To answer this question we needed randomized, controlled research. The latest study, sponsored by the National Institutes of Health, enrolled 16,608 healthy women from ages 50 to 79 and randomly assigned them to take hormone replacement therapy or a placebo. Much to everyone's surprise, after 5.2 years the study showed that the risks of hormone treatment outweighed the benefits in preventing disease. . . .   4

There is a bigger issue than simply hormone therapy, however. There is a ten-   5
dency, driven by wishful thinking combined with good marketing and media hype,
to jump ahead of the medical evidence. In the 1950's, it was DES, a drug given to
pregnant women to prevent miscarriages. It was many years later that a randomized, controlled study showed that it had no effect in preventing miscarriages.
Finally, in 1971 it was learned that daughters of women who took DES were at
increased risk of developing vaginal cancer.

In the 1990's, the bone marrow transplant—high-dose chemotherapy with   6
stem-cell rescue—was proposed to treat aggressive breast cancers. It was widely
used until four randomized, controlled studies showed it was no better than standard therapy, and had far more side effects. Arthroscopic surgery for osteoarthritis
was commonly performed but just last week a controlled study showed it had
no objective benefit. Hormone replacement therapy is just one more example of
this phenomenon. . . .

1. What is the difference between an observational study and a "randomized,
   controlled" study?

2. Identify the projected property, the target population, the sample, and the
   conclusion of the National Institutes of Health study of hormone replacement
   therapy, and then evaluate the reliability of the conclusion.

3. According to Dr. Love, why does medical practice "jump ahead of the medical
   evidence"? What other examples of this phenomenon, in addition to hormone
   replacement, does she cite? Can you add to this list?

EXERCISE 7K

Collecting Generalizations

Humorist James Thurber had fun exploiting our tendency to overgeneralize in his
essay "What a Lovely Generalization." Many of his examples are absurd, but some
suggest the dangers that can spring from such patterns of thought. For those interested in collecting generalizations, he suggests listening "in particular to women,
whose average generalization is from three to five times as broad as a man's." Was
he sexist or making a joke? He listed many others from his collection, labeling some
"true," some "untrue," others "debatable," "libelous," "ridiculous," and so on. Some
examples from his collection: "Women don't sleep very well," "There are no pianos in
Japan," "Doctors don't know what they're doing," "Gamblers hate women," "Cops off
duty always shoot somebody," "Intellectual women dress funny." And so his collection
ran, brimming with hasty generalizations.

Your task is to collect two "lovely generalizations" from the world around you,
comment on the accuracy, absurdity, and dangers of each, and discuss the implications of your generalizations for those who seem to be the target.

WRITING ASSIGNMENT 13

Questioning Generalizations

Add the two generalizations you chose for Exercise 7K, Collecting Generalizations, to the following list of generalizations and choose one to write a one-page paper in support of, or in opposition to. This list could be even longer and more diverse if your instructor collects the entire class's generalizations and makes them available to you.

1. Women are better dancers than men.
2. Men are better athletes than women.
3. Everyone is capable of being creative.
4. Nice guys finish last.
5. Appearances can be deceiving.
6. The purpose of a college degree is to prepare an individual for a career.
7. A college graduate will get a higher-paying job than a high school graduate.
8. A woman will never be elected president of the United States.
9. All people are created equal.
10. War is a necessary evil.

Audience

A reader who is not strongly invested in the proposition one way or another but who is interested in hearing your point of view.

Purpose

To cast a critical eye on a generalization that people tend to accept without question.

WRITING ASSIGNMENT 14

Conducting a Survey: A Collaborative Project

Conduct a survey at your school to determine something of significance about the student body and then write a report in which you state either a question or a hypothesis, describe the survey, and speculate on the results.

The class as a whole can brainstorm possible questions to ask the student body, the target population. What do students think about the current administration on campus or in Washington? Our nation's war on terrorism? Or a host of other political issues. How many students take a full academic load and work part-time as well? How many students expect to graduate in four years? There are many possibilities.

Choose five or six topics from these many possibilities and divide into groups around them. These groups will then create a survey—a questionnaire appropriate to the topic they are researching—and a strategy for distributing it to a representative sample.

The next step is to collect, tabulate, and discuss the data. Either each student can then write her own report or the group can write a single report, assigning a section to each member of the group.

The report will contain the following:

1. A description of the survey
   What questions did you ask?
   When and where did you ask them?

2. A description of the sample
   Whom did you ask?
   How many did you ask?

3. Evaluation of the survey
   Was the sample large enough?
   Was it representative?
   Were your questions unbiased?
   What could you do to make it better?

4. Analysis of the results
   How does it compare with what you expected the results to be before you began gathering the data?
   What do you imagine are the causes that led to these results?
   What are the implications of the results?

Audience

Your campus community—students, faculty, and staff.

Purpose

To inform your campus community about its student members.

SUMMARY

Inductive and deductive reasoning are distinct from one another in two ways:

1. In a **deductive argument**, the conclusion follows by necessity from the premises if the method of reasoning is valid. In an **inductive argument**, the conclusion can follow with only some degree of probability.

2. In a deductive argument, the inference moves from a generalization to a particular instance or example that fits that generalization. In an inductive argument, the inference usually moves from a series of specific instances to a generalization.

Induction and deduction are interdependent; it takes an interplay of the two thinking methods to arrive at our conclusions.

There are three possible relationships between classes: **inclusion**, **exclusion**, and **overlap**.

Both inductive and deductive reasoning often depend on supporting a conclusion on the basis of relationships between classes.

For a **categorical argument** to be sound, the structure of the argument must be valid and the premises acceptable.

For a **hypothetical argument** to be valid, the second, or minor premise, must either affirm the antecedent or deny the consequent.

The **statistical generalization**, based as it is on an inductive leap from some to all, is never as certain as a conclusion drawn from sound deductive reasoning.

The direction of inductive reasoning can vary. We may note specific instances and from them make general inferences, or we may begin with a general idea and seek specific examples or data to support it.

For a statistical generalization to be reliable, the sample must be adequate in size and representative of the target population.

With any generalization supported by specific examples, one **counterexample** can discredit the conclusion.

A **correlation** between two characteristics such as speaking English and having heart attacks does not mean that speaking English causes heart attacks.

KEY TERMS

Antecedent   the part of a hypothetical argument that establishes a condition.

Categorical syllogism   a deductive argument composed of three classes; the argument has two premises and one conclusion derived from the two premises.

Causation   anything that directly produces an effect.

Class   in logic all of the individual things—persons, objects, events, ideas—that share a determinate property.

Consequent   the part of a hypothetical argument that results from the antecedent.

Correlation   a mutual relationship or connection between two or more things, but not necessarily a direct cause–effect relationship

Deduction   a pattern of reasoning in which the conclusion follows of necessity from the premises if the reasoning is valid.

Epidemiology   a branch of medical research devoted to determining the incidence, distribution, and possible control of disease.

Exclusion   a relationship between classes in which classes share no members.

Hypothesis   a tentative generalization, an unproved theory or proposition we are interested in proving.

Hypothetical argument   a common type of deductive argument concerned with conditions.

Inclusion   a relationship between classes in which every member of one class is a member of another class.

Induction   a pattern of reasoning in which the conclusion follows only with some degree of probability.

Necessary condition   a condition without which the consequence cannot occur; for example, fire cannot occur without oxygen.

Overlap   a relationship between classes in which classes share at least one member.

Particular proposition   refers to some members of a designated class.

Predicate   includes everything being asserted about the subject.

Projected property   what is to be determined about the target population.

Sample   the surveyed members of the target population.

Soundness   describes a deductive argument whose premises are acceptable and whose structure is valid.

Statistical generalization   a prediction about the distribution of a particular feature in a given group.

Subject   that part of the sentence about which something is being asserted.

Sufficient condition   one condition, among others, that leads to a particular consequence; for example, a match is one way to start a fire but not the only way.

Target population   the group about which the conclusion will be drawn.

Universal proposition   refers to all members of a designated class.

Validity   the conclusion follows of necessity from the premises; the form of the argument is correct.

CHAPTER 8

The Language of Argument—Style

Style is the dress of thought.

—SAMUEL WESLEY

Some may dismiss style as ornament, as the decorative frills of writing, or as something limited to matters of correct grammar and usage. But an effective style can capture your reader's attention and possibly win the day for your argument. Style certainly includes a carefully proofread, grammatically correct final draft, but it also means **well-crafted sentences** that carry meaning gracefully to your readers.

We address well-crafted sentences in Chapters 3 and 4 when we discuss the importance of **logical joining** in argument, and in Chapter 5 when we present **appositives** as a technique for defining and describing terms within a sentence. In this chapter we introduce **parallel structure** and stress the use of **concrete and consistent sentence subjects** and **active voice verbs**. With these strategies, we emphasize the value of rhetorical repetition and the elimination of wordiness.

PARALLELISM

Parallel structure, used to organize items in a sentence and ideas in a paragraph, is another strategy for promoting coherence. The emphasis you achieve by harnessing your points into balanced grammatical structures increases the force of your written arguments.

The Structure of Parallelism

Parallel structure is simply a repetition of like grammatical units—a list of items—often joined by the conjunctions *and*, *but*, *or*, and *yet*.
Look at the following two sentences:

> *I came, I saw, I conquered.*
> *The president had three choices: war, diplomacy, or appeasement.*

Parallelism is a useful rhetorical device, providing a powerful means of emphasizing relationships by organizing ideas into predictable patterns. We hear a **repetition** and expect the pattern to continue. When our expectations are thwarted, we may falter briefly in our reading or even lose the thread of the writer's thought. In most cases, our ear tells us when a series is wandering off track, but sometimes it can be helpful to check the grammatical structure. Here is a strategy for examining your own sentences.

Think of **parallel structures as lists**; in the preceding case, it is a list of the president's options. We can illustrate this list and the need for it to conform to the principles of parallelism by placing parallel lines at the beginning of the list:

The president had three choices // *war, diplomacy, or appeasement.*

The conjunction *or* joins three nouns.

We can do the same thing to a more complicated sentence taken from writer Joan Didion's essay on Alcatraz, "Rock of Ages."

It is not an unpleasant place to be, out there on Alcatraz with only // the *flowers* and the *wind* and a bell *buoy* moaning and the *tide* surging through the Golden Gate. . . . [a list of nouns as direct objects of the preposition *with*]

Now read the next sentence (aloud if possible) and hear how the loss of expected balance or harmony offends the ear.

When I should be studying, I will, instead, waste time by // *watching television or daydream.*

The two verbs are not in the same form and are therefore not parallel. They can be made parallel by simply changing *daydream* to *daydreaming* to match *watching*.

EXERCISE 8A

Supplying Parallel Elements

A. Complete these sentences with a parallel element.

1. Writing a good paper is a task that demands // hard work, patience, and . . .

2. She // rushed home, threw her assorted debris into a closet, and . . .

3. Fewer Americans are saving these days // not because they don't think it's wise to save, but . . .

4. The first lady is a woman who // has an open mind but . . .

5. The first lady is a woman who has // an open mind and . . .

B. In the following sentences, identify the misfits—the element of the sentence that is not parallel—and revise the sentence so that all the elements of the list are parallel. Putting slashes where each series starts will help you see where the sentence goes off track.

1. Many influences shape a child's development: family, church, peer groups, economic, social, and school.

2. Michelle lives in a neighborhood where knife wounds, killings, and people are raped are as common as the sun rising in the morning.

3. He helped to wash the car and with cleaning out the garage.

4. Free inquiry in the search for truth sometimes necessitates the abandonment of law and order but which always demands freedom of expression.

5. Pineapple juice is my favorite because it is a good source of energy, it isn't artificially sweetened, and because of its low cost.

6. The mayor launched a campaign against drunk driving and promoting the use of seat belts.

C. Read the following passage taken from *The Road from Coorain* by Jill Ker Conway and note her effective use of parallel structure. Use our system of notation to mark off the different series or lists. How many did you find?

Those night train journeys had their own mystery because of the clicking of the rails, the shafts of light pouring through the shutters of the sleeping compartment as we passed stations, and the slamming of doors when the train stopped to take on passengers. In the morning there was the odd sight of green landscape, trees, grass, banks of streams—an entirely different palette of colors, as though during the night we had journeyed to another country. Usually I slept soundly, registering the unaccustomed sounds and images only faintly. This time I lay awake and listened, opened the shutters and scanned unknown platforms, and wondered about the future.

Logic of the Parallel Series

The items in a list, however, must not only be **grammatically** similar but also relate **logically** to one another. Sometimes faulty parallelism offends not only our ear but also our reason.

People who have "book smarts" usually work in places like // *libraries* or *assistants* to attorneys.

Though the writer has joined two nouns (grammatically compatible elements), an assistant of any kind cannot be a "place." The writer has lost control of the sentence because he has forgotten where the list begins. There is more than one way to fix this sentence, to make it logical and balanced. How would you correct it?

To understand further what we mean, look at the following sentence:

We will have to look at the language used in the text for sexism, racism, and bias.

The list in this sentence is "sexism, racism, and bias." The list is *grammatically* parallel because all three words in the list are nouns, but not *logically* parallel since sexism, racism, and bias are presented as three separate and distinct categories when in fact sexism and racism are particular forms of bias. They are included in what we can call the class or group of *bias*, not separate from it. (Remember class logic in Chapter 7.) One way to correct this faulty logic would be to replace *bias* with *other forms of bias* and thus illustrate the logical and actual relationship that exists between the three terms.

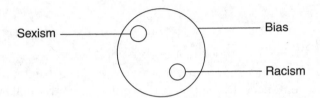

EXERCISE 8B

Editing the Illogical Series

Revise the following sentences for logical parallel structure.

1. In their attempt to excel, our employees often work extra hours and work through many lunch hours.
2. I have seen city ordinances that do not allow smoking popping up all over the place: in offices, in buildings.
3. I asked Linda if she had any materialistic aspirations such as living in a mansion, having a nice car, or being extremely wealthy.
4. The customers at the bank where I work are wealthy depositors, checking account holders, cooperative individuals, and those who are thoughtlessly rude to me.
5. For the most part, he is handsome, active, well dressed, and wears a suit and tie.

Emphasizing Ideas with Parallelism

Parallelism can be a powerful rhetorical device, especially in argument. Beyond the sentence, parallelism can provide emphasis and organize major ideas in a paragraph. Note how Robert F. Kennedy illustrates this technique (underlines are ours):

> Every time we turn our heads the other way <u>when we see</u> the law flouted, <u>when we tolerate</u> what we know to be wrong, <u>when we close</u> our eyes and ears to the corrupt because we are too busy or too frightened, <u>when we fail</u> to speak up and speak out, we strike a blow against freedom and decency and justice.

In a column on Israel, writer Thomas L. Friedman added force and passion to his prose with parallel structures. Read the passage aloud to hear the effect of his style.

. . . In sum, Israel should withdraw from the territories, not because it is weak, but because it must remain strong; not because Israel is wrong, but because Zionism is a just cause that the occupation is undermining; not because the Arabs would warmly embrace a smaller Israel, but because a smaller Israel, in internationally recognized boundaries, will be much more defensible; . . .

Listen for the **repetition** of the phrase "when we" in the Kennedy example and repetition of "not because" and "but because" in Friedman.

EXERCISE 8C

Creating Parallel Structure

In your next essay or in an assignment you are revising, construct a paragraph with a series of parallel sentences to emphasize a point you are making. The device may sound mechanical at first but may be useful in mounting your arguments, both written and spoken.

SHARPENING SENTENCES, ELIMINATING WORDINESS

He draweth out the thread of his verbosity finer than the staple of his argument.
—SHAKESPEARE, *LOVE'S LABOUR'S LOST*

We are all familiar with the confusion and obfuscation of much official prose—political, bureaucratic, academic. Some of this muddled language may be deliberate, to conceal meaning. But often it is inadvertent, a result of writers surrendering to the abstractness of language. (See Chapter 5 on abstract language.) Such writing tends to be wordy and unclear.

Look at this example.

Agreement on the overall objective of decision usefulness was a prerequisite to the establishment of a conceptual framework. Now, at least, we know where we are headed. (*The Week in Review*, newsletter of Deloitte Haskins & Sells)

Do we know where they are going?

Compare the following memo from the Internal Revenue Service and a possible revision.

Original
Advice has been requested concerning tax deductions for research expenses, including traveling expenses, incurred by college professors.

Revision
College professors have requested advice about tax deductions for their research expenses, including traveling expenses.

Which version is clearer, easier to read? We assume that the majority of readers will prefer the second. What are the differences? The revision is shorter by two words. This is one distinction. Are there others?

Calvin and Hobbes   by Bill Watterson

Concrete Subjects

Look at the grammatical subjects in the IRS examples above—*advice* in the first, *professors* in the second—and notice what kinds of nouns they are. One is an **abstract noun**, the other a **concrete noun**. Because the sentence subject tends to reflect what a passage is about, the subject is where the main point of emphasis usually sits. A concrete noun is capable of producing a visual picture and thus can also focus a reader's attention more closely. When that concrete noun is a person or people, readers can visualize an action and so more readily follow the precise progression of ideas in a sentence. Hence, *professors* as the subject of the second sentence is preferable to the *advice* of the original. The reader can see the *professor* but not the abstraction *advice*.

Active and Passive Verbs

Now look at the verbs. In the original sentence on tax deduction, the verb is *has been requested* while in the revision the verb is *has requested*. The first is **passive voice**, the second, **active voice**. The basic distinction is:

> **With a passive verb, the subject is acted upon; the subject is not doing anything in the sentence—it is passive.**

Advice is being requested, not doing the requesting.

> **When the verb is active, its subject is performing the action of the sentence.**

Thus the reader can see a subject **doing** something. The *professors* are doing the requesting.

We must wade through the original IRS memo to understand the point, whereas in the revision we see from the beginning that professors are requesting advice, people are doing something. Bureaucrats, often writing about vague or abstract subjects, can easily fall into the passive verb trap. They are rarely the ones actually *doing* anything they are writing about. Don't let your academic writing succumb to this danger.

Sentences written in the passive are easy to spot because they always follow a grammatical pattern:

subject + a form of the verb *to be* (*am, is, are, was, were, has been*)

+

the past participle of the verb (usually with an *-ed* ending) + a *by* phrase (sometimes implied) which contains the agent of the verb

(subject)	(to be)	(past participle)	(*by* phrase)
Advice	has been	requested	by college professors

The following two sentences say essentially the same thing, but catch how the change in the form of the verb shifts the emphasis from the concrete subject, *J. Robert Oppenheimer*, to the abstract, *elemental danger*.

Active: J. Robert Oppenheimer, one of the creators of the atom bomb, **felt** the elemental danger loosed on the earth.

Passive: The elemental danger loosed on the earth **was felt** by J. Robert Oppenheimer, one of the creators of the atom bomb.

Which version do you prefer? Why?

Passive Verbs and Evasion

When we want to avoid responsibility, we tend to rely on passive verbs to evade responsibility. Olympic swimming champion Michael Phelps turned to passive verbs when confronted with a photo of him smoking a marijuana pipe. Hoping to avoid attention, Phelps said, "You know, it happens. When stupid things **are done**, bad judgment **is made** and mistakes **are made**.

Phelps was trying to separate himself from his folly by leaving himself out of the sentence, thus avoiding the blame.

When the Passive Is Appropriate

Aiming for direct, assertive prose, careful writers usually prefer active verbs. But on occasion, when one wants to emphasize someone or something not performing the action in a sentence, the passive is useful. Scientists and social scientists, for example, must often focus on the content of their research rather than on themselves as researchers. Under such circumstances, the passive serves a useful purpose.

This research *was undertaken* with a grant from the National Science Foundation.

rather than

I *undertook* this research with a grant from the National Science Foundation.

Consistent Sentence Subjects

Central to a good **paragraph** is the logical progression of ideas. Read the following paragraph closely to see how research physician and writer Lewis Thomas maintains consistent sentence subjects, emphasizing the topic of the paragraph—how **we** relate to the concept of **death**. Note how the grammatical subjects provide a coherent line of reasoning even though at the heart of the passage lies an abstract idea.

> **We** continue to share with our remotest ancestors the most tangled and evasive attitudes about death, despite the great distance **we** have come in understanding some of the profound aspects of biology. **We** have as much distaste for talking about personal death as for thinking about it; it is an indelicacy, like talking in mixed company about venereal disease or abortion in the old days. **Death** on a grand scale does not bother us in the same special way; **we** can sit around a dinner table and discuss war, involving 60 million volatilized human deaths, as though **we** were talking about bad weather; **we** can watch abrupt bloody death every day, in color, on films and television, without blinking back a tear. But when the numbers of dead are very small, and very close, **we** begin to think in scurrying circles. At the very center of the problem is the naked cold **deadness** of one's own self, the only reality in nature of which **we** can have absolute certainty, and **it** is unquestionable, unthinkable. **We** may be even less willing to face the issue at first hand than our predecessors because of a secret new hope that maybe **it** will go away. **We** like to think, hiding the thought, that with all the marvelous ways in which **we** seem now to lead nature around by the nose, perhaps **we** can avoid the central problem if **we** just become, next year, say, a bit smarter.

Revising for well-crafted sentences and coherent paragraphs helps to maintain the clear, direct expression you and your readers demand, no matter what your academic or professional discipline. Keep in mind, however, that revising is often most effective at a late stage in the writing process. We may expect a first draft to have several wordy and unclear sentences and paragraphs. Look back at Chapter 1 to refresh your memory on the writing process and at Chapter 4 on abstract language.

EXERCISE 8D

Sharpening Sentences and Pruning Deadwood

A. Revise the following sentences, combining where appropriate for a smooth, logical flow of ideas. Think in terms of assertive sentences, ones that use active verbs and concrete subjects and say directly who is doing what. All these strategies will create clarity and eliminate wordiness.

Example:

First Draft
Feeling in good spirits, it was concluded by the students that Accounting 400 was a good class.

Revision
Feeling in good spirits, the students concluded that Accounting 400 was a good class.

1. A strike is used when employees want things their employers are unwilling to provide.
2. When it is seen that a criminal act is being committed, a call should be placed to the police.
3. Fear of brutality from customers is a concern many prostitutes have.
4. The leaders have determined that the spiritual initiate has no need of worldly things, so only minimum wages are paid.
5. There is a much bigger emphasis placed on the role of the individual in this generation than in our parents' generation.
6. Teenagers are easily influenced by TV. Specific violent acts have been committed by teenagers after such acts have been shown on prime time.
7. The people of this tribe are literate, given that they have twenty terms for *book*. There also may be several kinds of artwork they create, since they have nine words for *artist*.
8. Having developed a complex social order, cultural patterns have been shown by the people of this tribe. These patterns are reflected in their arts and their theatre.

B. Now try your hand at revising this student paragraph with the same strategies in mind. Note how difficult it is to follow the writer's reasoning in this poorly focused paragraph.

There are many ways to be a bad teacher. There are mistakes made by bad teachers that come in a variety of forms. Assignments are given unclearly so that when papers are graded it isn't known what students are graded on or what the grade means. Grading by the ineffective teacher is according to arbitrary standards, so students think their grades are unfair. There are problems with explanations given by bad teachers and understanding is hard to arrive at. This disorganization can be seen by students when the poor teacher fails to bring all materials to class. There are many explanations given, but the dissatisfaction of students is clearly not done away with. In such cases it is not clear who is responsible for a bad grade—the student or the teacher.

WRAP-UP ON WRITING STYLE

1. Use parallel structure to increase coherence, organize lists, and emphasize ideas.

2. When possible, use concrete, consistent grammatical subjects that reflect the subject you are writing about.

3. Choose active verbs that allow for direct, vigorous expression of your ideas, unless you have compelling reasons for preferring the passive voice.

Caution: Do not think about these writing strategies until you have completed a first draft. Content and organization come first.

SUMMARY

Style as well as correctness is an essential part of effective written argument.

Parallelism is a useful rhetorical device, providing a powerful means of emphasizing relationships by organizing ideas into predictable patterns.

For a vigorous and concise style, writers prefer **concrete, consistent subjects and active verbs**.

KEY TERMS

Active voice   a sentence construction in which the subject performs the action of the sentence. [Example: The Supreme Court ruled on the constitutionality of the 1991 civil rights legislation.]

Parallel structure   a repetition of like grammatical units, often joined by the conjunctions *and, but, or*, or *yet*.

Passive voice   a sentence construction in which the subject is acted upon, not doing anything in the sentence. [Example: The constitutionality of the 1991 civil rights legislation was ruled on by the Supreme Court.]

A QUICK GUIDE TO INTEGRATING RESEARCH INTO YOUR OWN WRITING

"Go ask your search engine."

In Chapter 4, you learned the value of narrowing your topic to a particular question at issue. This focus will make it much easier for you to conduct your research. We don't have the space available here to cover completely the topics of research and documentation. We focus instead on integrating research into your own writing. For a complete and thorough guide to conducting your research, finding sources, and documenting these sources, go to **MyCompLab.com**.

Where to Begin

Everyone today is familiar with Google and Wikipedia, and they can indeed be good places to begin your research, but these sites are not prescreened by professionals.

Librarians Index to the Internet (lii.org) is. The stated goal of this website is "to provide a well-organized point of access for reliable, trustworthy, librarian-selected internet resources." Your own college's library is a great resource, as it subscribes (at significant cost) to many indexes and databases covering a wide range of disciplines. Here are a few of the indexes and databases your library will most likely subscribe to:

> ***InfoTrac Expanded Academic.*** The Gale Group's general periodical index covering arts and humanities, the social sciences, and sciences as well as national news periodicals. It includes full-text articles.

> ***LexisNexis Academic.*** An index of news and business, legal and reference information, with full-text articles. ***LexisNexis*** includes international, national, and regional newspapers; newsmagazines; and legal and business publications.

> ***Wilson Databases.*** A collection of indexes including ***Business Periodicals Index, Education Index, General Science Index, Humanities Index, Readers' Guide to Periodical Literature,*** and ***Social Sciences Index.***

Three Options for Including Research

Once you have completed your research, you have three choices for incorporating it into your paper:

> **Direct quotation:** A word-for-word transcription of what an author says, requiring quotation marks and documentation. For the most part, keep quotations short. It is your paper, not the words of others that your instructor wants to read. Reserve direct quotations for those times when the author's precise language is important, either because it is colorful or exact or cannot be paraphrased without distorting the author's original intent.

> **Paraphrase:** A restatement of an idea in language that retains the meaning but changes the exact wording. Such references require documentation but not quotation marks.

> **Summary:** A short restatement in your own words of the main points in a passage, an article, or a book. (See Chapter 3.)

Blend Quotations and Paraphrases into Your Own Writing

If you want your paper to read smoothly, you must take care to integrate direct quotations and paraphrases into the grammatical flow of your sentences. Don't just "drop" them with a thud into a paragraph. Rely, rather, on a ready supply of introductory or signal phrases with which to slide them in gracefully; for example, "As Freud **discovered**," "Justice Scalia **notes**," and "**according to** the *Los Angeles Times*." What follows is a list (incomplete) of verbs with which to ease the ideas of others smoothly into your sentences:

believes

claims

comments

contends

describes

explains

illustrates

mentions

notes

observes

points out

reports

says

suggests

Make the Purpose Clear

As well as introducing quotations and paraphrases smoothly into the syntax of your sentence, you must also pay attention to the meaning of your sentence. Don't assume that the relevance of the quotation is self-evident. Make its relationship to your reasoning explicit. Is it an example? An appeal to authority? Premise support? A counterargument? A concession? Whatever the case, the purpose of the quotation—how it relates to the point you are making—should be made clear.

Punctuation and Format of Quotations

Periods and commas are placed *inside* quotation marks unless the quotation is followed by a parenthetical citation, in which case the period follows the citation.

> *"Writing, like life itself, is a voyage of discovery," said Henry Miller, author of* Tropic of Cancer.

> *"Thinking is the activity I love best, and writing to me is simply thinking through my fingers."*
> —ISAAC ASIMOV

> **"The true relationship between a leader and his people is often revealed through small, spontaneous gestures" (Friedman 106).**

Colons and semicolons go *outside* quotation marks.

> **Read Tamar Lewin's essay, "Schools Challenge Students' Internet Talk"; we'll discuss it at our next class meeting.**

Use single quotation marks [' '] for quotations within quotations.

> **"In coping with the violence of their city, Beirut also seemed to disprove Hobbes's prediction that life in the 'state of nature' would be 'solitary'" (Friedman 210).**

If the prose quotation is more than four lines long, it should be indented, about 10 spaces for MLA (Modern Language Association) format, 5 spaces for APA (American Psychological Association) format, and double-spaced as in the rest of the text. Drop the quotation marks when you indent.

Omitting Words from a Direct Quotation—Ellipsis

Sometimes we don't want to include all of a quotation, but just certain sections of it that apply to the point we are making. In this case, we may eliminate a part or parts of the quotation by the use of *ellipsis* dots: **three spaced periods that indicate the intentional omission of words**. If the *ellipses* conclude a sentence, add a final period.

1. Something left out at the beginning:

   ". . . a diploma from Harvard or Emory nearly guarantees a financially rewarding career," says columnist Cynthia Tucker of the *Atlanta Constitution*.

2. Something left out in the middle:

   Explaining the desperation of a writer, William Faulkner once said, "Everything goes by the board: honor, pride, decency . . . to get the book written. If a writer has to rob his mother, he will not hesitate; the 'Ode on a Grecian Urn' is worth any number of old ladies."

3. Something left out at the end:

   As Henry Louis Gates says, "The features of the Black dialect of English have long been studied and found to be not an incorrect or slovenly form of Standard English but a completely grammatical and internally consistent version of the language. . . . "

Plagiarism

In a summary, you paraphrase another writer's ideas, putting them into your own words. When writing a paper of your own, you must be circumspect in giving credit to the sources you consult and place quotation marks around the words of others. **To pass off someone else's ideas or words as your own is to plagiarize**. The word *plagiarism* is derived from the Latin *plagiarius*, meaning kidnapper. Now, there are ideas or facts that are part of the public domain—they belong to all of us, such as the Latin root of *plagiarism*. No one person "owns" that information; it's (almost) common knowledge. But if we went on to trace history's most famous cases of plagiarism, research would be required, and we would have to document all of our sources and place quotation marks around sentences taken from these sources.

The Internet, while it has been an enormous help to students and teachers alike in its ability to provide us with an abundance of information on any subject, also makes it easier for students, and others, to plagiarize. According to Donald L. McCabe, founder of the Center for Academic Integrity at Duke University, in 2003, 40 percent of college students admitted to Internet plagiarism, up from 10 percent in

1999. In response to the problem, colleges subscribe to websites that allow professors to submit students' papers, which are then analyzed for plagiarism.

Read the words of Gillian Silverman, an English professor at a public university, whose essay on plagiarism appeared in *Newsweek* magazine:

> **The thing my students don't seem to realize, however, is that as easily as they can steal language from the Web, I can bust them for it. All it takes is an advanced [Web] search. . . . Plug in any piece of questionable student writing and up pops the very paper from which the phrase originates.**

Silverman goes on to say that she uncovered eight cases of plagiarism in one semester, "a new record," and failed each of the offenders. (See MyCompLab.com for more on plagiarism and how to avoid it with appropriate documentation and citations.)

ADDITIONAL READINGS

Here are three essays, all of which present longer, more complex texts than we have included in Chapters 1 through 8. "Is Google Making Us Stupid?" comes from *The Atlantic Online*; "Blinded by Science" from the *Columbia Journalism Review*; and the final, shorter piece, "When Human Rights Extend to Nonhumans," from *The New York Times*.

We offer these essays not necessarily as models for your own written arguments, but as vehicles for thinking critically about issues and as springboards for your writing. We follow each essay with questions, some of which you may use as topics for a written argument.

Is Google Making Us Stupid?

NICHOLAS CARR

"Dave, stop. Stop, will you? Stop, Dave. Will you stop, Dave?" So the supercomputer HAL pleads with the implacable astronaut Dave Bowman in a famous and weirdly poignant scene toward the end of Stanley Kubrick's *2001: A Space Odyssey*. Bowman, having nearly been sent to a deep-space death by the malfunctioning machine, is calmly, coldly disconnecting the memory circuits that control its artificial "brain." "Dave, my mind is going," HAL says, forlornly. "I can feel it. I can feel it." 1

I can feel it, too. Over the past few years I've had an uncomfortable sense that someone, or something, has been tinkering with my brain, remapping the neural 2 circuitry, reprogramming the memory. My mind isn't going—so far as I can tell—but it's changing. I'm not thinking the way I used to think. I can feel it most strongly when I'm reading. Immersing myself in a book or a lengthy article used to be easy. My mind would get caught up in the narrative or the turns of the argument, and I'd spend hours strolling through long stretches of prose. That's rarely the case anymore. Now my concentration often starts to drift after two or three pages. I get fidgety, lose the thread, begin looking for something else to do. I feel as if I'm always dragging my wayward brain back to the text. The deep reading that used to come naturally has become a struggle.

I think I know what's going on. For more than a decade now, I've been spending   3
a lot of time online, searching and surfing and sometimes adding to the great databases of the Internet. The Web has been a godsend to me as a writer. Research that once required days in the stacks or periodical rooms of libraries can now be done in minutes. A few Google searches, some quick clicks on hyperlinks, and I've got the telltale fact or pithy quote I was after. Even when I'm not working, I'm as likely as not to be foraging in the Web's info-thickets reading and writing e-mails, scanning headlines and blog posts, watching videos and listening to podcasts, or just tripping from link to link to link. (Unlike footnotes, to which they're sometimes likened, hyperlinks don't merely point to related works; they propel you toward them.)

For me, as for others, the Net is becoming a universal medium, the conduit for   4
most of the information that flows through my eyes and ears and into my mind. The advantages of having immediate access to such an incredibly rich store of information are many, and they've been widely described and duly applauded. "The perfect recall of silicon memory," *Wired*'s Clive Thompson has written, "can be an enormous boon to thinking." But that boon comes at a price. As the media theorist Marshall McLuhan pointed out in the 1960s, media are not just passive channels of information. They supply the stuff of thought, but they also shape the process of thought. And what the Net seems to be doing is chipping away my capacity for concentration and contemplation. My mind now expects to take in information the way the Net distributes it: in a swiftly moving stream of particles. Once I was a scuba diver in the sea of words. Now I zip along the surface like a guy on a Jet Ski.

I'm not the only one. When I mention my troubles with reading to friends and   5
acquaintances—literary types, most of them—many say they're having similar experiences. The more they use the Web, the more they have to fight to stay focused on long pieces of writing. Some of the bloggers I follow have also begun mentioning the phenomenon. Scott Karp, who writes a blog about online media, recently confessed that he has stopped reading books altogether. "I was a lit major in college, and used to be [a] voracious book reader," he wrote. "What happened?" He speculates on the answer: "What if I do all my reading on the web not so much because the way I read has changed, i.e. I'm just seeking convenience, but because the way I THINK has changed?"

Bruce Friedman, who blogs regularly about the use of computers in medicine,   6
also has described how the Internet has altered his mental habits. "I now have almost totally lost the ability to read and absorb a longish article on the web or in print," he wrote earlier this year. A pathologist who has long been on the faculty of the University of Michigan Medical School, Friedman elaborated on his comment in a telephone conversation with me. His thinking, he said, has taken on a

"staccato" quality, reflecting the way he quickly scans short passages of text from many sources online. "I can't read *War and Peace* anymore," he admitted. "I've lost the ability to do that. Even a blog post of more than three or four paragraphs is too much to absorb. I skim it."

Anecdotes alone don't prove much. And we still await the long-term neuro- logical and psychological experiments that will provide a definitive picture of how Internet use affects cognition. But a recently published study of online research habits, conducted by scholars from University College London, suggests that we may well be in the midst of a sea change in the way we read and think. As part of the five-year research program, the scholars examined computer logs documenting the behavior of visitors to two popular research sites, one operated by the British Library and one by a U.K. educational consortium, that provide access to journal articles, e-books, and other sources of written information. They found that people using the sites exhibited "a form of skimming activity," hopping from one source to another and rarely returning to any source they'd already visited. They typically read no more than one or two pages of an article or book before they would "bounce" out to another site. Sometimes they'd save a long article, but there's no evidence that they ever went back and actually read it. The authors of the study report:

> It is clear that users are not reading online in the traditional sense; indeed there are signs that new forms of "reading" are emerging as users "power browse" horizontally through titles, contents pages and abstracts going for quick wins. It almost seems that they go online to avoid reading in the traditional sense.

Thanks to the ubiquity of text on the Internet, not to mention the popularity of text-messaging on cell phones, we may well be reading more today than we did in the 1970s or 1980s, when television was our medium of choice. But it's a different kind of reading, and behind it lies a different kind of thinking—perhaps even a new sense of the self. "We are not only *what* we read," says Maryanne Wolf, a develop- mental psychologist at Tufts University and the author of *Proust and the Squid: The Story and Science of the Reading Brain.* "We are *how* we read." Wolf worries that the style of reading promoted by the Net, a style that puts "efficiency" and "immedi- acy" above all else, may be weakening our capacity for the kind of deep reading that emerged when an earlier technology, the printing press, made long and com- plex works of prose commonplace. When we read online, she says, we tend to become "mere decoders of information." Our ability to interpret text, to make the rich mental connections that form when we read deeply and without distraction, remains largely disengaged.

Reading, explains Wolf, is not an instinctive skill for human beings. It's not etched into our genes the way speech is. We have to teach our minds how to trans- late the symbolic characters we see into the language we understand. And the media or other technologies we use in learning and practicing the craft of reading play an important part in shaping the neural circuits inside our brains. Experiments demonstrate that readers of ideograms, such as the Chinese, develop a mental cir- cuitry for reading that is very different from the circuitry found in those of us whose written language employs an alphabet. The variations extend across many regions of the brain, including those that govern such essential cognitive functions as memory and the interpretation of visual and auditory stimuli. We can expect as well that the circuits woven by our use of the Net will be different from those woven by our reading of books and other printed works.

Sometime in 1882, Friedrich Nietzsche bought a typewriter—a Malling-Hansen Writing Ball, to be precise. His vision was failing, and keeping his eyes focused on a page had become exhausting and painful, often bringing on crushing headaches. He had been forced to curtail his writing, and he feared that he would soon have to give it up. The typewriter rescued him, at least for a time. Once he had mastered touch-typing, he was able to write with his eyes closed, using only the tips of his fingers. Words could once again flow from his mind to the page. 10

But the machine had a subtler effect on his work. One of Nietzsche's friends, a composer, noticed a change in the style of his writing. His already terse prose had become even tighter, more telegraphic. "Perhaps you will through this instrument even take to a new idiom," the friend wrote in a letter, noting that, in his own work, his "'thoughts' in music and language often depend on the quality of pen and paper." 11

"You are right," Nietzsche replied, "our writing equipment takes part in the forming of our thoughts." Under the sway of the machine, writes the German media scholar Friedrich A. Kittler, Nietzsche's prose "changed from arguments to aphorisms, from thoughts to puns, from rhetoric to telegram style." 12

The human brain is almost infinitely malleable. People used to think that our mental meshwork, the dense connections formed among the 100 billion or so neurons inside our skulls, was largely fixed by the time we reached adulthood. But brain researchers have discovered that that's not the case. James Olds, a professor of neuroscience who directs the Krasnow Institute for Advanced Study at George Mason University, says that even the adult mind "is very plastic." Nerve cells routinely break old connections and form new ones. "The brain," according to Olds, "has the ability to reprogram itself on the fly, altering the way it functions." 13

As we use what the sociologist Daniel Bell has called our "intellectual technologies"—the tools that extend our mental rather than our physical capacities—we inevitably begin to take on the qualities of those technologies. The mechanical clock, which came into common use in the 14th century, provides a compelling example. In *Technics and Civilization*, the historian and cultural critic Lewis Mumford described how the clock "disassociated time from human events and helped create the belief in an independent world of mathematically measurable sequences." The "abstract framework of divided time" became "the point of reference for both action and thought." 14

The clock's methodical ticking helped bring into being the scientific mind and the scientific man. But it also took something away. As the late MIT computer scientist Joseph Weizenbaum observed in his 1976 book, *Computer Power and Human Reason: From Judgment to Calculation*, the conception of the world that emerged from the widespread use of timekeeping instruments "remains an impoverished version of the older one, for it rests on a rejection of those direct experiences that formed the basis for, and indeed constituted, the old reality." In deciding when to eat, to work, to sleep, to rise, we stopped listening to our senses and started obeying the clock. 15

The process of adapting to new intellectual technologies is reflected in the changing metaphors we use to explain ourselves to ourselves. When the 16 mechanical clock arrived, people began thinking of their brains as operating "like clockwork." Today, in the age of software, we have come to think of them as operating "like computers." But the changes, neuroscience tells us, go much deeper than metaphor. Thanks to our brain's plasticity, the adaptation occurs also at a biological level.

The Internet promises to have particularly far-reaching effects on cognition. In   17 a paper published in 1936, the British mathematician Alan Turing proved that a digital computer, which at the time existed only as a theoretical machine, could be programmed to perform the function of any other information-processing device. And that's what we're seeing today. The Internet, an immeasurably powerful computing system, is subsuming most of our other intellectual technologies. It's becoming our map and our clock, our printing press and our typewriter, our calculator and our telephone, and our radio and TV.

When the Net absorbs a medium, that medium is re-created in the Net's   18 image. It injects the medium's content with hyperlinks, blinking ads, and other digital gewgaws, and it surrounds the content with the content of all the other media it has absorbed. A new e-mail message, for instance, may announce its arrival as we're glancing over the latest headlines at a newspaper's site. The result is to scatter our attention and diffuse our concentration.

The Net's influence doesn't end at the edges of a computer screen, either. As   19 people's minds become attuned to the crazy quilt of Internet media, traditional media have to adapt to the audience's new expectations. Television programs add text crawls and pop-up ads, and magazines and newspapers shorten their articles, introduce capsule summaries, and crowd their pages with easy-to-browse info-snippets. When, in March of this year, *The New York Times* decided to devote the second and third pages of every edition to article abstracts, its design director, Tom Bodkin, explained that the "shortcuts" would give harried readers a quick "taste" of the day's news, sparing them the "less efficient" method of actually turning the pages and reading the articles. Old media have little choice but to play by the new-media rules.

Never has a communications system played so many roles in our lives—or   20 exerted such broad influence over our thoughts—as the Internet does today. Yet, for all that's been written about the Net, there's been little consideration of how, exactly, it's reprogramming us. The Net's intellectual ethic remains obscure.

About the same time that Nietzsche started using his typewriter, an earnest   21 young man named Frederick Winslow Taylor carried a stopwatch into the Midvale Steel plant in Philadelphia and began a historic series of experiments aimed at improving the efficiency of the plant's machinists. With the approval of Midvale's owners, he recruited a group of factory hands, set them to work on various metal-working machines, and recorded and timed their every movement as well as the operations of the machines. By breaking down every job into a sequence of small, discrete steps and then testing different ways of performing each one, Taylor created a set of precise instructions—an "algorithm," we might say today—for how each worker should work. Midvale's employees grumbled about the strict new regime, claiming that it turned them into little more than automatons, but the factory's productivity soared.

More than a hundred years after the invention of the steam engine, the Indus-   22
trial Revolution had at last found its philosophy and its philosopher. Taylor's tight
industrial choreography—his "system," as he liked to call it—was embraced by
manufacturers throughout the country and, in time, around the world. Seeking
maximum speed, maximum efficiency, and maximum output, factory owners
used time-and-motion studies to organize their work and configure the jobs of
their workers. The goal, as Taylor defined it in his celebrated 1911 treatise, *The
Principles of Scientific Management*, was to identify and adopt, for every job, the
"one best method" of work and thereby to effect "the gradual substitution of science for rule of thumb throughout the mechanic arts." Once his system was
applied to all acts of manual labor, Taylor assured his followers, it would bring
about a restructuring not only of industry but of society, creating a utopia of perfect efficiency. "In the past the man has been first," he declared; "in the future the
system must be first."

Taylor's system is still very much with us; it remains the ethic of industrial man-   23
ufacturing. And now, thanks to the growing power that computer engineers and
software coders wield over our intellectual lives, Taylor's ethic is beginning to govern the realm of the mind as well. The Internet is a machine designed for the efficient and automated collection, transmission, and manipulation of information,
and its legions of programmers are intent on finding the "one best method"—the
perfect algorithm—to carry out every mental movement of what we've come to
describe as "knowledge work."

Google's headquarters, in Mountain View, California—the Googleplex—is the   24
Internet's high church, and the religion practiced inside its walls is Taylorism.
Google, says its chief executive, Eric Schmidt, is "a company that's founded around
the science of measurement," and it is striving to "systematize everything" it does.
Drawing on the terabytes of behavioral data it collects through its search engine
and other sites, it carries out thousands of experiments a day, according to the
Harvard Business Review, and it uses the results to refine the algorithms that increas-
ingly control how people find information and extract meaning from it. What
Taylor did for the work of the hand, Google is doing for the work of the mind.

The company has declared that its mission is "to organize the world's informa-   25
tion and make it universally accessible and useful." It seeks to develop "the perfect
search engine," which it defines as something that "understands exactly what you
mean and gives you back exactly what you want." In Google's view, information is
a kind of commodity, a utilitarian resource that can be mined and processed with
industrial efficiency. The more pieces of information we can "access" and the faster
we can extract their gist, the more productive we become as thinkers.

Where does it end? Sergey Brin and Larry Page, the gifted young men who   26
founded Google while pursuing doctoral degrees in computer science at Stanford,
speak frequently of their desire to turn their search engine into an artificial intelligence, a HAL-like machine that might be connected directly to our brains. "The
ultimate search engine is something as smart as people—or smarter," Page said in
a speech a few years back. "For us, working on search is a way to work on artificial
intelligence." In a 2004 interview with *Newsweek*, Brin said, "Certainly if you had all
the world's information directly attached to your brain, or an artificial brain that

was smarter than your brain, you'd be better off." Last year, Page told a convention of scientists that Google is "really trying to build artificial intelligence and to do it on a large scale."

Such an ambition is a natural one, even an admirable one, for a pair of math   27 whizzes with vast quantities of cash at their disposal and a small army of computer scientists in their employ. A fundamentally scientific enterprise, Google is motivated by a desire to use technology, in Eric Schmidt's words, "to solve problems that have never been solved before," and artificial intelligence is the hardest problem out there. Why wouldn't Brin and Page want to be the ones to crack it?

Still, their easy assumption that we'd all "be better off" if our brains were   28 supplemented, or even replaced, by an artificial intelligence is unsettling. It suggests a belief that intelligence is the output of a mechanical process, a series of discrete steps that can be isolated, measured, and optimized. In Google's world, the world we enter when we go online, there's little place for the fuzziness of contemplation. Ambiguity is not an opening for insight but a bug to be fixed. The human brain is just an outdated computer that needs a faster processor and a bigger hard drive.

The idea that our minds should operate as high-speed data-processing   29 machines is not only built into the workings of the Internet, it is the network's reigning business model as well. The faster we surf across the Web—the more links we click and pages we view—the more opportunities Google and other companies gain to collect information about us and to feed us advertisements. Most of the proprietors of the commercial Internet have a financial stake in collecting the crumbs of data we leave behind as we flit from link to link—the more crumbs, the better. The last thing these companies want is to encourage leisurely reading or slow, concentrated thought. It's in their economic interest to drive us to distraction.

Maybe I'm just a worrywart. Just as there's a tendency to glorify technological   30 progress, there's a countertendency to expect the worst of every new tool or machine. In Plato's *Phaedrus*, Socrates bemoaned the development of writing. He feared that, as people came to rely on the written word as a substitute for the knowledge they used to carry inside their heads, they would, in the words of one of the dialogue's characters, "cease to exercise their memory and become forgetful." And because they would be able to "receive a quantity of information without proper instruction," they would "be thought very knowledgeable when they are for the most part quite ignorant." They would be "filled with the conceit of wisdom instead of real wisdom." Socrates wasn't wrong—the new technology did often have the effects he feared—but he was shortsighted. He couldn't foresee the many ways that writing and reading would serve to spread information, spur fresh ideas, and expand human knowledge (if not wisdom).

The arrival of Gutenberg's printing press, in the 15th century, set off another   31 round of teeth gnashing. The Italian humanist Hieronimo Squarciafico worried that the easy availability of books would lead to intellectual laziness, making men "less studious" and weakening their minds. Others argued that cheaply printed books and broadsheets would undermine religious authority, demean the work of scholars and scribes, and spread sedition and debauchery. As New York University professor Clay Shirky notes, "Most of the arguments made against the printing press were correct, even prescient." But, again, the doomsayers were unable to imagine the myriad blessings that the printed word would deliver.

So, yes, you should be skeptical of my skepticism. Perhaps those who dismiss   32 critics of the Internet as Luddites or nostalgists will be proved correct, and from our hyperactive, data-stoked minds will spring a golden age of intellectual discovery and universal wisdom. Then again, the Net isn't the alphabet, and although it may replace the printing press, it produces something altogether different. The kind of deep reading that a sequence of printed pages promotes is valuable not just for the knowledge we acquire from the author's words but for the intellectual vibrations those words set off within our own minds. In the quiet spaces opened up by the sustained, undistracted reading of a book, or by any other act of contemplation, for that matter, we make our own associations, draw our own inferences and analogies, foster our own ideas. Deep reading, as Maryanne Wolf argues, is indistinguishable from deep thinking.

If we lose those quiet spaces, or fill them up with "content," we will sacrifice   33 something important not only in our selves but in our culture. In a recent essay, the playwright Richard Foreman eloquently described what's at stake:

> I come from a tradition of Western culture, in which the ideal (my ideal) was the complex, dense and "cathedral-like" structure of the highly educated and articulate personality—a man or woman who carried inside themselves a personally constructed and unique version of the entire heritage of the West. [But now] I see within us all (myself included) the replacement of complex inner density with a new kind of self—evolving under the pressure of information overload and the technology of the "instantly available."

As we are drained of our "inner repertory of dense cultural inheritance," Foreman concluded, we risk turning into "'pancake people'—spread wide and thin as we connect with that vast network of information accessed by the mere touch of a button."

I'm haunted by that scene in *2001*. What makes it so poignant, and so weird, is   34 the computer's emotional response to the disassembly of its mind: its despair as one circuit after another goes dark, its childlike pleading with the astronaut—"I can feel it. I can feel it. I'm afraid"—and its final reversion to what can only be called a state of innocence. HAL's outpouring of feeling contrasts with the emotionlessness that characterizes the human figures in the film, who go about their business with an almost robotic efficiency. Their thoughts and actions feel scripted, as if they're following the steps of an algorithm. In the world of *2001*, people have become so machinelike that the most human character turns out to be a machine. That's the essence of Kubrick's dark prophecy: as we come to rely on computers to mediate our understanding of the world, it is our own intelligence that flattens into artificial intelligence.

Questions for Discussion

1. Carr writes "that boon comes at a price." What is the "boon"? What is the "price"?

2. What does Maryanne Wolf of Tufts University worry about?

3. What other revolutionary technologies does Carr discuss? What was their impact on individuals and society?

4. What impact does the computer have on other technologies?

5. What is Google's mission? Its ultimate goal? What is your reaction to this ultimate goal?

6. Near the end of his essay, Carr makes a concession and then presents a refutation. Briefly summarize both.

7. Do you agree or disagree with the question at issue: Is Google making us stupid? Support your answer with specific examples and details from the Carr piece and from your own experience and reading.

Blinded By Science: How "Balanced" Coverage Lets the Scientific Fringe Hijack Reality

CHRIS MOONEY

On May 22, 2003, the *Los Angeles Times* printed a front-page story by Scott Gold, its respected Houston bureau chief, about the passage of a law in Texas requiring abortion doctors to warn women that the procedure might cause breast cancer. Virtually no mainstream scientist believes that the so-called ABC link actually exists—only anti-abortion activists do. Accordingly, Gold's article noted right off the bat that the American Cancer Society discounts the "alleged link" and that anti-abortionists have pushed for "so-called counseling" laws only after failing in their attempts to have abortion banned. Gold also reported that the National Cancer Institute had convened "more than a hundred of the world's experts" to assess the ABC theory, which they rejected. In comparison to these scientists, Gold noted, the author of the Texas counseling bill—who called the ABC issue "still disputed"—had "a professional background in property management." 1

Gold's piece was hard-hitting but accurate. The scientific consensus is quite firm that abortion does not cause breast cancer. If reporters want to take science and its conclusions seriously, their reporting should reflect this reality—no matter what anti-abortionists say. 2

But what happened next illustrates one reason journalists have such a hard time calling it like they see it on science issues. In an internal memo exposed by the Web site LAobserved.com, the *Times*'s editor, John Carroll, singled out Gold's story for harsh criticism, claiming it vindicated critics who accuse the paper of liberal bias. Carroll specifically criticized Gold's "so-called counseling" line ("a phrase that is loaded with derision") and his "professional background in property management" quip ("seldom will you read a cheaper shot than this"). "The story makes a strong case that the link between abortion and breast cancer is widely discounted among researchers," Carroll wrote, "but I wondered as I read it whether somewhere there might exist some credible scientist who believes in it. . . . Apparently the scientific argument for the anti-abortion side is so absurd that we don't need to waste our readers' time with it." 3

Gold declined to comment specifically on Carroll's memo, except to say that it   4
prompted "a sound and good discussion of the standards that we all take very seriously." For his part, Carroll—now editing his third newspaper—is hardly so naïve as
to think journalistic "balance" is synonymous with accuracy. In an interview, he
nevertheless defended the memo, observing that "reporters have to make judgments about the validity of ideas" but that "a reporter has to be broad-minded in
being open to ideas that aren't necessarily shared by the crowd he or she happens
to be hanging around with." Carroll adds that in his view, Gold needed to find a
credible scientist to defend the ABC claim, rather than merely quoting a legislator
and then exposing that individual's lack of scientific background. "You have an
obligation to find a scientist, and if the scientist has something to say, then you can
subject the scientist's views to rigorous examination," Carroll says.

The trouble is, the leading proponent of the idea that abortions cause breast   5
cancer, Dr. Joel Brind of Baruch College at the City University of New York, under-
went a pro-life religious conversion that left him feeling "compelled to use science
for its noblest, life-saving purpose," as he put it in *Physician*, a magazine published
by a conservative religious group called Focus on the Family. Brind's dedication to
the ABC theory has flown in the face of repeated negative critiques of that theory
by his scientific peers. When the National Cancer Institute convened the world's
experts to assess the question in February 2003, Brind was the only dissenter from
the group's conclusions.

Nevertheless, a later article by Gold suggests he may have taken Carroll's les-   6
son to heart (though Gold says the piece "certainly wasn't a direct response, or an
attempt to change anything or compensate" following Carroll's memo). On
November 6, 2003, Gold reported on a push in Texas to revise the way biology
textbooks teach the scientific theory of evolution, which some religious conservatives don't accept. Gold opened with a glowing profile of one William Dembski,
described as a "scientist by trade" but "an evangelical Christian at heart who is
convinced that some biological mechanisms are too complex to have been created
without divine guidance." But according to his Web site, Dembski is a philosopher
and mathematician, not a biologist. Moreover, he's a leader of the new "intelligent
design" crusade against Darwin's theory, an updated form of creationism that evolutionary biologists have broadly denounced. (He recently took a job running the
Center for Science and Theology at the Southern Baptist Theological Seminary.)
The American Association for the Advancement of Science, the world's largest scientific society and publisher of *Science*, the highest-circulation general scientific
journal, has firmly stated that proponents have "failed to offer credible scientific
evidence to support their claim" that the intelligent design theory "undermines the
current scientifically accepted theory of evolution."

Scott Gold had it exactly right on abortion and breast cancer. Then he pro-   7
duced an article on "intelligent design" so artificially "balanced" it was downright
inaccurate and misleading.

The basic notion that journalists should go beyond mere "balance" in search of   8
the actual truth hardly represents a novel insight. This magazine, along with its
political Web site, *Campaign Desk*, has been part of a rising chorus against a preva-
lent but lazy form of journalism that makes no attempt to dig beneath competing

claims. But for journalists raised on objectivity and tempered by accusations of bias, knowing that phony balance can create distortion is one thing and taking steps to fix the reporting is another.

Political reporting hardly presents the only challenge for journalists seeking to   9
go beyond he said/she said accounts, or even the most difficult one. Instead, that distinction may be reserved for media coverage of contested scientific issues, many of them with major policy ramifications, such as global climate change. After all, the journalistic norm of balance has no corollary in the world of science. On the contrary, scientific theories and interpretations survive or perish depending upon whether they're published in highly competitive journals that practice strict quality control, whether the results upon which they're based can be replicated by other scientists, and ultimately whether they win over scientific peers. When consensus builds, it is based on repeated testing and retesting of an idea.

Journalists face a number of pressures that can prevent them from accurately   10
depicting competing scientific claims in terms of their credibility within the scientific community as a whole. First, reporters must often deal with editors who reflexively cry out for "balance." Meanwhile, determining how much weight to give different sides in a scientific debate requires considerable expertise on the issue at hand. Few journalists have real scientific knowledge, and even beat reporters who know a great deal about certain scientific issues may know little about other ones they're suddenly asked to cover.

Moreover, the question of how to substitute accuracy for mere "balance" in   11
science reporting has become ever more pointed as journalists have struggled to cover the Bush administration, which scientists have widely accused of scientific distortions. As the Union of Concerned Scientists, an alliance of citizens and scientists, and other critics have noted, Bush administration statements and actions have often given privileged status to a fringe scientific view over a well-documented, extremely robust mainstream conclusion. Journalists have thus had to decide whether to report on a he said/she said battle between scientists and the White House—which has had very few scientific defenders—or get to the bottom of each case of alleged distortion and report on who's actually right.

No wonder scientists have often denounced the press for giving credibility to   12
fringe scientific viewpoints. And without a doubt, the topic on which scientists have most vehemently decried both the media and the Bush administration is global warming. While some scientific uncertainty remains in the climate field, the most rigorous peer-reviewed assessments—produced roughly every five years by the United Nations' Intergovernmental Panel on Climate Change (IPCC)—have cemented a consensus view that human greenhouse gas emissions are probably (i.e., the conclusion has a fairly high degree of scientific certainty) helping to fuel the greenhouse effect and explain the observed planetary warming of the past fifty years. Yet the Bush administration has consistently sought to undermine this position by hyping lingering uncertainties and seeking to revise government scientific reports. It has also relied upon energy interests and a small cadre of dissenting scientists (some of whom are funded, in part, by industry) in formulating climate policy.

The centrality of the climate change issue to the scientific critique of the   13
press does not arise by accident. Climate change has mind-bogglingly massive

ramifications, not only for the future of our carbon-based economy but for the planet itself. Energy interests wishing to stave off action to reduce greenhouse gas emissions have a documented history of supporting the small group of scientists who question the human role in causing climate change—as well as consciously strategizing about how to sow confusion on the issue and sway journalists.

In 1998, for instance, John H. Cushman, Jr., of *The New York Times* exposed an   14
internal American Petroleum Institute memo outlining a strategy to invest millions to "maximize the impact of scientific views consistent with ours with Congress, the media and other key audiences." Perhaps most startling, the memo cited a need to "recruit and train" scientists "who do not have a long history of visibility and/or participation in the climate change debate" to participate in media outreach and counter the mainstream scientific view. This seems to signal an awareness that after a while, journalists catch on to the connections between contrarian scientists and industry. But in the meantime, a window of opportunity apparently exists when reporters can be duped by fresh faces.

"There's a very small set of people" who question the consensus, says *Science*'s   15
executive editor-in-chief, Donald Kennedy. "And there are a great many thoughtful reporters in the media who believe that in order to produce a balanced story, you've got to pick one commentator from side A and one commentator from side B. I call it the two-card Rolodex problem."

The Stanford climatologist Stephen Schneider echoes this concern. A scientist   16
whose interactions with the media on the subject of climate change span decades, Schneider has reflected at length on the subject, especially in his 1989 book *Global Warming*. Schneider's climate-change Web site also devotes a section to what he calls "Mediarology," where he notes that in science debates "there are rarely just two polar opposite sides, but rather a spectrum of potential outcomes, oftentimes accompanied by a considerable history of scientific assessment of the relative credibility of these many possibilities. A climate scientist faced with a reporter locked into the 'get both sides' mindset risks getting his or her views stuffed into one of two boxed storylines: 'we're worried' or 'it will all be okay.' And sometimes, these two 'boxes' are misrepresentative; a mainstream, well-established consensus may be 'balanced' against the opposing views of a few extremists, and to the uninformed, each position seems equally credible."

Academics have studied media coverage of climate change, and the results   17
confirm climate scientists' longstanding complaints. In a recent paper published in the journal *Global Environmental Change*, the scholars Maxwell T. Boykoff and Jules M. Boykoff analyzed coverage of the issue in *The New York Times*, *The Washington Post*, *The Wall Street Journal*, and the *Los Angeles Times* between 1988 and 2002. During this fourteen-year period, climate scientists successfully forged a powerful consensus on human-caused climate change. But reporting in these four major papers did not at all reflect this consensus.

The Boykoffs analyzed a random sample of 636 articles. They found that a   18
majority—52.7 percent—gave "roughly equal attention" to the scientific consensus view that humans contribute to climate change and to the energy-industry-supported view that natural fluctuations suffice to explain the observed warming.

By comparison, just 35.3 percent of articles emphasized the scientific consensus view while still presenting the other side in a subordinate fashion. Finally, 6.2 percent emphasized the industry-supported view, and a mere 5.9 percent focused on the consensus view without bothering to provide the industry/skeptic counterpoint.

Most intriguing, the Boykoffs' study found a shift in coverage between   19 1988—when climate change first garnered wide media coverage—and 1990. During that period, journalists broadly moved from focusing on scientists' views of climate change to providing "balanced" accounts. During this same period, the Boykoffs noted, climate change became highly politicized and a "small group of influential spokespeople and scientists emerged in the news" to question the mainstream view that industrial emissions are warming the planet. The authors conclude that the U.S. "prestige-press" has produced "informationally biased coverage of global warming . . . hidden behind the veil of journalistic balance."

In a rich irony, a UPI report on August 30, 2004, about the Boykoffs' study   20 covered it in—that's right—a thoroughly "balanced" fashion. The article gave considerable space to the viewpoint of Frank Maisano, a former spokesman for the industry-sponsored Global Climate Coalition and a professional media consultant, who called the Boykoffs' contentions "absolutely outrageous" and proceeded to reiterate many of the dubious criticisms of mainstream climate science for which the "skeptic" camp is so notorious. In the process, the UPI piece epitomized all the pathologies of U.S. coverage of climate change—pathologies that aren't generally recapitulated abroad. Media research suggests that U.S. journalists cover climate change very differently from their European counterparts, often lending much more credence to the viewpoints of "skeptics" like Maisano.

In an interview, Maxwell Boykoff—an environmental studies Ph.D. candidate   21 at the University of California at Santa Cruz—noted that if there's one American journalist who cuts against the grain in covering the climate issue, it's Andrew C. Revkin of *The New York Times.* That's revealing, because Revkin happens to be the only reporter at any of the major newspapers studied who covers "global environmental change" as his exclusive beat, which Revkin says means writing about climate change "close to half" of the time. Revkin has also been covering global warming since 1988 and has written a book on the topic. (This fall he began teaching environmental reporting as an adjunct at Columbia's Graduate School of Journalism.)

Revkin agrees with the basic thrust of the Boykoff study, but he also notes that   22 the analysis focuses only on the quantitative aspect of climate-change coverage, rather than more subtle qualitative questions such as how reporters "characterize the voices" of the people they quote.

After all, the issue isn't just how many column inches journalists give to the   23 perspective of climate-change "skeptics" versus the mainstream view. It's also how they identify these contrarian figures, many of whom have industry ties. Take a January 8, 2004, article by *The Washington Post*'s Guy Gugliotta, reporting on a study in the journal *Nature* finding that global warming could "drive 15 to 37 percent of living species toward extinction by mid-century." Gugliotta's story hardly suffered from phony balance. But when it did include a "skeptic" perspective—in a thoroughly subordinate fashion in the ninth paragraph—the skeptic's industry ties went unmentioned:

> One skeptic, William O'Keefe, president of the George C. Marshall Institute, a conservative science policy organization, criticized the *Nature* study, saying that the research 'ignored species' ability to adapt to higher temperatures' and assumed that technologies will not arise to reduce emissions.

What Gugliotta didn't say is this: the Marshall Institute receives substantial support   24
from oil giant ExxonMobil, a leading funder of think tanks, frequently conservative in orientation, that question the scientific consensus on climate change. Moreover, O'Keefe himself has chaired the anti-Kyoto Protocol Global Climate Coalition, and served as executive vice president and chief operating officer of the American Petroleum Institute. Senate documents from 2001 through 2003 also list him as a registered lobbyist for ExxonMobil. (To be fair, when I discussed this matter with O'Keefe while working on a previous article, he said that he registers as a lobbyist "out of an abundance of caution" and keeps his ExxonMobil and Marshall Institute work "separate.")

Asked about all of this, Gugliotta said he simply didn't know of O'Keefe's   25
industry connections at the time. He said he considered O'Keefe a "reasoned skeptic" who provided a measured perspective from the other side of the issue. Fair enough. His industry ties don't necessarily detract from that, but readers still should know about them. The point isn't to single out Gugliotta—any number of other examples could be found. And such omissions don't merely occur on the news pages. Some major op-ed pages also appear to think that to fulfill their duty of providing a range of views, they should publish dubious contrarian opinion pieces on climate change even when those pieces are written by nonscientists. For instance, on July 7, 2003, *The Washington Post* published a revisionist op-ed on climate science by James Schlesinger, a former secretary of both energy and defense, and a former director of Central Intelligence. "In recent years the inclination has been to attribute the warming we have lately experienced to a single dominant cause—the increase in greenhouse gases," wrote Schlesinger. "Yet climate has always been changing—and sometimes the swings have been rapid." The clear implication was that scientists don't know enough about the causes of climate change to justify strong pollution controls.

That's not how most climatologists feel, but then Schlesinger is an economist   26
by training, not a climatologist. Moreover, his *Washington Post* byline failed to note that he sits on the board of directors of Peabody Energy, the largest coal company in the world, and has since 2001. Peabody has resisted the push for mandatory controls on greenhouse gas emissions, such as those that would be required by the Kyoto Protocol. In a 2001 speech, the Peabody executive John Wootten argued that "there remains great uncertainty in the scientific understanding of climate," and that "imposition of immediate constraints on emissions from fossil-fuel use is not warranted." Funny, that's pretty much what Schlesinger argued.

For another group of scientists, the grievances with the press have emerged   27
more recently, but arguably with far greater force. That's because on an issue of great concern to these scientists—the various uses and abuses of somatic cell

nuclear transfer, or cloning—journalists have swallowed the claims of the scientific fringe hook, line, and sinker.

Consider the great 2002 cloning hoax. In the media lull following Christmas, one Brigitte Boisselier—the "scientific director" of Clonaid, a company linked to the UFO-obsessed Raelian sect, and already a semi-celebrity who had been profiled in *The New York Times Magazine*—announced the birth of the world's first cloned baby. At her press conference, covered live by CNN, MSNBC, and Fox, Boisselier could not even produce a picture of the alleged child—"Eve"—much less independent scientific verification of her claims. She instead promised proof within eight or nine days. Needless to say, the whole affair should have made the press wary. 28

Nevertheless, a media frenzy ensued, with journalists occasionally mocking and questioning the Raelians while allowing their claims to drive the coverage. CNN's medical correspondent, Sanjay Gupta, provided a case in point. When he interviewed Boisselier following her press conference, Gupta called Clonaid a group with "the capacity to clone" and told Boisselier, credulously, "We are certainly going to be anxiously awaiting to see some of the proof from these independent scientists next week." 29

Perhaps most outspoken in criticizing the press during the Clonaid fiasco was Arthur Caplan, the University of Pennsylvania biomedical ethicist. As one of the nation's most quoted bioethicists, Caplan had the advantage of actual access to the media during the feeding frenzy. Yet that familiarity made little difference. As Caplan complained in an MSNBC.com column following the Raelians' announcement, no one wanted to listen to his skepticism because that would have required dropping the story: "As soon as I heard about the Raelians' cloning claim, I knew it was nonsense," wrote Caplan. "The media have shown themselves incapable of covering the key social and intellectual phenomena of the 21st century, namely the revolution in genetics and biology." 30

Caplan observed that Clonaid had no scientific peer-reviewed publications to prove its techniques were up to snuff, and that cloning had barely worked in live animal species, and then only after countless initial failures. Nevertheless, Clonaid had implausibly claimed a stunning success rate—five pregnancies in ten attempts—in its experiments. 31

The Clonaid fiasco shows the media at their absolute worst in covering scientific issues. Reviewing the coverage two years later is a painful exercise. As even Gupta later admitted, "I think if we had known . . . that there was going to be no proof at this press conference, I think that we probably would have pulled the plug." Later on, even the Raelians themselves reportedly laughed at how easy it was to get free publicity. 32

But this wasn't just fun and games. The political consequences of the press's cloning coverage were considerable. Widespread fear of human cloning inevitably lends strength to sweeping legislation that would ban all forms of cloning, despite the fact that many scientists think the cloning of embryos for research purposes holds significant medical promise; it would allow for the creation of embryonic-stem-cell lines genetically matched to individual patients. Thus, on an issue where one side of the debate thrives on fear, the media delivered exactly what 33 these cloning-ban advocates desired. Where the press's unjustifiable addiction to "balance" on climate change produces a political stalemate on a pressing issue of global consequence, its addiction to cloning cranks provided a potent political weapon to the enemies of crucial research.

None of those examples of poorly "balanced" science reporting arise from pre- 34 cisely the same set of journalistic shortcomings. In Scott Gold's case at the *Los Angeles Times*, he appears to have known the scientific issues perfectly well. That gave his writing an authority that set off warning bells in an editor wary of bias. That's very different from the Clonaid example, where sheer credulousness among members of the media—combined with sensationalism and a slow news period—were the problem. And that's different still from the problem of false balance in the media coverage of climate change in the U.S., which has been chronic for more than a decade.

Yet in each case, the basic journalistic remedy would probably be the same. As 35 a general rule, journalists should treat fringe scientific claims with considerable skepticism, and find out what major peer-reviewed papers or assessments have to say about them. Moreover, they should adhere to the principle that the more out-landish or dramatic the claim, the more skepticism it warrants. *The Los Angeles Times*'s Carroll observes that "every good journalist has a bit of a contrarian in his soul," but it is precisely this impulse that can lead reporters astray. The fact is, non-scientist journalists can all too easily fall for scientific-sounding claims that they can't adequately evaluate on their own.

That doesn't mean that scientific consensus is right in every instance. There are 36 famous examples, in fact, of when it was proved wrong: Galileo comes to mind, as does a lowly patent clerk named Einstein. In the vast majority of modern cases, however, scientific consensus can be expected to hold up under scrutiny precisely because it was reached through a lengthy and rigorous process of professional skepticism and criticism. At the very least, journalists covering science-based policy debates should familiarize themselves with this professional proving ground, learn what it says about the relative merits of competing claims, and "balance" their reports accordingly.

Questions for Discussion

1. Why have scientists often denounced the press?

2. Why did the Bush administration present a special challenge for science journalists?

3. According to Mooney, what are the two difficulties journalists face when reporting on scientific stories?

4. What specific examples of balanced coverage does Mooney cite as being prob-lematic? What are the negative consequences of such balanced reporting?

5. What does Mooney urge journalists to do when reporting on stories about science?

6. At the end of his argument what concession does Mooney make and who are his examples?

When Human Rights Extend to Nonhumans

DONALD G. MCNEIL JR.

1   If you caught your son burning ants with a magnifying glass, would it bother you less than if you found him torturing a mouse with a soldering iron? How about a snake? How about his sister?

2   Does Khalid Shaikh Mohammed—the Guantánamo detainee who claims he personally beheaded the reporter Daniel Pearl—deserve the rights he denied Mr. Pearl? Which ones? A painless execution? Exemption from capital punishment? Decent prison conditions? Habeas corpus?

3   Such apparently unrelated questions arise in the aftermath of the vote of the environment committee of the Spanish Parliament last month to grant limited rights to our closest biological relatives, the great apes—chimpanzees, bonobos, gorillas and orangutans.

4   The committee would bind Spain to the principles of the Great Ape Project, which points to apes' human qualities, including the ability to feel fear and happiness, create tools, use languages, remember the past and plan the future. The project's directors, Peter Singer, the Princeton ethicist, and Paola Cavalieri, an Italian philosopher, regard apes as part of a "community of equals" with humans.

5   If the bill passes—the news agency Reuters predicts it will—it would become illegal in Spain to kill apes except in self-defense. Torture, including in medical experiments, and arbitrary imprisonment, including for circuses or films, would be forbidden.

6   The 300 apes in Spanish zoos would not be freed, but better conditions would be mandated.

7   What's intriguing about the committee's action is that it juxtaposes two sliding scales that are normally not allowed to slide against each other: how much kinship humans feel for which animals, and just which "human rights" each human deserves.

8   We like to think of these as absolutes: that there are distinct lines between humans and animals, and that certain "human" rights are unalienable. But we're kidding ourselves.

9   In an interview, Mr. Singer described just such calculations behind the Great Ape Project: he left out lesser apes like gibbons because scientific evidence of human qualities is weaker, and he demanded only rights that he felt all humans were usually offered, such as freedom from torture—rather than, say, rights to education or medical care.

Depending on how it is counted, the DNA of chimpanzees is 95 percent to 98.7 percent the same as that of humans.

10   Nonetheless, the law treats all animals as lower orders. Human Rights Watch has no position on apes in Spain and has never had an internal debate about who is human, said Joseph Saunders, deputy program director.

11   "There's no blurry middle," he said, "and human rights are so woefully protected that we're going to keep our focus there."

12   Meanwhile, even in democracies, the law accords diminished rights to many humans: children, prisoners, the insane, the senile. Teenagers may not vote, philosophers who slip into dementia may be lashed to their beds, courts can order

13   surgery or force-feeding.

Spain does not envision endowing apes with all rights: to drive, to bear arms 14 and so on. Rather, their status would be akin to that of children.

Ingrid Newkirk, a founder of People for the Ethical Treatment of Animals, con- 15 siders Spain's vote "a great start at breaking down the species barriers, under which humans are regarded as godlike and the rest of the animal kingdom, whether chimpanzees or clams, are treated like dirt."

Other commentators are aghast. Scientists, for example, would like to keep 16 using chimpanzees to study the AIDS virus, which is believed to have come from apes.

Mr. Singer responded by noting that humans are a better study model, and yet 17 scientists don't deliberately infect them with AIDS.

"They'd need to justify not doing that," he said. "Why apes?" 18

Spain's Catholic bishops attacked the vote as undermining a divine will that 19 placed humans above animals. One said such thinking led to abortion, euthanasia and ethnic cleansing.

But given that even some humans are denied human rights, what is the most 20 basic right? To not be killed for food, perhaps?

Ten years ago, I stood in a clearing in the Cameroonian jungle, asking a 21 hunter to hold up for my camera half the baby gorilla he had split and butterflied for smoking.

My distress—partly faked, since I was also feeling triumphant, having come 22 this far hoping to find exactly such a scene—struck him as funny. "A gorilla is still meat," said my guide, a former gorilla hunter himself. "It has no soul."

So he agrees with Spain's bishops. But it was an interesting observation for a 23 West African to make. He looked much like the guy on the famous engraving adopted as a coat of arms by British abolitionists: a slave in shackles, kneeling to either beg or pray. Below it the motto: Am I Not a Man, and a Brother?

Whether or not Africans had souls—whether they were human in God's eyes, 24 capable of salvation—underlay much of the colonial debate about slavery. They were granted human rights on a sliding scale: as slaves, they were property; in the United States Constitution a slave counted as only three-fifths of a person. As Ms. Newkirk pointed out, "All these supremacist notions take a long time to erode."

She compared the rights of animals to those of women: it only seems like a 25 long time, she said, since they got the vote or were admitted to medical schools. Or, she might have added, to the seminary. Though no Catholic bishop would suggest that women lack souls, it will be quite a while before a female bishop denounces Spain's Parliament.

But we're drifting from that most basic right—to not be killed for food. 26

Back to the clearing. As someone who eats foie gras and veal (made from tor- 27 tured animals) and has eaten whale (in Iceland), I don't know why I suddenly turned squeamish when offered a nibble of primate. On reflection, I probably faked that too. When I was young, my family used to drive over Donner Pass each year to go camping, and my mother would regale us with the history of the Donner Party. Even as a child, I had no doubt that, in extremis, I would have tucked in.

On our drive back to Cameroon's coast, my guide insisted that some of the 28 local Fang people, well known for cannibalism in the 19th century, still dug up bodies to eat. I believed him partly because in South Africa, where I then lived, murder victims were often found missing the body parts needed in traditional medicine.

Cannibalism is repugnant to the laws of all countries. But that repugnance is   29 not written in the extra tidbits of DNA that separate us from chimps. Quite the opposite: "pot polish" on human bones found in various archaeological sites suggests that some of our ancestors exited this world as stew. That too puts us in the "community of equals" with apes; female chimpanzees are known to eat rivals' babies.

But when human law does intervene in this primate-eat-primate world, it is   30 also on a sliding scale. Even animal cruelty laws have a bias toward big mammals like us. For example, in a slaughterhouse, chickens are sent alive and squawking into the throat-slitting machine and the scalding bath.

But under the federal Humane Slaughter Act, a cow must be knocked senseless   31 as painlessly as possible before the first cut can be made.

Which raises an interesting moral dilemma for the righteous Spanish Parlia-   32 ment: What about bullfighting?

As in all great struggles separating man from beast: a lot of it's in the cape-   33 work. Olé!

Questions for Discussion

1. What human qualities do apes possess?

2. What rights will be granted to apes if the Great Ape Project Bill passes?

3. Why do scientists and Catholic bishops object to the bill?

4. What analogy does McNeil draw between the West African and the baby gorilla the African killed, and what analogy between animals and people does Ingrid Newkirk draw? Are these analogies valid?

5. McNeil is a science reporter. In light of Chris Mooney's "Blinded by Science," is McNeil's reporting in this piece balanced and accurate? Support your answer with specific examples and references to "Blinded by Science."

6. If you were able to vote on this bill before the Spanish legislature, how would you vote and why? Make your argument specific and well developed.

TEXT CREDITS

INDEX

"Abortion Foes Entitled to Confront Patients. Supreme Court Says It's Free Speech" (Savage), 9
Abstraction ladder, 111–112
Abstractions
  concrete examples to illustrate, 111–112, 116
  evasion through use of, 114–115
  explanation of, 108–110
Abstract nouns, 205
Acknowledgment, in counterargument, 92
Active voice, 205–206, 209
Adelman, Clifford, 56–57
Ad hominem, 141–142, 155
Advertisements
  examination of, 41–42
  thinking critically about, 6
Agassiz, Louis, 158
Age of American Unreason, The (Jacoby), 116
Alchemy of Race and Rights, The (Williams), 63
Allen, Woody, 134, 160
Ambiguous argument, 60–61
American Enterprise Institute, 8
American Psychological Association (APA) format, 213
Analogy
  explanation of, 17–18, 21
  false, 137–138, 155
Antecedent, 176, 198
APA format, 213
AP Courses—Mounting Burden, Declining Benefit (Yan), 70–72
Appeal to authority, 132–133, 154
Appeal to fear, 133, 154
Appeal to pity, 133–134, 154
Appositives
  in argument, 118
  explanation of, 117, 130
  function of, 120
  punctuation of, 118–119
Argumentative edge, 77
Arguments
  ambiguous, 60–61
  appositives in, 118
  categorical syllogism as, 169
  checklist for, 102
  coherence in, 91–93
  conclusions in, 54–55, 84
  construction of, 37
  counterargument, 85–87, 91–92, 103 (*See also* Counterarguments)

deductive, 157–199 (*See also* Deductive arguments)
definition of, 53, 75
development of, 83–84
dialectical approach to, 85
examples of, 94–98
explanations vs., 72
fallacious, 131–156 (*See also* Fallacious arguments)
focus of, 77
hidden assumptions in, 62–68
hypothetical, 176–179
identifying your, 15
inappropriate issues for, 90–91
inductive, 157–199 (*See also* Inductive arguments)
introductions in, 82–83
issue in, 77–78
opinion vs., 53–54
parallelism in, 203–204 (*See also* Parallelism)
premises in, 54, 55, 84
rhetorical strategies for, 82
Rogerian strategy in, 87–88
standard form of, 56–58
steps to write, 81
structure of, 60–61
summaries in, 69–72
thesis in, 79–81
two-step process for, 98–101
valid, 169–170
written, 77–123 (*See also* Written arguments)
Aristotle, 82
Asimov, Isaac, 1, 212
Association, guilt by, 171–172
Assumptions. *See* Hidden assumptions
Audience
  awareness of hidden assumptions by, 68
  for essays, 37
  identifying your, 14–15
Authority, appeal to, 132–133, 154
Awareness, audience, 65
Ayers, Bill, 172

Bachar, John, 137
Background information, in essays, 37
Baker, Will, 44–45
Begging the question, 134–135, 154
Beloved (Morrison), 105
Benefit of the doubt, 61
Bennett, William, 122–123

Bias
  in news coverage, 7
  in online sources, 7–8
  in use of terms, 106
Bierce, Ambrose, 105
Bird by Bird: Some Instructions on Writing and Life (Lamott), 12
Blair, Jayson, 26
"Blinded By Science: How 'Balanced' Coverage Lets the Scientific Fringe Hijack Reality" (Mooney), 223–230
Blogs, 6, 7
Boston Globe, 7
"Boxing, Doctors—Round Two" (Cohn), 152–154
Brainstorming, 11, 21
Brodkey, Harold, 171
Brunch, John, 188
Bumiller, Elizabeth, 73
Bush, George W., 134
"Bush Remarks Roil Debate over Teaching of Evolution" (Bumiller), 73

Carr, Nicholas, 83, 215–222
Carroll, Jon, 4–5, 61, 142, 187
Carroll, Lewis, 104, 160
Carson, Rachel, 142
Cartoons, interpretation from, 24
"Case for Affirmative Action, A" (Tucker), 97–98
Categorical syllogisms. *See also* Deductive arguments
  classes of, 169
  explanation of, 169, 198
  soundness of, 171, 173–174
Causation
  correlation vs., 189–190
  explanation of, 189, 198
Chast, Roz, 166
"Child's Draft, The" (Lamott), 12–13
Ciardi, John, 17
Cicero, 1
Class
  exclusion and, 166
  explanation of, 164–165, 198
  inclusion and, 165
  overlap and, 166–167
Class logic
  explanation of, 164–165
  syllogism and, 168–173
Cochrane, Alfred, 131
Coherence, methods to achieve, 91–93
Cohn, Lowell, 152–154

"College Athletes—Special Admissions?" (student essay), 94–97
Colons, 212
Color Purple, The (Walker), 128
Columbia School of Journalism, 8
Commas, 212
Complete thesis, 81
Concessions
    examples of, 87–88, 91
    explanation of, 92, 103
Conclusions
    to argument, 54–55, 80, 84, 170
    to essays, 37
    explanation of, 54, 75
Concrete nouns, 205
Concrete objects
    explanation of, 109, 110
    to illustration abstract terms, 116–117
Conditions
    chains of, 178–179
    necessary, 177–178, 199
    sufficient, 178, 199
Confirmation, of argument position, 83
Conflict of interest, 191
Conjunctions
    coordinating, 92
    explanation of, 55, 91
    subordinating, 92
Connotation, 116, 130
Conrad, Barnaby, 55
Consequent, 176, 198
Coordinating conjunctions, 92
Correlation
    causation vs., 189–190
    explanation of, 189, 198
Cotton, John, 29–30
Could It Be That Video Games Are Good for Kids? (Johnson), 88–90
Counterarguments. *See also* Arguments
    explanation of, 85, 103
    method to address, 85–86, 91–92
    refutation and concession in, 86–87
Counterexamples, 187
Critical, 2
Critical reading, 34–37
Critical thinking
    about literature, 44
    about surveys and statistics, 188–192
    elements of, 17
    explanation of, 2, 21
    media literacy and, 6–9
    world view and, 3–4
CSI: Crime Scene Investigation, 23

Daily Kos, 8
Darwin, Charles, 2

Dawkins, Richard, 17
Days of Obligation (Rodriguez), 105–106
Dear Abby column, 138
Deduction, 198
Deductive arguments
    categorical syllogism as, 169, 171, 173–174, 198
    classes in, 168
    conclusions to, 170
    explanation of, 157
    hypothetical argument as, 176–179
    inference in, 158
Deductive reasoning
    class logic and, 164–175
    hypothetical, 176–179
    inductive vs., 157–160
    inference in, 158
Definitions
    alternative versions of, 126–128
    composing argument based on, 124–126
    extended, 120, 125
    information revealed in, 105–106
    shifts in, 106–107
    in social sciences and government, 108
    strategies for writing, 125
    in written argument, 116–126
Deitch, Edward, 7
Democracy, 5, 6, 112
Denotation, 130
Diagnosis (Sanders), 61
Dialectic, 103
Dialectical thinking, 85
Dickens, Charles, 33
Didion, Joan, 117
Dillard, Annie, 113
Direct quotations, 211
Doerr, Harriet, 118
Domino theory. *See* Slippery slope
Double standard, 135–136, 154
Douglas, Helen Gahagen, 171
Dowd, Maureen, 127–128
Drafts, first, 12–13
Dry Manhattan (Lerner), 28
Dulce Et Decorum Est (Owen), 182–183

Either/or reasoning. *See* False dilemma
Eliot, T. S., 2
Ellipsis, 213
E-mail, 15–16
Emotion, in argument, 133–134
Empathy, 87, 103
Epidemiology, 190, 198
Equivocation, 136–137, 155
Ergo propter hoc reasoning, 139, 155

Essays. *See also* Writing; Written arguments
    approach of, 36–37
    audience and purpose of, 37
    structure of, 37
    topic of, 36
Euler, Leonhard, 165
Euler diagrams, 165
Euphemism
    connotation and, 116
    explanation of, 115, 130
Evasion, 206
Examples
    concrete, 111–112
    counter-, 187
    specific, 112
Exclusion, 166, 198
Explanations
    for argument, 83
    argument vs., 72
    definition of, 75
Explicit, 44, 52, 62
Expository writing, 33

Facebook, 6
Facts
    balance between inferences and, 31–34
    explanation of, 24–25, 52
    interpretation of, 6
    journalism and, 25–26
"Facts of Media Life, The" (Frankel), 25–26
Fallacious arguments
    appeal to authority as, 132–133
    appeal to fear as, 133
    appeal to pity as, 133–134
    begging the question as, 134–135
    double standard as, 135–136
    equivocation as, 136–137
    explanation of, 131–132, 155
    false analogy as, 137–138
    false cause as, 139–140
    false dilemma as, 140–141
    faulty generalization as, 141
    personal attack as, 141–142
    poisoning the well as, 142
    red herring as, 142–143
    slippery slope as, 143
    straw man as, 144
    types and examples of, 154–156
False analogy, 137–138, 155
False cause, 139–140, 155
False dilemma, 140–141, 155
Farewell to Arms, A (Hemingway), 114
Faulkner, Shannon, 136
Faulty generalization, 141
Fear, appeal to, 133, 154
Fenster, Diane Lind, 139
Fiction, writing about, 44

Fish, Stanley, 109
Focus, of argument, 77
Four Quartets, The (Eliot), 2
Frankel, Max, 25
Frazier, Ian, 171
Freewriting, 11, 21
Friedman, Thomas L., 204
Fullam, Lisa, 73–75

Gates, Henry Louis, Jr., 3
Generalizations
  hasty, 141, 155, 187
  inductive reasoning and, 159,
    183–187
  inference in, 158
  statistical, 183, 185–187
Glass, Stephen, 26
Global warming, 4, 5, 8, 53, 78–80,
  133
Goodman, Ellen, 90–91, 140–141,
  144
Google, 6, 210
Grace Period (Baker), 44–45
Graham, Ben, 24
Greenblatt, Stephen, 33, 34
Greenhouse, Linda, 9
Greenpeace, 8
Guess clothing, 42, 43
Guilt by association, 171–172
Gutterson, David, 23

Hall, Rich, 128, 129
Hard Times (Dickens), 33
Hasty generalization, 141, 155,
  187
Hayakawa, S. I., 111, 112
Hayes, Stephen, 87–88
Helms, Jesse, 133
Hemingway, Ernest, 10, 48–51,
  114
Hidden agenda, 191
Hidden assumptions
  audience awareness and, 68
  dangers of, 64
  examples of, 63–64
  explanation of, 62–63, 75
  standard form and, 65
"High Court Upholds Buffer Zone
  of 15 Feet at Abortion Clin-
  ics (Greenhouse), 9
Hills Like White Elephants
  (Hemingway), 48–51
Holmes, Oliver Wendell, 170
Horace, 183n
Hostess (Mangum), 46–47
"How Colleges Are Gouging You"
  (Larson), 188
Howe, Geoffrey, 87
Hoyt, Clark, 38–41
Huffington Post, 9
Hurston, Zora Neale, 13
Hypothesis, 159, 184, 199

Hypothetical arguments
  chains of conditions in, 178–179
  in everyday reasoning, 179
  explanation of, 176, 199
  invalid, 177
  necessary and sufficient condi-
    tions and, 177–178
  validity of, 176, 179
Hypothetical chains, 178–179

Images, visual, 38–41
Implicit
  explanation of, 52, 62
  fiction as, 44
imply, 23
Inclusion, 165, 199
In Defense of Food (Pollan), 190
Induction, 199
Inductive arguments
  explanation of, 157–158
  inference in, 158
Inductive reasoning
  class logic and, 164–175
  deductive vs., 157–160
  direction of, 184–185
  explanation of, 83, 157–158
  generalization and, 159, 183–187
  surveys and statistics and,
    188–192
infer, 23, 24
Inference
  in deductive argument, 158
  in inductive argument, 158
Inferences
  about fiction, 44
  balance between facts and, 31–34
  based on facts, 24–26
  critical reading and, 34–37
  explanation of, 22–23, 52
  from images, 37–38, 41–42
  judgment and, 26–27
  language of, 23–24
  reliability of, 23
InfoTrac Expanded Academic, 211
In Our Time (Hemingway), 9
*In Search of Our Mothers'
  Gardens: Womanist Prose*
  (Walker), 128
Internet
  critical thinking about informa-
    tion on, 6–9
  e-mail and, 15–16
  plagiarism and, 214
  as research source, 210, 211, 213
Interpretation, of facts, 6
Introduction, to argument, 82–83
Is Google Making Us Stupid?
  (Carr), 83, 215–222
Issues
  explanation of, 77–78, 103
  questions at, 78
Ivins, Molly, 186

Jacoby, Susan, 116, 117
JAMA, 192
Jarvis, Jeff, 33
Jenkyns, Richard, 34
Johnson, Mark, 18, 68
Johnson, Samuel, 10
Johnson, Steven, 88–90
Joining words
  explanation of, 55, 76
  function of, 91–92
*Journal of the American Medical
  Association*, 165
Judgment, 26–27, 52
Julius Caesar (Shakespeare), 62

Kaminer, Wendy, 143
Kennedy, Robert F., 203
Kinsey, Alfred C., 188–189
Kinsey Report, The (Kinsey),
  188–189
Kluckhohn, Clyde, 36
Kushner, Tony, 17

Lakoff, George, 18, 68
Lakoff, Robin, 2
Lamott, Anne, 12
Language
  as abstract system of symbols,
    108–116
  for definition, 104–108, 116–128
  evasive, 114–115
  inventive use of, 128–129
Larson, Erik, 188
LaSalle, Mick, 140
"Leave Marriage Alone" (Bennett),
  122–123
Lebowitz, Fran, 2
Lerner, Michael A., 28
"Let Gays Marry" (Sullivan),
  121–122
Levine, Philip, 31
Lexis/Nexis Academic, 211
Limbo, 52
Literacy, media, 6–9
Loaded questions, 135, 154
"Loneliness of Being White, The"
  (Schoenfield), 32
Love, Susan, 194–195
"Love One, Hate the Other"
  (LaSalle), 140
Lux, Thomas, 110–111

"Maker's Eye, The" (Murray), 13
Mangum, Donald, 46–47
Manjoo, Farhad, 3–4
Marvell, Andrew, 180–182
Martin, Steve, 160
McCabe, Donald L., 213
McCarthy, Joseph, 171
McNeil, Donald G., Jr., 231–233
"Mechanics' Logic" (Pirsig),
  160–163

Media literacy, 6–9
Media Research Center, 8
Meillet, Antoine, 104
Menand, Louis, 3, 85
Metaphors, 17, 18, 21
Metaphors We Live By (Lakoff & Johnson), 18, 68
Mill, John Stuart, 85
Miller, Henry, 10
Miss Manners column, 138
MLA format, 213
Modern Language Association (MLA) format, 213
Modus ponens, 176
Modus tollens, 176
Mooney, Chris, 91, 223–230
Morrison, Toni, 104–105
Murray, Donald, 13, 14
MySpace, 6

Nabokov, Vladimir, 113
Narrative, in introductions, 82–83
National Assessment of Education Progress, 16
National Review, 8
Necessary conditions, 177–178, 199
Necessity, probability vs., 157–158
New England Journal of Medicine, 192
Newlove, Donald, 171
News coverage, bias in, 7
News Hour (PBS), 4, 7
Newspapers, 6, 7
New York Times, 6, 7, 16, 185
New York Times Book Review, 139
Nixon, Richard, 171
Non sequitor, 132
Nouns, 205
Nunberg, Geoffrey, 124, 143

Obama, Barack, 87–88, 172
Obfuscation, 114
Occam's razor, 61, 76
"Of God and the Case for Unintelligent Design" (Fullam), 73–75
"On Date Rape" (Paglia), 152
On Me! (Levine), 31
Onthemedia.org, 8–9
Open mind, 2, 3
Open thesis, 81
Opinion
    argument vs., 53–54
    explanation of, 53, 76
Opposing views, in introductions, 83
Orenstein, Peggy, 105
Orwell, George, 115
Overlap, 166–167, 199
Owen, Wilfred, 182–183

Paglia, Camille, 152
"Painful Images of War, The" (Hoyt), 38–41
Parallelism
    emphasizing ideas with, 203–204
    logic and, 202–203
    structure of, 200–201
Parallel structure, 200, 209
Paraphrases, 211–212
Paré, Ambroise, 158
Particular proposition, 173, 199
Pascal, Blaise, 17
Passive voice
    appropriate use of, 206–207
    explanation of, 205–206, 209
Paul Mitchell Hair Products, 42, 43
Periods, 212
Personal attack, 141–142, 155
Persuasion, 38
Phaedrus (Plato), 83, 84
Phelps, Michael, 206
Piaget, Jean, 85
Pirelli, 41, 42
Pirsig, Robert, 160
Pity, appeal to, 133–134, 154
Plagiarism, 213–214
Plath, Sylvia, 30–31
Plato, 83, 84, 105
Poisoning the well, 142, 156
"Politics and the English Language" (Orwell), 115
Pollan, Michael, 190
Polonius, 134
Post hoc reasoning, 139–140, 155
Predicate, 169, 199
Premises
    conclusions vs., 55
    explanation of, 54, 76
    to support argument, 83–84
    true or acceptable, 170, 171
"Preventive Medicine, Properly Practiced" (Love), 194–195
Price, Hilary B., 166
Probability, necessity vs., 157–158
Problems of Philosophy, The (Russell), 157
"Problem with New Data, The" (Carroll), 4–5
Process, writing as, 10–11
Projected property, 183, 199
Project for Excellence in Journalism, 8
Propublica.org, 9
Punctuation
    of appositives, 118–119
    of quotations, 212–213
Purpose
    of essays, 37
    identifying your, 15

Question at issue, 77, 78, 103
Question-begging epithet, 154

Questions, loaded, 135, 154
Quotation marks, 212, 213
Quotations
    direct, 211
    in introductions, 83
    punctuation and format of, 212–213
    in research papers, 211

"Radical [1] (student essay), 126
"Radical [2] (student essay), 127
Reading, critical, 34–37
Reasoning. *See* Deductive reasoning; Inductive reasoning
Red herring, 142–143, 156
Refutation
    in counterargument, 85, 86, 91
    examples of, 87–88
    explanation of, 83
    function of, 85
Renfrew, Charles, 33
Repetition, 200–201, 204
Research papers
    avoiding plagiarism in, 213214
    options for including, 211
    resources for beginning, 210–211
    use of quotations and paraphrases in, 211–213
Revision, 13–14
Rhetoric, 82, 103
Rich, Frank, 106
Rodriguez, Richard, 105–106
Rogerian strategy, 87–88, 103
Rogers, Carl H., 87
Roosevelt, Eleanor, 85
Rowan, Carl, 142
Rushdie, Salmon, 87
Russell, Bertrand, 77, 157

Safire, William, 143
Salon.com, 3, 69
Sample, 183, 199
Sanders, Lisa, 61
Satanic Verses, The (Rushdie), 87
Savage, David G., 9
Sayles, John, 52
Schell, Orville, 114
Schoenfield, Bruce, 32
Schopenhauer, Arthur, 144
Second Amendment, 5, 27, 83, 120
Self-defense, in critical thinking, 2
Semicolons, 212
Shakespeare, William, 62, 105, 204
Shattered Glass, 26
Sierra Club, 8
Silent Spring (Carson), 142
Silverman, Gillian, 214
Slippery slope, 143, 156
"Slut" (Dowd), 127–128
Snob appeal, 154
Snow Falling on Cedars (Gutterson), 23

Socially constructed views, 3
Social networks, 6, 21
Soundness
  of categorical syllogisms, 171,
    173–174
  explanation of, 170, 199
Special pleading. *See* Double
    standard
Specific examples, 112
Spell checks, 14
Standard form
  argument in, 56–57
  explanation of, 56, 76
  hidden assumptions and, 65
Staples, Brent, 16
Statistical generalizations
  criteria for evaluating, 185–187
  explanation of, 183, 199
Statistics, 188–192
Steinem, Gloria, 106
"Straw Feminist, The"
    (Goodman), 144
Straw man, 144, 156
Structure, of essays, 37
Style
  parallelism and, 200–204
  to sharpen sentences and elimi-
    nate wordiness, 204–206
Subjects
  concrete, 205
  consistence in, 207
  explanation of, 169, 199
Subordinating conjunctions, 92
Sufficient conditions, 178, 199
Sullivan, Andrew, 121–122
Summaries
  example of, 70
  explanation of, 69
  research paper, 211
  strategies for writing, 69–70
Supporting paragraphs, 37
Surveys, 188–192
Syllogisms. *See also* Deductive
    arguments
  categorical, 169, 171,
    173–174, 198
  class logic and, 168–173
  unreliable, 171
  validity and, 169–170
Symbols, words as, 108–110

*Talking Power: The Politics of Lan-
    guage* (Lakoff), 2
Target population, 183, 186, 199
Text messages, 16
Thesis
  complete, 81
  explanation of, 79–81, 103
  formulation of, 11
  function of, 93

open, 81
  statement of, 82
Thesis statements, 81
Thinking. *See also* Critical thinking
  connection between writing
    and, 1–2
  dialectical, 85
  discovering weaknesses and
    contradictions in, 86
Thomas, Lewis, 207
Thurber, James, 195
To His Coy Mistress (Marvell),
    181–182
Topics, 36, 78
*Traffic: Why We Drive the Way
    We Do (and What It Says
    About Us)* (Vanderbilt), 28
Transitional words/phrases, 55, 91
Transition phrases, 91
*True Enough: Learning to Live
    in a Post-Fact Society*
    (Manjoo), 3–4
Tucker, Cynthia, 97–98, 136
Tu quoque, 142, 156
Twain, Mark, 139
Twitter, 6

*Under Fire: The NRA and the
    Battle for Gun Control*
    (Kaminer), 143
Universal proposition, 173, 199

Validity
  of argument, 169–170, 179
  explanation of, 199
Vanderbilt, Tom, 28
Visual images
  in advertisements, 41–43
  effects of, 38–41
Voice, active and passive,
    205–207, 209
"Voice You Hear When You Read
    Silently, The" (Lux),
    110–111
Voltaire, 104
Vonnegut, Kurt, 14

Waiting for Daisy (Orenstein), 105
Walker, Alice, 128
Websites, 6–9. *See also* Internet
Wesley, Samuel, 200
"What a Lovely Generalization"
    (Thurber), 195
*When Human Rights Extend to
    Nonhumans* (McNeil),
    231–233
White, E. B., 112
Whitehead, Alfred North, 157
"Who Needs Alzheimer's Testing?"
    (University of California), 101

Wikipedia, 6, 210
Wilbur, Richard, 19–20
William of Occam, 61
Williams, Glanville, 143
Williams, Patricia J., 63
Will in the World (Greenblatt),
    33, 34
Willis, Ellen, 104
Wilson Databases, 211
Wordiness, 204–205
Words. *See also* Definitions
  inventing new, 128–129
  joining, 55, 76, 91–92
  as symbols, 108–110
World view
  examining your, 3–4
  explanation of, 3, 21
"Writer, The" (Wilbur), 19–20
Writing
  audience and purpose
    for, 14–15
  connection between thinking
    and, 1–2
  e-mail and text message, 15–16
  expository, 33
  first drafts for, 12–13
  generating ideas for, 11–12
  using a critical mind to revise,
    13–14
Writing process
  correction stage in, 13–14
  creation stage in, 11–12
  overview of, 10–11
  shaping stage in, 12–13
Written arguments. *See also*
    Arguments
  addressing counterargument
    in, 85–87 (*See also*
    Counterarguments)
  checklist for, 102
  coherence in, 91–93
  conclusions in, 84
  definition in, 116–126
  development of, 83–84
  dialectical approach to, 85
  examples of, 94–98
  inappropriate issues
    for, 90–91
  introductions in, 82–83
  Rogerian strategy in, 87–88
  thesis in, 79–81
  two-step process for complete,
    98–101

Yan, Nathan, 70–72, 120

*Zen and the Art of Motorcycle
    Maintenance* (Pirsig),
    160–163
Ziff, Larzer, 118